European Consumers in the Digital Era

Consumers make purchasing decisions every day, taking into account their needs, preferences, and beliefs which may change due to various determinants: some depending on the consumers themselves and others on the organizations acting in the market. What determinants are inducing these changes in consumers' needs, perceptions, attitudes, values, and, finally, purchasing behaviour? This edited collection offers a comprehensive description of the consumer behaviour process and the determinants that affect it in the era of digitalization.

This book offers a holistic perspective of consumer behaviour in the 21st century in different European cultures that are characterized by new technologies, including smartphones, augmented reality (AR), the Internet of Things (IoT), Artificial Intelligence (AI), and social media, as well as cultural changes and the Covid-19 pandemic. The first part of this book is devoted to characteristic phenomena in consumer behaviour in the era of digitalization, such as changes in the consumer buying decision-making processes, e-commerce, and prosumers' and consumers' attitudes towards innovations. The second part will describe the consumers, their decision-making processes, with examples from almost all geographical regions in Europe, including Germany, Spain, Italy, Finland, Poland, and Russia. Both individually and collectively, the contributors provide discussion points and practical implications resulting from the changes observed in consumer behaviour in each country.

European Consumers in the Digital Era provides a comprehensive overview of digital consumer behaviour, offering timely insights for scholars and researchers. It will also appeal to postgraduate students of related fields, including marketing, innovation, and sociology.

Małgorzata Bartosik-Purgat is a Professor in the Department of International Management at Poznań University of Economics and Business, Poland. Her research addresses cultural aspects in international business, cross-cultural communication, cross-cultural consumer behaviour, consumer ethnocentrism, acceptance of innovations in the consumers' decisions, and significance of new media in marketing and personal communication. She is a member of

EIBA – European International Business Association, IAIR – International Academy for Intercultural Research, ABC – Association for Business Communication, SIETAR Poland – Society for Intercultural Education Training and Research, IT&FA – International Trade and Finance Association, and AIB – Academy of International Business. She is an author and co-author of publications in *International Journal of Emerging Markets*, *European Journal of International Management*, *Technology Analysis & Strategic Management*, *Entrepreneurial Business and Economics Review*, and *Economics and Business Review*.

Nela Filimon is an Associate Professor – Serra Húnter Fellow in the Department of Business at the Universitat de Girona, Spain. Her research interests are related to consumer behaviour, market research, social media, wellbeing and ICTs, sociology of consumption, marketing in cultural industries, and quantitative research methods. She has published her research in international journals such as *Social Science Computer Review*, *Journal of Cultural Economics*, *Poetics*, *Advances in Sociology Research*, *Sociological Review*, *Sustainability*, *International Journal of Environmental Research and Public Health*, *Regional Science Inquiry*, and *Economics and Business Review*, among others.

Routledge Studies in Marketing

This series welcomes proposals for original research projects that are either single or multi-authored or an edited collection from both established and emerging scholars working on any aspect of marketing theory and practice and provides an outlet for studies dealing with elements of marketing theory, thought, pedagogy and practice.

It aims to reflect the evolving role of marketing and brings together the most innovative work across all aspects of the marketing 'mix' – from product development, consumer behaviour, marketing analysis, branding, and customer relationships, to sustainability, ethics, and the new opportunities and challenges presented by digital and online marketing.

21 **Information Asymmetry in Online Advertising**
Jan W. Wiktor and Katarzyna Sanak-Kosmowska

22 **Evaluating Social Media Marketing**
Social Proof and Online Buyer Behaviour
Katarzyna Sanak-Kosmowska

23 **Charity Marketing**
Contemporary Issues, Research and Practice
Edited by Fran Hyde and Sarah-Louise Mitchell

24 **The Dynamics of Influencer Marketing**
A Multidisciplinary Approach
Edited by José M. Álvarez-Monzoncillo

25 **Consumer Ethnocentrism, Country of Origin and Marketing**
Food Market in Poland
Paweł Bryła and Tomasz Domański

26 **European Consumers in the Digital Era**
Implications of Technology, Media and Culture on Consumer Behavior
Edited by Małgorzata Bartosik-Purgat and Nela Filimon

27 **Artificial Intelligence for Marketing Management**
Edited by Park Thaichon and Sara Quach

28 **Sustainable Marketing and Customer Value**
Edited by Subrata Chattopadhyay, Sundeep Singh Sondhi and Arunava Dalal

For more information about this series, please visit: www.routledge.com/Routledge-Studies-in-Marketing/book-series/RMKT

European Consumers in the Digital Era

Implications of Technology, Media and Culture on Consumer Behavior

Edited by
Małgorzata Bartosik-Purgat
and Nela Filimon

Routledge
Taylor & Francis Group
LONDON AND NEW YORK

First published 2023
by Routledge
4 Park Square, Milton Park, Abingdon, Oxon OX14 4RN

and by Routledge
605 Third Avenue, New York, NY 10158

Routledge is an imprint of the Taylor & Francis Group, an informa business

British Library Cataloguing-in-Publication Data
A catalogue record for this book is available from the British Library

ISBN: 978-1-032-20461-1 (hbk)
ISBN: 978-1-032-20466-6 (pbk)
ISBN: 978-1-003-26368-5 (ebk)

DOI: 10.4324/9781003263685

Typeset in Bembo
by codeMantra

Contents

Figures

Tables

Contributors

Olga Alkanova, PhD, is a Senior Lecturer in the Marketing Department at St. Petersburg State University, Russia.

Małgorzata Bartosik-Purgat, PhD, Habilitation, is Full Professor in Social Sciences at the Poznań University of Economics and Business, Poland. Her research addresses cross-cultural communication and consumer behaviour, acceptance of innovations in the consumers' decisions, and significance of new media in marketing and personal communication.

Joanna Bednarz, PhD, Habilitation, is an Associate Professor at the Faculty of Economics. She is Head of the Department of International Business and a member of the Publishing Council of the University of Gdańsk, Poland.

Karina Bogatyreva, PhD, is an Associate Professor in the Department of Strategic and International Management, Director of the Center for Entrepreneurship, Saint Petersburg State University, Russia.

Nela Filimon, PhD, Serra Húnter, is an Associate Professor in the Department of Business, Commercialization and Market Research area, University of Girona, Spain.

Alberto Frigerio, PhD in Management and Development of Cultural Heritage from IMT – Lucca (Italy), is currently working as Dean of the School of Politics and Law at Almaty Management University, Kazakhstan, where he is also Professor of International Relations.

Francesc Fusté-Forné is a Lecturer and Researcher in the Department of Business, University of Girona, Spain. He is undertaking research on culinary and rural heritages from a marketing and travel perspective.

Margarita Galagan is a PhD candidate in International Relations at Kazakh Ablai Khan University of International Relations and World Languages, Kazakhstan. She is currently working as an Assistant to the Dean of the School of Politics and Law at Almaty Management University, Kazakhstan.

Ksenia Golovacheva is a Senior Lecturer in the Marketing Department at Saint Petersburg State University, Russia

Tomasz Grzegorczyk, PhD, is an Assistant Professor in the Department of International Management at Poznań University of Economics and Business, Poland. He specialises in consumers' acceptance of emerging technologies and behavioural aspects of consumer interaction with artificial intelligence

Michael Hinner, PhD, MA, State University of New York at Stony Brook, is a Professor Emeritus at the TU Bergakademie Freiberg, Germany. His research and publications focus on the impact of culture and communication on human behaviour and interaction in business contexts.

Barbara Jankowska, PhD, Habilitation, is Full Professor in Social Sciences at the Poznań University of Economics and Business, Poland. Her research areas include international business, Industry 4.0, and business clusters. He is the author of research papers in journals such as *International Business Review, European Planning Studies,* and *Journal of Intellectual Capital.*

Jaana Kivivuori, MA, is a Senior Lecturer in Finnish and Communication, focusing on developing students´ competence in interaction and reporting skills in various faculties of Turku University of Applied Sciences, Finland. Kivivuori has been developing materials and approaches to teaching in different projects considering diverse students´ needs.

Agata Linkiewicz, MA, is an Assistant in the Department of International Competitiveness at the Poznań University of Economics and Business, Poland. Her research areas include consumer behaviour, digital tools, and marketing communication.

Ewa Mińska-Struzik, PhD, Habilitation, is an Associate Professor in the Department of International Economics at the Poznań University of Economics and Business, Poland. Her main research area is international trade, with a particular focus on the linkage between exporting activity of a firm and its innovative potential.

Maria Smirnova, PhD, is an Associate Professor, Marketing Department Chair, Head of the Research Center for Strategic Marketing and Innovations, Saint Petersburg State University, Russia.

Monica Tamminen, Master of Science (Economics and Business Administration), Certified Senior Team Coach, is a Senior Lecturer in Service Development at the Turku University of Applied Sciences, Finland, focusing on future development and strategically detecting changes, e.g. in consumer behaviour and advances in technology.

The general circumstances of digital consumer behaviour in Europe

Małgorzata Bartosik-Purgat and Nela Filimon

The period since the turn of the Millenium has been full of rapid changes in people's lives thanks to the development of technology (Bianchi, 2021; Srivastava et al., 2021). Innovations in the Internet, digital tools, and mobile devices have impacted almost all individuals, companies, and other institutions' daily activities (Bianchi, 2021; Chen et al., 2021). The changes in information and communication technologies (ICT) have contributed to changes in personal needs, a system of values, style of living, preferences, final purchasing behaviour, and consumer decisions. Kemp's newest report, *Digital audiences swell, but there may be trouble ahead,* indicates that 60.9% of the global population are now Internet users, 66.9% are mobile device users, and 56.8% use social media (Kemp, 2021). Many European states appear close to the top of the list of countries with the highest Internet usage, e.g. Denmark (99%), the United Kingdom (98%), Sweden (97%), Switzerland (96%), the Netherlands (95.7%), Germany (95%), Spain (93%), Belgium (92%), and Ireland (92%) (Kemp, 2021), whilst many other are above the world average (60.9%), e.g. Austria, France, Poland, Portugal, Italy, Greece, and others (Kemp, 2021). Such a high percentage of the population using the Internet undoubtedly contributes to the development and popularity of various tools available through Internet, e.g. social media, online shops, the instruments of artificial intelligence (such as augmented and virtual reality, the Internet of Things, etc.).

Given this, as can be expected, many European countries rank high in development and innovation rankings. For example, according to the *Global Innovation Index 2020*, as many as seven of the top ten are from Europe (Switzerland, Sweden, Germany, United Kingdom, the Netherlands, Denmark, and Finland) (Dutta et al., 2020). According to the *IMD World Digital Competitiveness Ranking* (which looks at the capacity and readiness of 63 world economies to adopt digital technologies in relation to economic, business, government, and society in general), six European economies made it to the top ten in 2020: Denmark, Sweden, Switzerland, the Netherlands, Norway, and Finland (IMD, 2020).

The COVID-19 pandemic, which led to lockdowns in many world's regions, has had a significant impact on the increasing use of the Internet and

DOI: 10.4324/9781003263685-1

its various tools, which, in turn, has caused the transfer of 'real-life' to the Internet in many European countries. Schools were closed and children participated in distance learning using various communication platforms, such as Zoom, MS Teams, and Google Meets. Many shops (apart from e.g. grocery stores, pharmacies), as well as service and cultural venues (e.g. restaurants, swimming pools, cinemas, theatres), were temporarily closed. People also dealt with administrative matters via the Internet. It is also in purchasing patterns where changes were most acutely seen, especially given the closure of shops and other social-distancing measures. Results from Kemp's newest (2021) report show that nearly 77% of Internet users (aged 16–64) said that they bought something online each month. The Covid-19 pandemic thus accelerated the process of digitalisation of consumers and changed their habits. Even people who have previously used e-commerce sporadically or at all, started to shop online. However, there are still significant differences between generational cohorts of consumers, and the age diversity of consumers is a big challenge for the e-commerce industry (Bianchi, 2021). On the one hand, there is Gen Z, most of whom do not remember the world without the Internet. On the other hand, there is the silver generation (Baby Boomers), for whom the Internet is still a largely undiscovered sphere. The differences are significant not only in terms of digital tools' usage but also in their ways of online decision-making. For example, younger generations usually buy spontaneously, which is dictated by temporary and rapidly changing trends and the strong impact of influencers advertising products. By contrast, older groups of consumers tend to make more thoughtful purchases. Apart from the generational gap, the report produced by the International Telecommunication Union (ITU, 2021) on ICT trends in Europe in the period 2017–2020 reveals the persistence of the gender gap and of the digital divide between urban and rural areas: thus, in 2019, only 80.1% of the women used the Internet against 85.1% of men; likewise, the percentage of rural households with access to the Internet (77.9%) was lower than in the case of urban households (87.9%). The evidence invites governments and telecommunication companies to continue investing in the digital development of the European regions with lower Internet penetration rates. ICT skills also play a role in explaining the behaviour of digital consumers, and ITU (2021, p. 10) reports heterogeneous statistics on the three levels of the ICT skills – basic, standard, and advanced – measured across Europe in the period 2017–2020; thus, in most countries, the levels of basic and standard ICT skills acquired range from 40 to 50% of the Internet users.

All of these circumstances influence the need for changes and adjustments in global value chains (Schmidt et al., 2020; Vadana et al., 2020) and companies that want to be competitive in the market must constantly monitor the domestic and foreign environment in order to be able to change and adapt quickly (Chen et al., 2021; Rossato & Castellani, 2020). Furthermore, retailers should monitor the market and try to keep up-to-date with the latest technological e-commerce solutions (Hagberg et al., 2016). They also have to recognise consumers' needs and the level of acceptance of new technologies before implementing adequate digital devices. For example, using virtual assistants or chatbots instead of messaging with consumers, a virtual window for online shopping, e-store mobile apps, advanced payment methods, etc. The flexibility and agility of companies (both producers and retailers) have been crucial during the COVID-19 pandemic and will continue to be so in the coming years. For many companies, the COVID-19 pandemic has turned out to be a catalyst for digital solutions and contributed to the development of the organisation. Therefore, companies are trying to focus on improving customer experience and developing omnichannel processes (Srivastava et al., 2021; Yuruk-Kayapinar, 2020), and in doing so have changed the way they communicate with consumers as well as the key channels of reaching them. This has translated into the creation of a holistic and consistent experience (Cheng & Guo, 2021), independent of the selected sales channel. It has also led to the development of new types of commerce, such as social commerce, where social media platforms are used for buying and selling activities.

This book concerns consumers and the changes explaining their behaviour in the digital era. The main aims of this book are three-fold and attempt to answer the following questions:

- What are the main distinguishing traits characterising consumer behaviour in different European countries in the 21st century?
- What are the determinants of the changes in consumers' perceptions, needs, and buying decisions in the digital era (taking into account: the development of new ICTs, new media/social media, new marketing activities such as social marketing or mobile marketing, and the impact of the COVID-19 pandemic) and how do they influence consumers' behaviour?
- What are the main patterns of consumption emerging from the increasing adoption and usage of the IoT (e.g. house automation, intelligent voice assistants, etc.) in consumers' everyday life?
- What are the practical implications associated with consumers' decisions in digital times? What should companies know about their actual and potential clients (e.g. the digital tools they use) to be able to adapt products and promotional offers to better meet their needs and expectations?

This book offers a holistic perspective of consumer behaviour in the 21st century in different European countries, taking into account new technologies [including smartphones, autonomous products, augmented reality (AR), the Internet of Things (IoT), Artificial Intelligence (AI), and social media, amongst others], cultural and generational changes, and the COVID-19 pandemic. The first part of this book (Chapters 1–4) offers a more general and theoretical approach, while the second part, a more empirical one, builds on the topics from the first part and presents consumer behaviour in selected European countries. The chapters from the second part (Chapters 5–10) cover almost all geographical regions in Europe, e.g. West – Germany; South – Spain and Italy; North – Finland; Central – Poland; and East – Russia. These countries vary in terms of the degree of socio-economic development, culture, and acceptance of ICT. However, they all represent significant marketplaces for the development of new forms of selling and consuming goods.

The contributing authors applied diverse research methods, and worked both with primary and secondary data, in order to achieve the goals of particular parts of this book, e.g. literature analyses using the SALSA method (*Search, Appraisal, Synthesis, and Analysis*), narrative description of literature, online surveys, qualitative semi-structured interviews, multivariate quantitative methods, and others. Furthermore, each chapter outlines the general socio-cultural and generational background in the presented countries. Several authors also underline the influence of the COVID-19 pandemic on online consumer behaviour. Lastly, the above-mentioned changes to consumer needs, attitudes, preferences, and decisions have consequences for both producers and retailers. Thus, in each of the chapters in Part 2, the authors highlight the business implications of their analyses, as well as indicate potential future trends and patterns.

As mentioned earlier, the COVID-19 pandemic, which reached Europe in the first months of 2020, has accelerated digitalisation and in doing so completely changed the image of the consumers, consumer behaviours, and trade. However, consumer purchasing patterns started changing as far back as the 1990s, which was a period of rapid development of the Internet and the beginning of the emergence of online stores all around the world (e.g. Amazon, e-bay, Rakuten, Allegro, Mercado Libre, Alibaba, and others). This led to the appearance of new models of consumer behaviour (e-consumer, online shopping), processes, and effects of this behaviour, e.g. ROPO effect (*Research Online, Purchase Offline*) and reverse ROPO (*Research Offline, Purchase Online*). These general issues related to changes in e-consumer behaviour are presented in the first chapter of this book.

Next, the development of ICT in form of social media changed methods of communication between producers/retailers and final buyers. Thanks to new digital tools, one-way communication has been turned into two-way communication (Bartosik-Purgat, 2019) and nowadays consumers actively participate in the communication process with producers, i.e., they are no longer merely passive recipients of information, but can instead react at any time and share their experiences about the usage of products with producers (and, indeed, other consumers). Besides this, modern consumers are active and eager to participate in the production process of goods. Many of them have become prosumers (i.e., *pro*ducers and con*sumers*) who contribute to the development of products. Such behaviour is connected with the desire for personalisation and having nonstandard products. These three phenomena – prosumerism, co-creation, and personalisation – are the focus of Chapter 2.

The purpose of Chapter 3 is to identify the factors which determine the consumer acceptance of those technologies. Consumer behaviour in the digital century is dependent on the development of technological innovations and their acceptance by consumers. The most significant innovations that influence consumers' decisions are, among others, AI, IoT, and AR. However, they evoke diverse attitudes (both positive and negative) among consumers that certainly affect their behaviour.

The determinants and trends presented above have affected the development of e-commerce, which is discussed in Chapter 4. The authors describe the facilitators which led to the development and rapid growth of e-commerce, in particular ICT (e.g. social media, mobile devices). In this chapter, the authors present the development and implementation of new technological solutions within a broader context of particular phases of the online purchasing process (e.g. the determinants impacting online shopping, the devices used in this process, the categories of products bought online, methods of payments and delivery, etc.). In addition, the chapters take into account the impact of the COVID-19 pandemic on the increase in online purchases, as well the importance of demographic factors related to age and gender in understanding online consumer behaviour.

In the second part of this book, the authors develop the issues concerning the acceptance and usage of ICT in consumer behaviour, in particular, of European countries. Some of the chapters (e.g. Chapters 5, 6, and 7) also present a general situation concerning the level of digilatisation in the presented countries. Elsewhere, other authors present specific online tools and their influence on consumer decisions, e.g. social media (Chapters 6 and 8), mobile devices (Chapter 8), and IoT, with a special focus on the usage of virtual voice assistants (VVA), devices used to employ them, activities performed with VVA, and the digital consumption patterns of the VVA users (Chapter 10). In turn, the authors of Chapter 9 focus on consumer competencies regarding two types of digital information: product information and personal data. These include posts, comments, and brand reviews generated by online consumers.

In the final chapter of this book, the authors attempt to present predictions and forecasts for the future impact of ICTs on European consumer behaviour, paying particular attention to communication between producers, retailers, and consumers; the adoption of IoT by consumers; the impact of the IoT on the interaction between consumers and brands; gathering information about consumers and the needs for offer personalisation; eco-consumers and green marketing; the development of payments and delivery methods in e-commerce; and cross-border e-commerce and international e-consumers, among others.

References

Bartosik-Purgat, M. (2019). *New media in the marketing communication of enterprises in the international market*. WN PWN Publishers.

Bianchi, C. (2021). Exploring how internet services can enhance elderly well-being. *Journal of Services Marketing*, Vol. ahead-of-print No. ahead-of-print. https://doi.org/10.1108/JSM-05-2020-0177.

Chen, Y., Visnjic, I., Parida, V., & Zhang, Z. (2021). On the road to digital servitization – The (dis)continuous interplay between business model and digital technology. *International Journal of Operations & Production Management, 41*(5), 694–722. https://doi.org/10.1108/IJOPM-08-2020-0544.

Cheng, V.T.P., & Guo, R. (2021). The impact of consumers' attitudes towards technology on the acceptance of hotel technology-based innovation. *Journal of Hospitality and Tourism Technology*, Vol. ahead-of-print No. ahead-of-print. https://doi.org/10.1108/JHTT-06-2020-0145.

Dutta, S., Lanvin, B., & Wunsch-Vincent, S. (eds.) (2020). *Global innovation index 2020: Who will finance innovation?* Cornell University, INSEAD, and WIPO.

Hagberg, J., Sundstrom, M., & Egels-Zandén, N. (2016). The digitalization of retailing: an exploratory framework. *International Journal of Retail & Distribution Management, 44*(7), 694–712. https://doi.org/10.1108/IJRDM-09-2015-0140.

IMD. (2020). *World digital competitiveness ranking.* https://www.imd.org/centers/world-competitiveness-center/rankings/world-digital-competitiveness/.

ITU. (2021). *Digital trends in Europe 2021. ICT trends and developments in Europe, 2017–2020.* ITU Publications. https://www.itu.int/en/ITU-D/Regional-Presence/Europe/Documents/Publications/Digital-Trends_Europe-E.pdf

Kemp, S. (2021, July 21). *Digital audiences swell, but there may be trouble ahead.* https://wearesocial.com/blog/2021/07/digital-audiences-swell-but-there-may-be-trouble-ahead.

Rossato, C., & Castellani, P. (2020). The contribution of digitalisation to business longevity from a competitiveness perspective. *The TQM Journal, 32*(4), 617–645. https://doi.org/10.1108/TQM-02-2020-0032.

Schmidt, M.-C., Veile, J.W., Müller, J.M., & Voigt, K.-I. (2020). Ecosystems 4.0: Redesigning global value chains. *The International Journal of Logistics Management*, Vol. ahead-of-print No. ahead-of-print. https://doi.org/10.1108/IJLM-03-2020-0145.

Srivastava, V., Kishore, S., & Dhingra, D. (2021). Technology and the future of customer experience. In S. Popli & B. Rishi (Eds.), *Crafting customer experience strategy* (pp. 91–116). Emerald Publishing Limited. https://doi.org/10.1108/978-1-83909-710-220211006.

Vadana, I.-I., Torkkeli, L., Kuivalainen, O., & Saarenketo, S. (2020). Digitalization of companies in international entrepreneurship and marketing. *International Marketing Review, 37*(3), 471–492. https://doi.org/10.1108/IMR-04-2018-0129.

Yuruk-Kayapinar, P. (2020). Digital consumer behavior in an omnichannel world. In T. Dirsehan (Ed.), *Managing customer experiences in an omnichannel world: Melody of online and offline environments in the customer journey* (pp. 55–73). Emerald Publishing Limited. https://doi.org/10.1108/978-1-80043-388-520201007.

Part I

Trends in consumer behaviour in digital centuries

1 Changes in consumer behaviour in the digital age

Agata Linkiewicz and Małgorzata Bartosik-Purgat

Introduction

Observing the changes in society taking place around the world and their impact on the lifestyles and shopping habits of consumers, it is difficult to resist the impression that people buy differently now than in the latter decades of the 20th century. Consumers' attitudes are shaped by many factors: political, economic, socio-cultural, and technological (Adam & Dzang Alhassan, 2021; Luna & Forquer Gupta, 2001). The latter factors are also related to the role of the media and access to the Internet, which contribute to shaping social attitudes and creating a person's vision of the world. One significant determinant impacting lifestyles, including consumer behaviour, is the technological revolution, which has led to the interpenetration of the virtual and real worlds. This is an era of changes caused by the development of computerisation and modern technologies which, in turn, lead to digital inclusion (Adam & Dzang Alhassan, 2021). This phenomenon can be characterised by rapid technological progress, widespread digitalisation, and its impact on all areas of life. Due to the changes brought about by the digital revolution, a new social formation has emerged, known as the information society, which includes digital consumers. For members of such a society, knowledge (including consumer knowledge) is a strategic resource, with the collection, processing, creation, and distribution of information now essential for consumers (Castells, 1999). Thanks to rapid technological development, it is possible to collect copious amounts of information using more and more advanced tools. As a consequence, information can be transmitted not only directly but also through a host of modern communication tools which, in turn, necessitate consumers to modify their behaviour, including their decision-making processes.

The use of the Internet and its tools may differ among consumers as far as their proficiency, frequency, attitude, and expectations are concerned, with the key variable being age. People of similar age have common experiences and memories, which transfer into a shared perspective, approach to work, life, and decision-making process (McCrindle, 2014). They also differ in terms of attitudes towards, and use of new technologies. The youngest generations are usually the most positive about using Internet resources, mobile

DOI: 10.4324/9781003263685-3

devices, applications, and new e-commerce solutions. Younger generations are also more eager to buy online shops and use the Internet to search for information about products (Dorie & Loranger, 2020; Hall, 2017; Helal et al., 2018). Many older consumers still prefer to buy in stationary stores and use the Internet to obtain information about products. However, because of the restrictions and lockdowns concerning, e.g. the closing of many stationary shops, the Covid-19 pandemic has caused many older consumers to use the Internet and mobile devices more.

The following chapter offers a theoretical analysis on the subject of consumer and consumer behaviour in the digital era (21st century). As such, it attempts to focus on the interdisciplinary nature of the concept of the consumer as well as changing features in consumers' decision-making processes, with specific regard to the development of information technology.

The authors use a narrative description method to report on a literature review of primarily secondary sources (mainly, important scientific publications such as papers, monographs, web sources) available on different scientific databases such as Emerald, Elsevier, and Taylor and Francis. The main keywords used to search the most suitable sources were "consumer", "consumer behaviour", "consumer behaviour process", "digital consumer", "e-consumer", "ROPO effect", and "ZMOT". The literature study is also supported by the analysis of empirical data and data from reports and studies of various institutions available in the aforementioned databases. This knowledge about changes in consumer behaviour as a result of the development of the Internet and communication and information technologies (ICT) is then systematised.

The chapter is structured as follows: first, the traditional versus "digital" processes of consumer behaviour are presented, second, the specifics of Zero Moment of Truth (ZMOT), Research Online, Purchase Offline (ROPO), and Research Offline, Purchase Online (Reverse ROPO) effects are described, and, finally, the authors present the business implications of the results and predictions for future trends.

Consumers and consumer behaviour: traditional and new aspects

The concept of the consumer has been investigated by researchers in a wide range of academic fields, e.g. economics, psychology, sociology, and anthropology (MacInnis & Folkes, 2010), although it should be noted that each of these fields focuses on different features of the term. For example, biologists and anthropologists claim that individual behaviour is influenced by the survival of the individuals, i.e. being a consumer is in part about survival in one's surroundings (Neal et al., 2006). Elsewhere, motivation is a crucial factor for psychologists as it triggers an individual to take action. Such researchers look for an explanation of the connection between the influence of the state of the person on behaviour (Mowen, 2000). By contrast, sociologists focus on the manner of meeting the needs of consumers and the societal impact on the behaviour of an individual. In economic papers, a consumer is understood as a person focused on their decisions regarding the maximum satisfaction of their consumer needs, i.e. maximisation of utility (from an economic point of view, maximum utility proves rational consumer decisions) (Bartosik-Purgat, 2011).

The term "consumer" very often encompasses the decision-maker, the buyer, and the ultimate user – and these may not necessarily be the same person. However, many researchers underline the importance of differentiating between such terms as a buyer, recipient, customer, or payer (Linkiewicz & Bartosik-Purgat, 2017). For example, Bon and Pras (1984) identify differences between a buyer, consumer, and payer. According to them, an individual who uses a product or service is a consumer, and a buyer buys a product or service, while a payer reimburses the expenses. The consumer is not required to buy the product personally and even though an individual is a buyer, they may not be the consumer of the product or service. Examples of such individuals are children that do not cover the costs of the products that they consume and their parents who purchase products or services to be consumed by their offspring. Using the terms "consumer" and "customer" interchangeably is incorrect according to Aldridge (2005). The needs of the consumer are often created by the surroundings and their satisfaction also depends on external factors that impact the decisions made by the consumer, while the customer's needs are chosen by the customer himself. Thus, the concept of a consumer is broader than that of a buyer who acquires goods via monetary exchange. The consumer performs additional activities such as making decisions, purchasing a good or service, and disposing of it (MacInnis & Folkes, 2010). These issues may be developed by the description of the broader element which is consumer behaviour.

Initially, some scholars used the term consumer behaviour to emphasise the relationship between "consumers and producers at the time of purchase" (Solomon, 2018, p. 29). However, exploratory economic models do not take into account non-economic factors and the issues connected with the decision-making process (MacInnis & Folkes, 2010). Thus, some researchers developed integrated models of consumer behaviour that take into account the process itself as well as socio-psychological and cultural factors. Such consumer behaviour models were researched, among others, by Andreasen (1965), Nicosia (1966), Howard and Sheth (1969), as well as Engel et al. (1978). Most of the consumer behaviour models comprise of various stages in which an individual makes a selection of the most suitable product or service, then buys, uses, and, in the end, disposes of it. Consumption is one of the stages of the process (Bartosik-Purgat, 2011) and consumer decision-making is one of the elements that determine consumer behaviour, which is why it is analysed by many researchers (Linkiewicz & Bartosik-Purgat, 2017).

Nicosia (1966) identified the fundamental areas of consumer behaviour as mass communication, exploration and choice, consumption, and the relationship between them. Andreasen (1965) emphasised the importance of consumers receiving information from many sources, which is then filtered and may influence different stages of consumer behaviour. According to this idea, consumer choices are impacted by reference groups as well as interactions between consumers (Zalega, 2012). Next, the model created by Howard and Sheth (1969) includes a perceptual conception of receiving and processing information that is indispensable for an individual to make a final decision about a purchase. Similarly, in the model developed by Engel et al. (1978), it is the central control unit that receives advertising stimuli and indicates and solves problems. The authors also underlined the significance of the environment in determining the behaviour of the consumer.

Changes in a consumer's environment also affect their behaviour. Some such factors are the development of the Internet and information and communication technologies (ICTs), especially with regard to searching for information about products, places, and services, as well as the methods of purchase transactions (see, e.g. Vinerean et al., 2013). The possibilities that arise according to the above changes may include, e.g. the ability to store large amounts of information at no charge, the ability to inexpensively search for, organise, and disseminate information; interactivity and on-demand information sharing; direct peer-to-peer communication with other consumers; the ability to transact online; access to product offerings from around the world; and relatively low operating costs for those wishing to sell their products via the Internet (Vinerean et al., 2013).

Modern consumers make decisions in an environment dominated by new technologies, online tools (e.g. social media) that significantly influence their behaviour (Sreejesh et al., 2020). The second and third decade of the 21st century has been characterised by consumers that are spending more time online (Kemp, 2021; Skiera et al., 2015) and consumers are increasingly skilled in using modern tools to communicate and obtain information. Online communication channels (e-mail, consumer reviews, social networking sites, Internet forums, blogs, and microblogs) have been added to the traditional manners of communication, i.e. a direct conversation with the manufacturer's representatives, a salesperson, or users of the product (Lovett et al., 2013; Vithayathil et al., 2020). This is influenced not only by more permanent access to the Internet but also by the development of mobile devices that allow communication at almost any time, while their users, through the Internet, have constant access to current information (Borrero et al., 2014; Hou & Elliott, 2021; Wang et al., 2021). Mobile applications allow consumers to search for information, products, and services at a time and place convenient for them. Such use of the Internet and mobile devices causes changes in the needs and expectations of consumers towards producers and they now expect omnichannel entities with seamless integration between all the channels – offline, online, and mobile. It is also worth mentioning the increasing numbers of consumers that opt to use mobile phones to make purchases (Malter et al., 2020). Next, not only can social media provide full product information, but such data can be obtained very easily and at negligible cost. What is more, such information is usually seen to be trustworthy, because it is delivered not only by the producer but also by other consumers (Geng et al., 2021; Vithayathil et al., 2020). Widespread access to social media and e-commerce platforms makes such information available to a group of potential consumers that are searching for reviews that are not professionally written but rather shared by other Internet users (Moran et al., 2014). Furthermore, a shopping experience using e-commerce platforms is smooth, can provide a considerable amount of product data, and is more and more secure. These factors allow consumers to more quickly evaluate alternatives before making the final decision (Dijesh et al., 2020; Grewal et al., 2017).

In light of the abovementioned circumstances, terms such as "digital consumer" and "digital consumer behaviour" have appeared (e.g. Malchenko et al., 2020; Yuruk-Kayapinar, 2020). "Digital consumer" is a term that could be defined in a broad sense as a consumer using the Internet to search for information on products or services and afterwards making the purchase decision, often online, as well as using the content that is available online. In the more narrow sense, "digital consumer" refers to consumers using mobile devices. Their preferences change quickly as they are conditioned by their frequent use of technology. Furthermore, they are not satisfied with being a passive recipient of information but rather expect interaction, hence their frequent use of social media (Tkaczyk, 2016).

ZMOT, ROPO, and reverse ROPO effect – changes in the consumer decision process

The rapid development of technology and its increasing availability to the consumer has prompted changes in the characteristics of today's consumers. As a consequence, the existing models of consumer behaviour needed to be reassessed as they did not take into consideration the changes in consumer needs or competencies, or the new, online contexts (Linkiewicz & Bartosik-Purgat, 2017).

The Engel-Kollat-Blackwell (EKB) model is one of the traditional, integrated models of consumer behaviour established by Engel, Kollat, and Blackwell in the second half of the 20th century (Engel et al., 1978). According to the researchers, the purchase of a product or a service is one of the stages of the decision-making process. In order to have insight into the whole process from start to finish, it is important to analyse what happens before and after the purchase (Engel et al., 1978). Especially taking into consideration the importance of examining the environment that impacts the purchase behaviour of an individual.

Engel et al. (1978) identified five stages in consumer behaviour, including pre- and post-purchase actions. Problem recognition is the first stage of this process. An internal stimuli (e.g. thirst or hunger) or external stimuli (e.g. inspiration caused by observation of others) generate a need in an individual.

In the next phase, one searches for information on how to satisfy this need. First, the individual searches for a solution using their knowledge. If this turns out to be insufficient, they turn to external sources of information: asking for advice among their immediate circle of family, friends, and acquaintances. Afterwards, if their search is unsuccessful, the consumer expands their search to such sources of information as commercial (e.g. advertising), public (e.g. mass media), and experimental (personal testing of goods) (Kotler & Keller, 2012).

Once a consumer has all the information they have managed to gather, the options assessment stage begins (Engel et al., 1978) in which consumers evaluate the advantages and disadvantages from the perspective of their needs. The final buying decision is often made when visiting a stationary shop, where the consumer can compare all the available offers at once, which may cause them to change their mind on the spot, despite the previously conducted verification of options. Making a purchase decision is the fourth stage of the EKB model (Linkiewicz & Bartosik-Purgat, 2017). The last stage of the model focuses on consumer behaviour after the purchase, where, regardless of a positive or negative opinion, the consumer can share their views with a circle of friends (Engel et al., 1978; Kotler & Keller, 2012).

Each stage of the traditional consumer behaviour process is based predominantly on face-to-face communication. In the first phase, the external stimuli are usually created by the observation of the closest family and friends. The search for information also focuses on people that an individual can consult for opinion (family, friends, colleagues) or for more specific information (salesperson is the principal information source). The final decision is usually made in a stationary shop (Kotler & Keller, 2012). Similarly, the final opinion after using the product or service is usually shared with the consumer's inner circle.

In the second decade of the 21st century, while studying the consumer decision-making process, experts from Procter & Gamble (Lecinski, 2011), identified the mental marketing moment when an individual visits a stationary store. This is the moment where a person compares the available offers, taking into consideration the previously gathered information to make the final decision. They named it the *First Moment of Truth* (FMOT) (Figure 1.1). In the EKB model, this is the fourth stage of the decision-making process. Following this research, the *Second Moment of Truth* (SMOT) originates when the

Figure 1.1 Three-step marketing model by Procter & Gamble

consumer uses the product to form a positive or negative opinion (Kreutzer & Land, 2014; Lecinski, 2011). This phase corresponds to the fifth stage of the EKB model (Linkiewicz & Bartosik-Purgat, 2017).

Further analysis of the decision-making process and consumer behaviour models was necessitated by the development of the Internet, social media, and various new tools (Linkiewicz & Bartosik-Purgat, 2017). The emergence of desktop computers and the possibility of Internet access at home triggered significant changes in the information search which is a crucial part of many consumer behaviour models. Internet access at home allows for researching a huge amount of sources of information whenever it suits the consumer (Grunert & Ramus, 2005), i.e. knowledge of a product or service specifications are not limited to manufacturer's representatives or salespeople. Such a situation has only expedited the implementation of multichannel strategies of companies, e.g. adding Internet stores and other online services to serve potential consumers (Zarei et al., 2019).

Such knowledge along with the ability to quickly compare prices, product variants, and brands is causing consumers to become increasingly interested in manufacturers' offerings (Linkiewicz & Bartosik-Purgat, 2017). They see more and more value in online information sources, which, in turn, has led to the rapid development of e-commerce and many other company activities (e.g. social media profiles, online advertising) and mobile applications (Jamil & Qayyum, 2021; Li et al., 2020). In turn, it also encourages the consumers to write reviews and share their feelings regarding their purchases (Wang et al., 2019).

The development of social media and mobile technologies has created new modes of interaction for consumers (Wang et al., 2021). They now have access to a wide variety of social media, while mobile devices facilitate access to these platforms from any place (Pan et al., 2020). Consumers are allowed to share their opinions and assessments of products or services without any constraints, which is why both social media and mobile technology have become significant channels of information (Ju et al., 2021; Zhang et al., 2017). These changes need to be taken into account when analysing the next stage in the transformation of the consumer decision-making model.

Social media created a breakthrough as far as the World Wide Web is concerned. At first, websites were mostly used by businesses (e-commerce) and institutions. Then forums and personal websites became available. However, the effortlessness offered by social media is unprecedented. Every person that has the desire to share their opinion with their peers can do it without much effort (Jamil & Qayyum, 2021) and, connected to this, the number of people who can access a review about a given product is significantly growing (Tang & Wu, 2021) – a review, comment, or opinion posted online is available to any user searching for information and, as a consequence, it can influence a consumer's decision (Cheung et al., 2008; Choi et al., 2017). The moment of distribution of an opinion about goods or services on the Internet employing social media has been defined as the *Third Moment of Truth* (TMOT) (Ashby et al., 2002) (Figure 1.2).

As the consumer can spend more time researching various options to satisfy their needs, a purchase decision is often made before the consumer enters the store, online or offline. This moment has been defined as the *Zero Moment Of Truth* (ZMOT) by Google experts (Figure 1.2), thus expanding the decision-making process proposed by Procter & Gamble (Lecinski, 2011). Most significantly, this model shifts the moment of the purchase decision in comparison to the EKB model, where the purchase decision was dependent on the store visit (i.e. the FMOT). The ZMOT model suggests that because of Internet access, in general, and the use of social media, in particular, the initial purchase decision is already made while checking online recommendations, before the actual act of buying the product or service.

In addition to this, the visibility of the brand on the web certainly influences a consumer's purchasing decision. Another important step to "winning" a ZMOT is therefore the fostering of excellent communication with the client (potential buyer). Moreover, companies should cultivate positive reviews that will attract buyers, as well as a transparent website that will facilitate decision-making and encourage repeat visits to the website. As Bilgihan et al. (2016) claim, skillfully created content is simply a response to what the client is looking for.

As mentioned above, the World Wide Web allows people to access huge amounts of information, and find significantly more alternatives to a particular product or service before making the final decisions. Thus, consumers now search for more information online than offline (Jamil & Qayyum, 2021; Kulviwat et al., 2004) as it allows the consumer to conduct a comprehensive analysis of the current offers on the market before a purchase decision. These developments have led to the emergence of the ROPO (*Research Online, Purchase Offline*) effect (Figure 1.3), which accentuates the significance

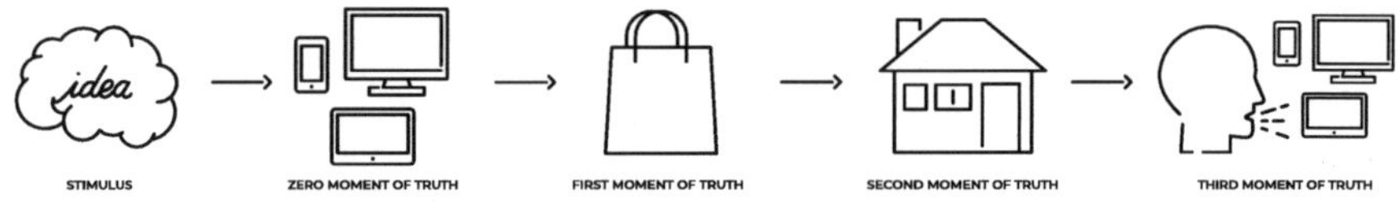

Figure 1.2 ZMOT – a purchase decision-making model

Figure 1.3 ROPO effect

of online sources of information. The ROPO effect recognises that despite seeking information about a product or service online, a consumer will still often decide to visit a stationary store to buy a product or service (Heinrich & Thalmair, 2013).

In other words, when consumers need to make a choice, they can easily use the online sources whenever and wherever they prefer (webrooming). They do not need to turn to their family, friends, or a salesperson (as in the traditional purchasing decision model) for information before making the final purchase. Furthermore, in contrast to Internet communication, face-to-face communication is time and place sensitive. Focusing on online research means that consumers can experience the three stages of the EKB model without any offline interaction, such as visiting a store or asking people in their closest circle about their opinions. The results of the research conducted by Gemius and published in their "E-commerce in Poland 2020" report indicate that the ROPO effect is particularly pronounced for food products (48% of respondents underlined this way of buying), construction, and decorating materials (48%), furniture and interior design (46%), footwear (46%) (Gemius, 2020). For example, shoes can be very pretty in a photo on an online store but be uncomfortable to wear. Footwear manufacturers are already trying to develop helpful online tools to address this matter (e.g. phone applications that allow you to take a scan of the foot before making a purchase). However, for many customers, there is no substitute for trying on shoes in the store as it is less time-consuming than ordering shoes online and sending them back in the case of the wrong size.

The ROPO effect does not have to mean losses for online stores, but it does significantly shape sales. The analysis of the ROPO effect allows marketers to reach a group of valuable customers who are at the stage of comparing offers and just before making a purchase decision. Many stores maintain a balance between offline and online sales and thus do not feel the negative effects of ROPO.

The opposite phenomenon to ROPO is known as a *reverse* ROPO effect (*Research Offline, Purchase Online*) (Figure 1.4). This is when a consumer visits stores to look for a product (information about it) but the final purchase is made online. Such a phenomenon is also defined as showrooming (Verhoef

Figure 1.4 Reverse ROPO effect

et al., 2015). For example, they try on clothes, check the capabilities and parameters of a smartphone, experience the softness of an armchair, or smell perfumes in a stationary shop but they finalise the transaction online. One of the advantages of *reverse* ROPO is the opportunity to see, feel, smell, touch, and try the item, and check if it meets all the needs of an individual. The decision to buy the goods online may stem from a lower price offered online, as well as the possibility of using websites that allow price comparison (Fedorko et al., 2021). In this case, the two stages of the decision-making process – the information search and the evaluation of available options – are experienced without the need to use modern technology. Whilst this process displays a similarity to traditional models of consumer behaviour, the final purchase is made online, which enhances the importance of e-commerce.

Consumers often combine both offline and online shopping, taking into consideration the fact of which is more suitable for them on a case-by-case basis. Online shopping prevails when speed and wider choice are of utmost importance, while offline shopping is the better option in situations where personal service and the opportunity to try the item are crucial (Fedorko et al., 2021). What is more, thanks to mobile devices with Internet access, it is possible to visit a bricks-and-mortar store to see the product in reality while at the same time researching the product online (Rapp et al., 2015). For example, 82% of users of mobile phones search for information on the item they plan to buy while at the store and 45% read online reviews (Loupiac & Goudey, 2019).

One consequence of technological development and new information tools is a change in the moment of making a purchase decision. A visit to a stationary store does not represent the final purchase decision, but rather it is the moment when a consumer gathers enough information about a product to make a final decision. The manner of gathering the information can combine online sources (e.g. ROPO effect, ZMOT) as well as offline (e.g. *reverse* ROPO effect). It should be mentioned that these assumptions may not apply to all consumer segments. The degree of use of online resources varies according to a person's aptitude for using the Internet, social media, and search engines, including very busy people, young people, and people who spend a lot of time in front of the computer.

Conclusions, business implications, and predictions for future

The analysis conducted for this chapter has shown the development of consumers and consumer behaviour in light of substantial ICT advances. Many circumstances, such as the increasingly accessible Internet and the growth of Internet users (Kemp, 2021), generational differences and these generation's attitudes towards new technologies, the Covid-19 pandemic, etc., have meant that the average world consumer has become an e-consumer.

Analysing the changes in consumer behaviour, it should be pointed out that because of increasing access to the Internet many consumers now make purchases in online shops and search for information about products from online sources. This does not mean that they do not visit stationary shops anymore, but it does mean that the process of making purchasing decisions has changed. This issue was developed in the chapter through the description of ROPO and the subsequent ROPO effect (Kowalczuk, 2018). The particular modes of buying decisions are clearly associated with certain categories of products. As a result, producers and retailers should identify the ways of purchasing that consumers use for the particular type of products and should then implement marketing strategies and instruments to encourage consumers to buy their products online and in their shops.

With regard to the ROPO effect, it is worth emphasising that it is very difficult (from the seller's point of view) to precisely and unambiguously indicate which Internet user purchases in a stationary store. However, it is very important to be aware of the existence of the ROPO effect and the reverse ROPO. Data on consumer behaviour available on databases should be analysed and appropriate decisions should be made on this basis. In the case of the ROPO effect among purchasers of certain products, it is worth trying to convince them to buy online. The availability of the product on the Internet in places where the consumer looks for it plays a very important role here. In addition, the product card is also important, as it should convey all the important benefits of the product and satisfy the consumer's curiosity in such a way that they do not feel the need to go to a stationary shop. Online retailers can use rich content, including, for example, extensive product descriptions presented in a simple and friendly way (e.g. infographics, tables), and attractive photos, videos, or graphics presenting the product from every angle and how it can be used. In addition, to build the company or brand's image, other tools are available, such as: providing advice on the use of the product, answering questions, posting other users' opinions about products they have purchased, the use of multiple communication channels, presence on portals used by potential buyers, and advertising, reminders about visiting the website or an abandoned cart and many others.

In the case of the reverse ROPO effect, the key issue is to offer products at attractive prices in online stores. Research conducted by Gemius (2020) shows that the main advantage of online stores is competitive prices, which attract people who first look for products in stationary stores. Therefore, it is worth following the offline competition's prices and modifying the price offer in the online store on an ongoing basis. Promotions and sales in online stores can also be added to the marketing mix.

Second, the generational changes, the attitudes of young consumers towards usage of digital and mobile devices, and finally their e-purchasing behaviour will continue to develop (Verma et al., 2021). Gen Z is becoming a very important consumer segment for retailers and their needs differ from the older purchasers for which companies previously modelled their activities (Calvo-Porral & Pesqueira-Sanchez, 2020; Lissitsa & Laor, 2021). Both producers and retailers should research Gen Z's needs and preferences and try to adapt their offers and services accordingly. These needs will probably develop towards the usage of the newest technologies at each step of the consumer behaviour process (from searching information about products, through online shopping, and using digital methods of payment). However, it is not only the youngest consumers that have positive attitudes towards becoming e-consumers; the older generational cohorts (from Gen Y to X) are also trying to follow technological novelties in e-commerce and use them in practice (Lissitsa & Laor, 2021). Thus, online retailers should follow new trends within each consumer segment and use the devices expected by potential buyers.

Third, the Covid-19 pandemic has contributed to the even greater use of online tools, not only in e-commerce but also in other spheres of life, e.g. e-learning, e-communication, e-working (Aissaoui, 2021; El Refae et al., 2021). The new modes of living, working, and shopping are likely to continue to some extent after the coronavirus pandemic has lessened somewhat. This is because many people found out and learned how to use digital technologies to facilitate the performance of many daily activities and tasks, as well as save time and costs associated with moving to and from work, school, stationary stores, etc. (Lang, Dolan et al., 2021). Many people, even those previously sceptical about using new technologies, cannot imagine their lives without these technologies. As a result, ICT infrastructure improvements should be implemented and continuously upgraded by businesses that want to be up to date with their offer and the needs of buyers.

The issue of consumer behaviour and predictions about it for the future are extremely complex and difficult to present in one chapter. This is due to a number of different factors related to various spheres of people's lives, including economic, social, and technological. The elements outlined above can certainly increase online shopping and the growth of e-commerce in total commerce. Moreover, technological progress may lead to products being increasingly modified and created by the ultimate buyers (Eckhardt et al., 2019; Ritzer & Jurgenson, 2010). The conduit through which this happens and will still develop is the Internet and social media (Alhashem et al., 2021; Chung et al., 2020).

Consumers not only buy products but also experience the specific emotions that the brand evokes in them. In the case of online trading, this role will be increasingly taken over by a virtual adviser, i.e. a chatbot or virtual assistant based on artificial intelligence (AI) that conducts a conversation with the user in their native language (Hsieh & Lee, 2021; Lei et al., 2021). Such a virtual adviser can check the price and availability of the product or the date of order fulfillment (Jiménez-Barreto et al., 2021; Lei et al., 2021). The implementation of chatbots is one of the elements of an omnichannel strategy, which consists of combining online and offline communication channels (Lei et al., 2021). However, companies need to be vigilant because the inevitable surfeit of modernity may cause a return of past habits and a longing for more traditional shopping experiences (Lao et al., 2021). Especially when consumers are likely to want to demonstrate independence from the mainstream of mass culture and emphasise their originality and individualism.

Next, consumers are likely to pay more and more attention to a healthy lifestyle, organic food, natural products, and friendly places (Chung et al., 2020; Matharu et al., 2020). The COVID-19 epidemic has made consumers even more likely to choose ecological food products and the health-promoting trend influences shopping choices. However, shopping for bio and eco products is not the only reason. Adopting a pro-ecological or ethical attitude is possible throughout the whole purchasing process (Onel & Mukherjee, 2016). Consumers' awareness of the importance of ecology and care for the natural environment is significantly increasing and is especially noticeable among young buyers. Conscious consumers choose ecological goods such as ecological cars, products made from ecologically-friendly substances, and even houses (Onel & Mukherjee, 2016). Producers have also begun to pay more attention to avoiding overproduction, and the produced goods have become more ecological. This awareness and consumer behaviour change have contributed to the rapid development of sharing economy activities (Lang, Kemper et al., 2021; Matharu et al., 2020), which in part has been possible thanks to the spread of ICTs. The sharing economy concerns connecting people through online platforms and applications, enabling them to provide services or share assets, resources, time, skills, or capital without transferring ownership rights. It is one of the key manifestations of universal digitalisation and is an area for increasing prosumer activity among average consumers, i.e., almost every consumer can become a producer by using widely available online platforms (Eckhardt et al., 2019; Lang, Kemper et al., 2021; Matharu et al., 2020).

In conclusion, it should be underlined that the development of new technologies, especially the Internet and ICTs, will play a significant role in the behaviour of consumers. It shapes and will continue to shape new modes of purchasing decisions and other activities, as well as people's attitudes (e.g. eco-awareness, pro-sumerism, and others) in the future.

Bibliography

Adam, I.O., & Dzang Alhassan, M. (2021). Bridging the global digital divide through digital inclusion: The role of ICT access and ICT use. *Transforming Government: People, Process and Policy*, Vol. ahead-of-print No. ahead-of-print. https://doi.org/10.1108/TG-06-2020-0114.

Aissaoui, N. (2021). The digital divide: A literature review and some directions for future research in light of COVID-19. *Global Knowledge, Memory and Communication*, Vol. ahead-of-print No. ahead-of-print. https://doi.org/10.1108/GKMC-06-2020-0075.

Aldrigde, A. (2005). *Consumption*. Polity.

Alhashem, M., Moraes, C., & Szmigin, I.T. (2021). Use and social value in peer-to-peer prosumption communities. *European Journal of Marketing, 55*(1), 193–218. https://doi.org/10.1108/EJM-03-2019-0235.

Andreasen, A.R. (1965). Attitudes and customer behavior: A decision model. In L.E. Preston (ed.), *New research in marketing* (pp. 1–16). University of California, Institute of Business and Economic Research.

Ashby, M.D., Miles, S.A., & Heidrick and Struggles. (2002). *Leaders talk leadership: Top executives speak their minds*. Oxford University Press.

Bartosik-Purgat, M. (2011). *Kulturowe uwarunkowania zachowań konsumentów na przykładzie młodych Europejczyków*. Wydawnictwo Uniwersytetu Ekonomicznego.

Bilgihan, A., Kandampully, J., & Zhang, T.(C). (2016). Towards a unified customer experience in online shopping environments: Antecedents and outcomes. *International Journal of Quality and Service Sciences, 8*(1), 102–119. https://doi.org/10.1108/IJQSS-07-2015-0054.

Bon, J., & Pras, B. (1984). Dissociation of the roles of buyer, payer and consumer. *International Journal of Research in Marketing, 1*(1), 7–16. https://doi.org/10.1016/0167-8116(84)90004-1.

Borrero, J.D.Y., Yousafzai, S., Javed, U., & Page, K.L. (2014). Perceived value of social networking sites (SNS) in students' expressive participation in social movements. *Journal of Research in Interactive Marketing, 8*(1), 56–78. https://doi.org/10.1108/jrim-03-2013-0015.

Calvo-Porral, C., & Pesqueira-Sanchez, R. (2020). Generational differences in technology behaviour: Comparing millennials and Generation X. *Kybernetes, 49*(11), 2755–2772. https://doi.org/10.1108/K-09-2019-0598.

Castells, M. (1999). Information technology, globalization and social development. *UNRISD Discussion Papers,* 144.

Cheung, C.M.K., Lee, M.K.O., & Rabjohn, N. (2008). The impact of electronic word-of-mouth. *Internet Research, 18*(3), 229–247. https://doi.org/10.1108/10662240810883290.

Choi, Y.K., Seo, Y., & Yoon, S. (2017). E-WOM messaging on social media: Social ties, temporal distance, and message concreteness. *Internet Research, 27*(3), 495–505. https://doi.org/10.1108/IntR-07-2016-0198.

Chung, C.H., Chiu, D.K.W., Ho, K.K.W., & Au, C.H. (2020). Applying social media to environmental education: Is it more impactful than traditional media?. *Information Discovery and Delivery, 48*(4), 255–266. https://doi.org/10.1108/IDD-04-2020-0047.

Dijesh, P., Babu, S.S., & Vijayalakshmi, Y. (2020). Enhancement of e-commerce security through asymmetric key algorithm. *Computer Communication, 153*, 125–134. https://doi.org/10.1016/j.comcom.2020.01.033.

Dorie, A., & Loranger, D. (2020). The multi-generation: Generational differences in channel activity. *International Journal of Retail & Distribution Management, 48*(4), 395–416. https://doi.org/10.1108/IJRDM-06-2019-0196.

Eckhardt, G.M., Houston, M.B., Jiang, B.J., Lamberton, C., Rindfleisch, A., & Zervas, G. (2019). Marketing in the sharing economy. *Journal of Marketing, 83*(5), 5–27. https://doi.org/10.1177/0022242919861929.

El Refae, G.A., Kaba, A., & Eletter, S. (2021). Distance learning during COVID-19 pandemic: Satisfaction, opportunities and challenges as perceived by faculty members and students. *Interactive Technology and Smart Education*, Vol. ahead-of-print No. ahead-of-print. https://doi.org/10.1108/ITSE-08-2020-0128.

Engel, J.F., Kollat, D.T., & Blackwell, R.D. (1978). *Consumer behaviour: A European perspective* (3rd ed.). Holt, Reinhart and Winston.

Fedorko, R., Bačík, R., Rigelský, M., & Oleárová, M. (2021). ROPO and reverse ROPO effect in gender-generation characteristics. *GATR Journal of Management and Marketing Review, 6*(1), 24–35. https://doi.org/10.35609/jmmr.2021.6.1(3).

Gemius. (2020, June 30). *E-commerce w Polsce 2020.* https://www.gemius.pl/wszystkie-artykuly-aktualnosci/e-commerce-w-polsce-2020.html.

Geng, S., Yang, P., Gao, Y, Tan, Y., & Yang, C. (2021). The effects of ad social and personal relevance on consumer ad engagement on social media: The moderating role of platform trust. *Computers in Human Behavior, 122*, 106834. https://doi.org/10.1016/j.chb.2021.106834.

Grewal, D., Roggeveen, A.L., & Nordfält, J. (2017). The future of retailing. *Journal of Retailing, 93*(1), 1–6. https://doi.org/10.1016/j.jretai.2016.12.008.

Grunert, K.G., & Ramus, K. (2005). Consumers' willingness to buy food through the Internet: A review of the literature and a model for future research. *British Food Journal, 107*(6), 381–403. https://doi.org/10.1108/00070700510602174.

Hall, A., Towers, N., & Shaw, D.R. (2017). Understanding how Millennial shoppers decide what to buy. *International Journal of Retail and Distribution Management, 45*(5), 498–517.

Heinrich, B., & Thalmair, A. (2013). Online social networks – New sales channel for individual customer approach for financial service providers?. *Banking and Information Technology, 14*(2), 49–63. https://doi.org/10.5283/epub.28974.

Helal, G., Ozuem, W., & Lancaster, G. (2018). Social media brand perceptions of millennials. *International Journal of Retail and Distribution Management, 46*(10), 977–998.

Hou, J., & Elliott, K. (2021). Mobile shopping intensity: Consumer demographics and motivations. *Journal of Retailing and Consumer Services, 63*, 102741. https://doi.org/10.1016/j.jretconser.2021.102741.

Howard, J.A., & Sheth, J.N. (1969). *The theory of buyer behavior.* Wiley.

Hsieh, S.H., & Lee, C.T. (2021). Hey Alexa: Examining the effect of perceived socialness in usage intentions of AI assistant-enabled smart speaker. *Journal of Research in Interactive Marketing, 15*(2), 267–294. https://doi.org/10.1108/JRIM-11-2019-0179.

Jamil, R.A., & Qayyum, A. (2021). Word of mouse vs word of influencer? An experimental investigation into the consumers' preferred source of online information. *Management Research Review*, Vol. ahead-of-print No. ahead-of-print. https://doi.org/10.1108/MRR-03-2021-0184.

Jiménez-Barreto, J., Rubio, N., & Molinillo, S. (2021). "Find a flight for me, Oscar!" Motivational customer experiences with chatbots. *International Journal of Contemporary Hospitality Management*, Vol. ahead-of-print No. ahead-of-print. https://doi.org/10.1108/IJCHM-10-2020-1244.

Ju, X., Chocarro, R., & Martín Martín, O. (2021). Value creation in mobile social media: A systematic review and agenda for future research. *Baltic Journal of Management*, Vol. ahead-of-print No. ahead-of-print. https://doi.org/10.1108/BJM-04-2021-0157.

Kemp, S. (2021, July 21). *Digital audiences swell, but there may be trouble ahead.* https://wearesocial.com/blog/2021/07/digital-audiences-swell-but-there-may-be-trouble-ahead.

Kotler, P., & Keller, K.L. (2012). *Marketing.* Rebis Publishers.

Kowalczuk, J. (2018). The evolvement of online consumer behavior: The ROPO and reverse ROPO effect in Poland and Germany. *Central European Management Journal, 26*(3), 14–29. https://doi.org/10.7206/jmba.ce.2450-7814.233.

Kreutzer, R.T., & Land, K. (2014). *Digital Darwinism: Branding and business models in Jeopardy*. Copernicus.

Kulviwat, S., Guo, C., & Engchanil, N. (2004). Determinants of online information search: A critical review and assessment. *Internet Research, 14*(3), 245–253. https://doi.org/10.1108/10662240410542670.

Lang, B., Dolan, R., Kemper, J., & Northey, G. (2021). Prosumers in times of crisis: Definition, archetypes and implications. *Journal of Service Management, 32*(2), 176–189. https://doi.org/10.1108/JOSM-05-2020-0155.

Lang, B., Kemper, J., Dolan, R., & Northey, G. (2021). Why do consumers become providers? Self-determination in the sharing economy. *Journal of Service Theory and Practice*, Vol. ahead-of-print No. ahead-of-print. https://doi.org/10.1108/JSTP-09-2020-0220.

Lao, A., Vlad, M., & Martin, A. (2021). Exploring how digital kiosk customer experience enhances shopping value, self-mental imagery and behavioral responses. *International Journal of Retail & Distribution Management, 49*(7), 817–845. https://doi.org/10.1108/IJRDM-09-2020-0357.

Lecinski, J. (2011). *Winning the zero moment of truth: ZMOT.* https://www.thinkwithgoogle.com/future-of-marketing/emerging-technology/2011-winning-zmot-ebook/.

Lei, S.I., Shen, H., & Ye, S. (2021). A comparison between chatbot and human service: Customer perception and reuse intention. *International Journal of Contemporary Hospitality Management*, Vol. ahead-of-print No. ahead-of-print. https://doi.org/10.1108/IJCHM-12-2020-1399.

Li, Y., Liu, H., Lee, M., & Huang, Q. (2020). Information privacy concern and deception in online retailing: The moderating effect of online–offline information integration. *Internet Research, 30*(2), 511–537. https://doi.org/10.1108/INTR-02-2018-0066.

Linkiewicz, A., & Bartosik-Purgat, M. (2017). Konsument oraz proces decyzyjny w warunkach globalizacji. In M. Bartosik-Purgat (ed.), *Zachowania konsumentów. Globalizacja, nowe technologie, aktualne trendy, otoczenie społeczno-kulturowe* (pp. 15–27). PWN Publishers.

Lissitsa, S., & Laor, T. (2021). Baby boomers, generation X and generation Y: Identifying generational differences in effects of personality traits in on-demand radio use. *Technology in Society, 64*, 101526. https://doi.org/10.1016/j.techsoc.2021.101526.

Loupiac, P., & Goudey, A. (2019). How website browsing impacts expectations of store features. *International Journal of Retail & Distribution Management, 48*(1), 92–108. https://doi.org/10.1108/ijrdm-07-2018-0146

Lovett, M.J., Peres, R., & Shachar, R. (2013). On brands and word of mouth. *Journal of Marketing Research, 50*(4), 427–444. https://doi.org/10.1509/jmr.11.0458.

Luna, D., & Forquer Gupta, S. (2001). An integrative framework for cross-cultural consumer behavior. *International Marketing Review, 18*(1), 45–69. https://doi.org/10.1108/02651330110381998.

MacInnis, D., & Folkes, V. (2010). The disciplinary status of consumer behavior: A sociology of science perspective on key controversies. *Journal of Consumer Research, 36*(6), 899–914. https://doi.org/10.1086/644610.

Malchenko, Y., Gogua, M., Golovacheva, K., Smirnova, M., & Alkanova, O. (2020). A critical review of digital capability frameworks: A consumer perspective. *Digital Policy, Regulation and Governance, 22*(4), 269–288. https://doi.org/10.1108/DPRG-02-2020-0028.

Malter, M.S., Holbrook, M.B., Kahn, B.E., Parker, J.R., & Lehmann, D.R. (2020). The past, present, and future of consumer research. *Marketing Letters, 31*, 137–149. https://doi.org/10.1007/s11002-020-09526-8.

Matharu, M., Jain, R., & Kamboj, S. (2020). Understanding the impact of lifestyle on sustainable consumption behavior: A sharing economy perspective. *Management of Environmental Quality, 32*(1), 20–40. https://doi.org/10.1108/MEQ-02-2020-0036.

McCrindle, M. (2014). *The ABC of XYZ. Understanding the global generations.* McCrindle Research Pty Ltd.

Moran, G., Muzellec, L., & Nolan, E. (2014). Consumer moments of truth in the digital context. *Journal of Advertising Research, 54*(2), 200–204. https://doi.org/10.2501/jar-54-2-200-204.

Mowen, J.C. (2000). *The 3M model of motivation and personality.* Springer Publishing.

Neal, C., Quester, P.G., & Hawkins, D.I. (2006). *Consumer behaviour: Implications for marketing strategy.* McGraw-Hill Irwin.

Nicosia, F.M. (1966). *Consumer decision process: Marketing and advertising implications.* Prentice-Hall.

Onel, N., & Mukherjee, A. (2016). Consumer knowledge in pro-environmental behavior: An exploration of its antecedents and consequences. *World Journal of Science, Technology and Sustainable Development, 13*(4), 328–352. https://doi.org/10.1108/WJSTSD-01-2016-0004.

Pan, Z., Lu, Y., Gupta, S., & Hu, Q. (2020). You change, I change: An empirical investigation of users' supported incremental technological change in mobile social media. *Internet Research, 31*(1), 208–233. https://doi.org/10.1108/INTR-06-2019-0226.

Rapp, A., Baker, T.L., Bachrach, D.G., Ogilvie, J., & Beitelspacher, L.S. (2015). Perceived customer showrooming behavior and the effect on retail salesperson self-efficacy and performance. *Journal of Retailing, 91*(2), 358–369. https://doi.org/10.1016/j.jretai.2014.12.007.

Ritzer, G., & Jurgenson, N. (2010). Production, consumption, prosumption: The nature of capitalism in the age of the digital 'prosumer'. *Journal of Consumer Culture, 10*(1), 13–36. https://doi.org/10.1177/1469540509354673.

Skiera, B., Hinz, O., & Spann, M. (2015). Social media and academic performance: Does the intensity of Facebook activity relate to good grades? *Schmalenbach Business Review, 67*(1), 54–72. https://doi.org/10.1007/bf03396923.

Solomon, M.R. (2018). *Consumer behavior: Buying, having, and being.* Pearson.

Sreejesh, S., Paul, J., Strong, C., & Pius, J. (2020). Consumer response towards social media advertising: Effect of media interactivity, its conditions and the underlying mechanism. *International Journal of Information Management, 54.* 102155. https://doi.org/10.1016/j.ijinfomgt.2020.102155.

Tang, M.-C., & Wu, P.M. (2021). Reconciling the effects of positive and negative electronic word of mouth: Roles of confirmation bias and involvement. *Online Information Review*, Vol. ahead-of-print No. ahead-of-print. https://doi.org/10.1108/OIR-01-2020-0026.

Tkaczyk, J. (2016). Digital consumer: Trends and challenges. In G. Mazurek & J. Tkaczyk (Eds.), *The impact of the digital world on management and marketing* (pp. 353–367). Poltext, & Akademia Leona Koźmińskiego.

Verhoef, P.C., Kannan, P.K., & Inman, J.J. (2015). From multi-channel retailing to omni-channel retailing. *Journal of Retailing, 91*(2), 174–181. https://doi.org/10.1016/j.jretai.2015.02.005.

Verma, D., Tripathi, V., & Singh, A.P. (2021). From physical to digital: What drives generation Z for mobile commerce adoption?. *Journal of Asia Business Studies*, Vol. ahead-of-print No. ahead-of-print. https://doi.org/10.1108/JABS-05-2020-0207.

Vinerean, S., Cetina, I., Dumitrescu, L., & Tichindelean, M. (2013). The effects of social media marketing on online consumer behavior. *International Journal of Business and Management, 8*(14), 66–79. https://doi.org/10.5539/ijbm.v8n14p66.

Vithayathil, J., Dadgar, M., & Osiri, K.J. (2020). Social media use and consumer shopping preferences. *International Journal of Information Management, 54*, 102117. https://doi.org/10.1016/j.ijinfomgt.2020.102117.

Wang, L., Wang, Z., Wang, X., & Zhao, Y. (2021). Explaining consumer implementation intentions in mobile shopping with SEM and fsQCA: Roles of visual and technical perceptions. *Electronic Commerce Research and Applications, 49*, 10108. https://doi.org/10.1016/j.elerap.2021.101080.

Wang, W.M., Wang, J.W., Li, Z., Tian, Z.G., & Tsui, E. (2019). Multiple affective attribute classification of online customer product reviews: A heuristic deep learning method for supporting Kansei engineering. *Engineering Applications of Artificial Intelligence, 85*, 33–45. https://doi.org/10.1016/j.engappai.2019.05.015.

Yuruk-Kayapinar, P. (2020). Digital consumer behavior in an omnichannel world. In T. Dirsehan (Ed.), *Managing customer experiences in an omnichannel world: Melody of online and offline environments in the customer journey* (pp. 55–73). Emerald Publishing Limited.

Zalega, T. (2012). *Konsumpcja: Determinanty, teorie, modele.* PWE Publications.

Zarei, G., Asgarnezhad Nuri, B., & Noroozi, N. (2019). The effect of Internet service quality on consumers' purchase behavior: The role of satisfaction, attitude, and purchase intention. *Journal of Internet Commerce, 18*(2), 197–220. https://doi.org/10.1080/15332861.2019.1585724.

Zhang, T.C., Abound Omran, B., & Cobanoglu, C. (2017). Generation Y's positive and negative eWOM: Use of social media and mobile technology. *International Journal of Contemporary Hospitality Management, 29*(2), 732–761. https://doi.org/10.1108/ijchm-10-2015-0611.

2 Who is a consumer in the digital era? Still a consumer or a prosumer?

Joanna Bednarz

Models of communication and building relations between producer and consumer in the digital era (from monologue to integrated marketing dialogue)

Marketing communication has always played an important role in the functioning of institutional entities, in particular enterprises, and building relationships with stakeholders – consumers, investors, suppliers, and employees. This process is two-way and consists of the transmission of the message by the sender (company) and its reception by the recipient (present and future buyer). Recipients of this message can then provide feedback to the sender (Danaher & Rossiter, 2011; Gabrielli & Balboni, 2010). Entrepreneurs communicate with the environment in order to establish a dialogue (Keller, 2001), send, receive and exchange information. As senders, they can inform about the detailed attributes of the offered products services, brands (Keller, 2001), pricing and distribution policy, as well as promotional activities. In return, they receive feedback on the needs, preferences, and expectations of buyers.

Marketing communication has transformed, with significant changes taking place on the market. The emergence of new marketing instruments, the development of the Internet, and new technologies played an especially significant role in this context. Various communication models can be found in the literature that shows a noteworthy evolution in this area. Hoffman and Novak (1996) present three communication schemes: an interpersonal marketing communication model ("one-to-one"), a model of mass marketing communication ("one-to-many"), and a model of marketing communication in the Internet environment ("many-to-many").

Among the above-mentioned models, the "one-to-one" interpersonal communication model is the simplest. It is of a basic nature, and it illustrates the direct relationship between the sender of the message and its recipient, e.g. seller and buyer. It expresses the essence of communication: informing and obtaining feedback; there is a question–answer interaction. On the seller's side, this may apply to such situations as informing about the product offer, presenting a new product, whereas on the side of the potential buyer: enquiring about the price and other terms of purchase. Communication can take place through a variety of channels, media, and devices.

DOI: 10.4324/9781003263685-4

The mass marketing communication model is a "one-to-many" process where the sender transmits the same information (content) to a wide audience. An example would be a company that wants to offer its products and services to many potential buyers. For this purpose, an entrepreneur may use different channels and media to convey the same message. It is a one-way communication model, meaning that the level of feedback is negligible, and interaction is excluded. The lack of reaction is most often due to the use of mass media, such as television, radio, press, or outdoor advertising.

The model of marketing communication in the Internet environment can be described as a "many-to-many" model. It uses both mass and interpersonal communication. Senders and recipients become active partners in the entire communication process since they have the opportunity to express themselves freely, publish comments, and express their own opinions. The specificity of this form of communication lies in the ability of recipients to independently search for information that best meets their needs. They can also be initiators in this communication process. An example of such a model of marketing communication are promotional activities carried out by producers and sellers, aimed at a specific segment of potential and actual buyers of products. This model is also well suited for communication in the business-to-business (B2B) market.

Communication models evolve rapidly along with the development of the market, media channels, and the implementation of new technologies. Finne and Grönroos (2017) state that today's customers regularly use several online devices, have access to multiple forms of media, and can interact with several of them at the same time. They can be active in some media and passive in others at the same time (Finne & Grönroos, 2017). Producers and sellers who are message senders have to face up to the challenge of reaching the recipients with a given message through a variety of media. These messages are addressed to a specific segment of final consumers or are personalised (Gurău, 2008). It was noticed that in order to achieve effective marketing communication, it is necessary to coordinate various communication tools and channels so that the message sent by the company is coherent (Bednarz & Orelly, 2020; Pluta-Olearnik, 2018).

The first conceptual ideas of integrated marketing communication (IMC) were published by Schultz et al. in 1993. Kliatchko (2005) reviewed the IMC definitions proposed in research in the extant literature. The term "integration" is understood as the implementation of horizontal coordination mechanisms (Schultz et al., 1993) where multiple messages and many communication activities are merged into a consistent marketing communication mix in order to send to the target market a clear message about a company and its market offer (Bednarz & Orelly, 2020; Danaher & Rossiter, 2011; Gabrielli & Balboni, 2010). Finne and Grönroos (2017, p. 449) summarise the IMC approach as follows: "its goal is synergy as the company tries to integrate all outgoing messages with one voice". It is "the result of aligning activities, procedures, messages and goals" for coherent communication

(Gabrielli & Balboni, 2010, p. 277). Porcu et al. (2017, p. 694) argue that the IMC "allows for the possibility of continuous dialogue by communicating consistent and transparent messages through all media to foster long-term beneficial relationships that create value". These authors also add that "integration involves the corporate, marketing and communication levels" and "highlight the importance of stakeholder-orientation and not just that of customer-orientation". Researchers do not agree entirely on the orientation of the IMC. Contrary to Porcu, Kliatchko and Schultz (2014, pp. 381–382) emphasise that IMC relates to consumer centricity that requires a profound understanding of consumers, their engagement as well as continuous contacts. Moreover, the use of multiple channels "involves the coordination of messages and media channels to create and deliver one-sight, one-sound, clear messages to achieve synergy". Finally, IMC requires "the involvement of the entire business process, not just marketing communication".

Batra and Keller (2016) highlight that when designing a well-integrated marketing communication process, three main aspects come into play: consistency, complementarity, and the interaction between media and communication options. Porcu et al. (2017) extend those to include four dimensions of the IMC construct: message consistency, interactivity, stakeholder-centred strategic focus, and organisational alignment. Interactivity is related to digital technologies, which play a key role in the implementation of an integrated approach (Kliatchko & Schultz, 2014). According to Gurău (2008) the synergy of Internet communication enables the integration and coordination of three main elements: three models of marketing communication presented above, various types of information, and complex information flows between the organisational intranet and the Internet.

Based on a review of the literature, Alameda García et al. (2019) state that IMC is a strategic element in building lasting relationships of companies with customers and other stakeholders. Kitchen and Burgmann (2010, p. 4) also confirm that "a well-established relationship between the company and the customer is necessary". It relates to the concept of relationship marketing. Morgan and Hunt (1994, p. 22) specify that "relationship marketing refers to all marketing activities directed toward establishing, developing and maintaining successful relational exchanges". Relationship marketing is characterised by concern, trust, commitment, and service (Buttle, 1996). Abosag et al. (2006) define relationship commitment as a persistent desire to maintain a relationship that plays a central role in long-lasting networks. Trust is about having confidence in or relying on the other party. It is based on reliability and credibility in fulfilling promises, as well as on feelings and emotions generated by empathy, politeness, similarity, and concern for the other party manifested in their interactions (Nikodemska-Wołowik & Bednarz, 2019).

Even though researchers analyse different types of relationships, the dominant emphasis is on relationships with external customers. The relationship marketing literature is focused on the concept of the value of the individual customer (Itani et al., 2019). Building business relationships with customers is fundamental in today's dynamic and interactive environment. The seller no longer has a dominant influence. It is buyers who play an increasingly active role in building commitment and trust in those relationships (Brodie, 2017). Customers are referred to as "associates or partners enmeshed in alliances or partnerships with companies" (Buttle, 1996, p. 4). The reason why entrepreneurs focus their attention on building marketing relationships is obvious – "the longer the relationship between the company and the customer, the more profitable the relationship becomes for the company" (Buttle, 1996, p. 5). Effective relationship marketing can be established based on several important requirements: mutual cooperation and interdependence between the customer and the seller; the development of new organisational structures and internal marketing; the availability of an advanced customer database to provide information and allow understanding of customer expectations (Buttle, 1996).

It is worth adding that, apart from relationship marketing, researchers also discuss relationship communication. Finne and Grönroos (2009, p. 193) define relationship communication as "any type of marketing communication that influences the receiver's long-term commitment to the sender by facilitating meaning creation through integration with the receiver's time and situational context".

Relationship marketing can be conducted offline and online. The scope of the research presented in this chapter includes online relationships which are understood as "relational exchanges mediated by Internet technology that occur in a human-to-technology environment" (Steinhoff et al., 2019, p. 370). As underlined by Kull (2017), the Internet provides an ideal environment for conducting marketing and communication relationships.

Development of new technologies and their impact on consumers

Even if traditional communication channels (television, radio, newspapers, telemarketing, and door-to-door sales) are still present in the daily lives of consumers, researchers argue that they are expected to decline (Danaher & Rossiter, 2011; Duffett, 2017). Nowadays, a diverse choice of other media channels, known as new media, are an integral part of people's work and home life: the Internet channel's banner ads, websites, e-mail and blogs, mobile phone communications SMS, MMS, cell phone TV, digital television, e-books, computer games, DVDs, social media (Bartosik-Purgat, 2019), and cloud computing (Klepek & Starzyczna, 2018). Bartosik-Purgat (2019) defines new media as instruments that use the latest Internet technologies for the creation of messages and content, their conversion, submission, transmission, and communication to appropriate recipients. The author emphasises that new media are distinguished by flexibility and accessibility, as users have the ability to adjust the form and time of using them. In addition, new media have five main characteristics: creation, content, conversion, circulation, and central storage, and several others: individualisation, interactivity, multimedia, accessibility, immateriality, no fees, speed of relation, and durability (Bartosik-Purgat, 2019).

Kaplan and Haenlein (2010, p. 61) define social media as "a group of Internet-based applications that build on the ideological and technological foundations of Web 2.0, and that allow the creation and exchange of User Generated Content". Social media, such as Facebook, Twitter, LinkedIn, YouTube, WhatsApp, Instagram, Tumblr, Pinterest, WeChat, and Google+ (Duffett, 2017), provides the ability "to connect with customers through richer media with greater reach" (Sashi, 2012, p. 255), so the cost is relatively lower and the level of efficiency higher than can be achieved with more traditional communication tools (Kaplan & Haenlein, 2010). Zajc (2015, pp. 29–44) recognises five major groups of attributes of social media: "prevalence of subject position, arbitrariness of physical position, highly structured online self, the importance of individuals' activities and the individual as the sole bearer of authenticity". Kietzmann et al. (2011) distinguish seven functional building blocks of social media: identity, conversations, sharing, presence, relationships, reputation, and groups.

New media plays an increasingly significant role in marketing communication between companies and consumers, provides interactions between actors, ensures the opportunity to engage in dialogue throughout the relationship life cycle (Iankova et al., 2018). New media represents the "many-to-many" marketing communication model. Consumers are able to contact, discuss and communicate with the producers, express their opinions, give advice to producers on how to adjust the offer to be more competitive (Bartosik-Purgat & Bednarz, 2021). Due to the fact that new media is a customer-centric tool, entrepreneurs have "greater access to customer information directly through company-customer interactions or indirectly through customer-customer interactions" (Trainor et al., 2014, p. 1203). Both sellers and buyers become co-creators of value (Iankova et al., 2018; Sashi, 2012).

Building relationships with active consumers – prosumers

Nowadays, companies develop strategies for the use of new media in online communication channels and encourage consumers not only to search for information but to actively cooperate. They take "a proactive-reactive attitude in online communication and combine consistency and continuity with flexibility and customisation" (Gurău, 2008, p. 180). The degree of consumer's involvement, "motivation (desire), ability, and opportunity to process a communication determine the intensity and direction of this cooperation and the resulting outcomes that occur" (Batra & Keller, 2016, p. 130). Finne and Strandvik (2012) distinguished various degrees and modes of buyers' activity. Client activity can be viewed as mental activity, which means that the message is interpreted and integrated with other information related to the context. The behavioural activity of recipients consists in taking initiatives, searching for information, reacting to communication messages, and initiating communication with others. Passive clients respond to specific stimuli only by accepting the message in accordance with its intended purpose.

Customers' relationships with enterprises are active, based on collaboration, co-participation, co-design, and the creation of social networks around the enterprise (Bartosik-Purgat & Bednarz, 2021; Tapscott & Williams, 2006). Companies use the engagement experiences of individuals and communities to co-create value (Brodie et al., 2011; Harrigan et al., 2018; Hollebeek et al., 2019; Itani et al., 2019; Ramaswamy, 2009). Sashi (2012) proposes seven stages of the customer engagement cycle: connection, interaction, satisfaction, retention, commitment, advocacy, and engagement. Engagement changes customers from transactional customers through delighted and loyal ones to fans (Sashi, 2012).

The development of new technologies has created the possibility of close cooperation between producers and consumers. This contributed to the emergence of a new type of consumer. Prosumption, co-production, and co-creation are terms used in the literature to describe the types of consumer participation in the production of goods and services (Alhashem et al., 2021).

Alvin Toffler introduced the concept of prosumption in the late 1970s (Toffler, 1981). The term prosumption was created by combining two words: production and consumption. Prosumption results from customer involvement, defined as "a psychological state that occurs by virtue of interactive, co-creative customer experiences with a focal agent/object (e.g. a brand) in focal service relationships" (Brodie et al., 2011).

Prosumers are involved in designing new products, their features, improving materials, product reliability and durability, designing packaging or graphic product elements, production processes (self-service activities), commercialisation of products and services, consulting in communication and designing promotional campaigns, e.g. advertising slogans or campaigns, etc., managing customer service, trying out the product and offering an opinion, sharing own content and data via social media (APQC, 2019; Bartosik-Purgat & Bednarz, 2021; Dusi, 2017; Ziemba et al., 2019). The possibility of co-creation is very attractive to consumers, especially young ones because it gives them a chance to get involved in the company's activities and the possibility of having a real impact on the final shape of the market offer. The idea of co-creation is closely related to the concept of crowdsourcing. It is based on constant cooperation with consumer environments and uses the knowledge and skills of their participants in order to obtain creative content, generate new ideas, and collect user opinions about a product, service, or brand. This is possible thanks to the implementation of new information technologies.

With the development of new media, consumers are radically changing the way they use media, including finding information. Their approach is dominated by multitasking, divisive attention, simultaneous activity, and passivity in various media (Batra & Keller, 2016; Finne & Grönroos, 2017). Alameda

García et al. (2019, p. 243) use the term crossumer pointing out that consumers are "much more informed, demanding and have greater power against the brands". The role of the Internet in the development of prosumption is substantial. "Social media permit young users to create personalised online pages, communicate and interact with friends, as well as exchange content that they have created themselves (user-generated content) and/or information from other brand-related sources" (Duffett, 2017, p. 20).

As the age differences in using the Internet are disappearing, it is currently difficult to determine which generation the prosumers belong to. The equalisation process was accelerated by the COVID-19 pandemic, which contributed to the digitisation of societies not only in the sphere of entertainment and games but also in science and business. Currently, not only the so-called generation Y, but also known as "millennials" or the digital generation, is associated with the prosumption trend.

Undoubtedly, prosumers are a very diverse, heterogeneous group of consumers; however, there is a certain set of features, motivations, values, and attitudes that distinguishes this group and implies their participation in these processes. Maciaszczyk and Kocot (2021) characterise a new generation of online prosumers, highlighting their strong need for liberty and freedom of choice. Prosumers "tailor the available offer to their own needs and strive for individualisation, dialogue, and entertainment. This generation is characterised by innovation and a tendency to make joint decisions" (Maciaszczyk & Kocot, 2021, p. 3). Prosumers are critical consumers who have doubts and concerns about many aspects of everyday life in today's world. They do not trust institutions or the media. They rarely watch TV and read newspapers and printed press. The main source of information for them is the Internet. For them, the main tool of functioning and communication is social media. They strive for individual development; they manifest their own emotions, feelings, preferences, and views. This is facilitated by the variety of styles that are a source of inspiration. The individualisation of tastes and needs is also strengthened by the appreciation of the importance of free time, which gives the possibility of self-fulfilment. The COVID-19 pandemic has increased the ability to work from home and combine it with consumer activities. The search for individual identity leads to the creation of a community of small groups, which additionally contribute to strengthening the will to create, develop mutual contacts, build closeness, transfer knowledge, share results and know-how. Prosumers are open and active, involved in the product life cycle, acting as advisers and reviewers for other users. They are also professional consumers who expect professional services. Prosumers invest in themselves, acquire knowledge, skills, and experience. They are demanding, conscious of their rights, paying more and more attention to the reliability of information (Bednarz, 2017; de Pourbaix, 2016; Maciaszczyk & Kocot, 2021).

Prosumers are referred to as the generation C; the "C", however, may stand for different traits. Hardey (2011) points out the behaviour that is characterised by the letter C: content creation, creativity, casual collapse, control, and celebrity. Other researchers of this phenomenon search for additional connotations associated with the "C": connected, communicating, content-centric, computerised, community-oriented, and always clicking. C may also stand for: co-creation, celebrity, conversation, change, collaboration, cyber collective (de Pourbaix, 2016).

Sustainable consumption and sharing economy as an ecosystem of prosumers' activities

Prosumption and sustainable consumption are the opposites of the present model of consumerism (mass consumption) understood as excessive consumption, unjustified by actual human needs and not taking into account social, ecological, and individual costs (Bednarz, 2017). The trend of sustainable consumption is strongly developing, mainly due to the growing environmental awareness of consumers, especially in terms of irreversible effects on the natural environment and the problem of using non-renewable resources. This is fuelled by the tendency to rationalise consumption for the sake of human health, a sense of weariness and disappointment with excessive consumption, and the increasingly frequent adherence to the belief that the purpose of one's life is not merely to purchase and consume things. The development of sustainable consumption is also fostered by the widespread increase in the importance of such values as health, youth, good appearance, physical fitness. Contemporary consumers care about their physical and mental development, want to prevent the development of civilisation diseases, and are keen on building immunity. They are interested in purchasing natural, unprocessed, organic products and the so-called functional food.

There are two trends in sustainable consumption, namely: conscious and collaborative consumption. Conscious (ethical, responsible) consumption is understood as making consumer choices based on knowledge about their social, ecological, and political consequences. Customers make purchasing decisions in a rational, thoughtful, and responsible manner. This involves issues such as social consumption, ecological consumption, fair trade, cruelty-free and green products. In turn, collaborative consumption (also called: collaborative economy, sharing economy, access economy, peer-to-peer economy, platform economy, and community-based economy) is based on the idea of sharing and an approach to using the product without having to own it (Bednarz, 2017; Maciaszczyk & Kocot, 2021). "Collaborative consumption is people coordinating the acquisition and distribution of a resource for a fee or other compensation" like bartering, trading, renting and swapping, which involve giving and receiving non-monetary compensation (Belk, 2014, p. 1597; Hossain, 2020, p. 4). In this way, consumers gain access to the goods and pay for the experience of accessing them temporarily.

Consumers may share different products, such as apartments, bicycles, cars, music, films, photos, videogame consoles, clothes, portable tools. The satisfaction with using collective consumption is positively influenced by the knowledge, trust, and usefulness of the service. Consumers enjoy the fact of sharing, the sense of togetherness, and the social experience involved (Barbu, 2018). Hossain (2020) lists strong motivators to participate in collective consumption: convenience, flexibility, home benefits, interaction, local authenticity, sharing economy ethos, community, and economic benefit such as savings. Kim and Jin (2020) discover dimensions that characterise consumer motivations for collaborative consumption of consumer goods:

- concern for sustainability (consumers are environmentally conscious with respect to the issue of waste reduction, especially from first world countries),
- social dimension (virtual communities are created on the online platforms and marketplaces where consumers can interact and socialise),
- cost-saving dimension (for the price-conscious consumers looking for the economic benefits of saving funds),
- variety-seeking dimension (consumers choose collaborative consumption practices to access a wide range of products),
- fun (consumers can benefit from the hedonistic value, resulting from searching for and finding unique items and receiving emotional rewards from smart shopping and saving money).

Park and Armstrong (2017) add one more dimension to this list – convenience explained as product availability, pricing model, specifically billing mechanisms, as well as time and cost savings.

Without a doubt, the Internet has contributed to the development of large-scale sharing. Many collaborative consumption practices are carried out by bilateral online platforms and mobile communication technologies that build trust and reduce the perceived risk (Jiang & Tian, 2016). Within these web platforms and communication technologies, a decentralised many-to-many model is being implemented. Belk (2014) argues that sharing makes great practical and economic sense for the consumer, the environment, and the community, as it demonstrates pro-social intentions and actions that connect people with others. It may also make sense for companies that are flexible, innovative, and forward-thinking. Finally, it is worth adding that while many companies (iTunes, Rhapsody, Pandora, and Spotify) have been successful in offering legal downloads or streaming of music, movies, and TV shows, unfortunately, in practice, some movie and music downloads, as well as software, e-books, and games are illegal (Belk, 2014).

Personalisation and customisation as a key trend in consumer behaviour in the digital age

With the growing need for individualisation displayed by modern consumers, entrepreneurs were forced to attempt the difficult task of reconciling these expectations with the economics involved in the production of mass goods (higher costs of design, production, flexibility, logistics, warehousing, etc.). This was also influenced by such factors as diversified demand, high consumer awareness, short product life cycle, market maturity (Bardakci & Whitelock, 2003) as well as new production and information technologies (Pędzik et al., 2020). As previously emphasised, today's consumers are very demanding, critical, impatient, and individual. Bardakci and Whitelock (2003, p. 468) even stress that "the fragmentation of demand has reached such a peak that even the niches are too broad to satisfy the consumers".

Personalisation, also called one-to-one marketing, individualisation, tailoring, derives from relationship marketing. The idea of personalisation is "to offer the right products and services at the right time and in the right place to the right customers" (Sunikka & Bragge, 2012, p. 10050). In this situation, there is an exceptional segmentation where there is one segment in which there can only be one buyer (Pędzik et al., 2020). The essence is the satisfaction of each client who is treated as an individual (Tseng et al., 2010). It is to meet customers' individual needs and maximise customer-perceived value (Du et al., 2006). Hart (1996) stresses that customised products and services are offered to customers at the price of standardised mass-produced alternatives, however, "customers are willing to pay more for products that match their individual size, tastes, styles, needs and expression" (Du et al., 2006, p. 396). It is worth adding that some researchers treat personalisation and customisation as synonyms, while others notice the differences. For Tseng et al. (2010) personalisation of products operates at the level of an individual customer, while customisation differentiates products for market segments. They explain also that "in terms of design, personalisation differs from customisation mainly in two respects: expanding product design space and embracing intangible customer experience". Contrary, Sunikka and Bragge (2012, p. 10054) perceive customisation as "an activity controlled by users, for example: configuring the content of a website". Mass customisation is a basic production paradigm that allows the production of highly variant products and services at costs close to those of mass production. Tapscott and Williams (2006) emphasise that it is possible that customers gain the ability to customise products for specific applications, while companies can maintain the economy of large-scale production.

Personalisation is about creating products and services tailored to individual consumers, in accordance with their needs and expectations. Piller (2004, p. 315) argues that "customers are integrated into value creation by defining, configuring, matching, or modifying an individual solution". It should be seen as an important element of product differentiation. This is to give the customer a sense of uniqueness in the process of purchasing a co-designed product. It may refer to three areas: style (consumers' willingness to adapt to trends, fashion, uniqueness), fit and comfort (sizing), and functionality (product features, interface, and application) (Piller, 2004). However, personalisation is about more than just delivering a personalised product, service, or marketing communication method. It provides consumers with personalised added value (Vesanen, 2007). In addition to creating products, personalisation is also a way of maintaining a dialogue between the producer and the consumer, the aim of which is to strengthen commitment, which then contributes to increasing the trust and loyalty of buyers. As a result of co-design, an individual contact between the manufacturer and the client is created, which gives the opportunity to build a lasting relationship (Piller, 2004).

Personalisation is a process consisting of four phases:

- identification of the customers' potential,
- determining their needs and values for the company,
- interacting with customers to get to know them better,
- customising products, services, and communications to individual customers.

When analysing personalisation, one can notice similarities with the concept of design thinking. The key point at the stage of data collection is their proper selection and then getting to know the consumers. In-depth understanding of customers' heterogeneous and independent preferences is essential to preparing and delivering a personalised offer, and then operationalising the results and measuring the impact of personalisation (Sunikka & Bragge, 2012). Enterprises can personalise their offers thanks to Big Data management and adaptive personalisation systems. The approach to adaptive personalisation is done automatically using algorithms, requires no proactive effort on the part of the customer, observes customer behaviour, and adjusts the product over time (Chung et al., 2016). Customer involvement in the product preparation and production process includes three components. The first is to familiarise the customer with the spectrum of the product offer, existing product attributes, and their options. The customers are then asked to prioritise the desired attributes according to their individual requirements. The third component concerns utility exploration to reflect the desirability of each attribute level (Du et al., 2006).

Hu (2013) lists new concepts and technologies that enable mass customisation, including product family architecture (developing a product portfolio in which some functional modules are common, while others are delivered in several variants), reconfigurable manufacturing systems (allows for quick modification of production in response to sudden changes in the market), and delaying differentiation (reduces costs as processes and assemblies are common up to the moment of product differentiation). This co-design process is enabled by an open product architecture (the consumer can create their personalised product from common and custom modules), personalisation design (design and integration of new interfaces as well as visualisation tools are needed), on-demand manufacturing systems (provide flexibility in production), and responsive cyber-physical system involving user participation in design, product simulation, manufacturing, supply, and assembly processes that meet consumer needs and preferences (Hu, 2013, pp. 6–7).

In conclusion, it should be stated that prosumption, personalisation, and customisation all develop to a different extent depending on the industry. The most susceptible to this trend is the IT industry in its broadest sense, where buyers can create a product in accordance with their needs and preferences. Another good example is e-commerce, banking services, the tourism industry, and real estate portals. The apparel industry is also developing in this direction, enabling consumers to stand out through personalised products, expressing their values and beliefs. The food industry is an example of an industry where prosumption is growing rather slowly. This is due to the fact that food is produced in a uniform and standardised way, and then purchased and consumed on a massive and permanent basis. Nevertheless, activities involving buyers in the co-creation of products, marketing messages, and methods of communication can be noticed here as well. One should not forget that consumers are increasingly involved in the production of food at home – they bake bread and cakes, make jams and vegetable preserves. This is a clear economic and health-promoting trend.

Therefore, there is no doubt that prosumption, personalisation, and customisation are trends that will be supported by producers. Contemporary enterprises operate in a highly competitive environment in which acquiring new and retaining existing customers require offering them goods and services tailored to their needs and expectations. This makes it possible to build close relations between producers and consumers, as well as consumer satisfaction and loyalty, especially among young people. This trend will be fostered by the further development of new information and communication technologies.

Bibliography

Abosag, I., Tynan, C., & Lewis, C. (2006). The commitment-trust theory: The British and Saudi Arabian cross-national perspectives. Paper presented at the 22nd Industrial Marketing and Purchasing Conference, Milan, Italy. https://www.researchgate.net/publication/228436168_The_Commitment-Trust_Theory_The_British_and_Saudi_Arabian_Cross-National_Perspectives.

Alameda García, D., Carcelén García, S., Pintado Blanco, T., & Sánchez, J. (2019). Integrated marketing communication in the digital environment. Advertiser attitudes towards online communication techniques. *Communication Studies, 29*, 241–258. https://doi.org/10.25768/FAL.EC.N29.A15.

Alhashem, M., Moraes, C., & Szmigin, I.T. (2021). Use and social value in peer-to-peer prosumption communities. *European Journal of Marketing, 55*(1), 193–218. https://doi.org/10.1108/EJM-03-2019-0235.

APQC. (2019). *Process classification framework 7.2.1.* American Productivity and Quality Center. https://www.apqc.org/resource-library/resource-listing/apqc-process-classification-framework-pcf-cross-industry-pdf-8.

Barbu, C.M., Florea, D.L, Ogarcă, R.F., & Barbu, M.C.R. (2018). From ownership to access: How the sharing economy is changing the consumer behavior. *Amfiteatru Economic, 20*(48), 373–387. https://doi.org/10.24818/EA/2018/48/373.

Bardakci, A., & Whitelock, J. (2003). Mass-customisation in marketing: The consumer perspective. *Journal of Consumer Marketing, 20*(5), 463–479. https://doi.org/10.1108/07363760310489689.

Bartosik-Purgat, M. (2019). *New media in the marketing communication of enterprises in the international market.* PWN Publishing.

Bartosik-Purgat, M., & Bednarz, J. (2021). The usage of new media tools in prosumer activities – A corporate perspective. *Technology Analysis & Strategic Management, 33*(4), 453–464. https://doi.org/10.1080/09537325.2020.1820475.

Batra, R., & Keller, K.L. (2016). Integrating marketing communications: New findings, new lessons, and new ideas. *Journal of Marketing, 80*, 122–145. https://doi.org/10.1509/jm.15.0419.

Bednarz, J. (2017). Prosumpcja jako rezultat zmian zachodzących w zachowaniach konsumentów na przykładzie przemysłu spożywczego. Współczesny konsument w strategiach przedsiębiorstw międzynarodowych (eng. Prosumption as a result of changes in consumer behaviour on the example of the food industry. Contemporary consumer in the strategies of international companies). *Studia Oeconomica Posnaniensia, 5*(1), 7–24. https://doi.org/10.18559/SOEP.2017.1.1

Bednarz, J., & Orelly, P. (2020). The importance of social media on the FMCG market in Bangladesh. *International Journal of Management and Economics, 56*(3), 230–242. https://doi.org/10.2478/ijme-2020-0019.

Belk, R. (2014). You are what you can access: Sharing and collaborative consumption online. *Journal of Business Research, 67*(8), 1595–1600. https://doi.org/10.1016/j.jbusres.2013.10.001.

Brodie, R.J. (2017). Enhancing theory development in the domain of relationship marketing: How to avoid the danger of getting stuck in the middle. *Journal of Services Marketing, 31*(1), 20–23. https://doi.org/10.1108/JSM-05-2016-0179.

Brodie, R.J., Hollebeek, L.D., Jurić B., & Ilić A. (2011). Customer engagement: Conceptual domain, fundamental propositions, and implications for research. *Journal of Service Research, 14*(3), 252–271. https://doi.org/10.1177/1094670511411703.

Buttle, F. (1996). *Relationship marketing: Theory and practice.* SAGE Publications Ltd.

Chung, T.S., Wedel, M., & Rust, R.T. (2016). Adaptive personalization using social networks. *Journal of the Academy of Marketing Science, 44*, 66–87. https://doi.org/10.1007/s11747-015-0441-x.

Danaher, P.J., & Rossiter, J.R. (2011). Comparing perceptions of marketing communication channels. *European Journal of Marketing, 45*(1/2), 6–42. http://dx.doi.org/10.1108/03090561111095586.

de Pourbaix, P. (2016). Prosumer of the XXI century – New challenges to commerce and marketing. *Acta Scientiarum Polonorum, Oeconomia, 15*(1), 89–97.

Du, X., Jiao, J., & Tseng, M.M. (2006). Understanding customer satisfaction in product customization. *The International Journal of Advanced Manufacturing Technology, 31*, 396–406. https://doi.org/10.1007/s00170-005-0177-8.

Duffett, R.G. (2017). Influence of social media marketing communications on young consumers' attitudes. *Young Consumers, 18*(1), 19–39. https://doi.org/10.1108/YC-07-2016-00622.

Dusi, D. (2017). Investigating the exploitative and empowering potential of the prosumption phenomenon. *Sociology Compass, 11*(6), 1–11. https://doi.org/10.1111/soc4.12488.

Finne, Å., & Grönroos, C. (2009). Rethinking marketing communication: From integrated marketing communication to relationship communication. *Journal of Marketing Communications, 15*(2–3), 179–193. https://doi.org/10.1080/13527260902757654.

Finne, Å., & Grönroos, C. (2017). Communication-in-use: Customer-integrated marketing communication. *European Journal of Marketing, 51*(3), 445–463. https://doi.org/10.1108/EJM-08-2015-0553.

Finne, Å., & Strandvik, T. (2012). Invisible communication: A challenge to established marketing communication. *European Business Review, 24*(2), 120–133. https://doi.org/10.1108/09555341211203991.

Gabrielli, V., & Balboni, B. (2010). SME practice towards integrated marketing communications. *Marketing Intelligence & Planning, 28*(3), 275–290. https://doi.org/10.1108/02634501011041426.

Gurău, C. (2008). Integrated online marketing communication: Implementation and management. *Journal of Communication Management, 12*(2), 169–184. https://doi.org/10.1108/13632540810881974.

Hardey, M. (2011). Generation, C: Content, creation, connections and choice. *International Journal of Market Research, 53*(6), 749–770. http://doi.org/10.2501/IJMR-53-6-749-770.

Harrigan, P., Evers, U., Miles, M.P., & Daly, T. (2018). Customer engagement and the relationship between involvement, engagement, self-brand connection and brand usage intent. *Journal of Business Research, 88*, 388–396. https://doi.org/10.1016/j.jbusres.2017.11.046.

Hart, C.W. (1996). Made to order. *Marketing Management, 5*(2), 12–22.

Hoffman, D.L., & Novak, T.P. (1996). Marketing in hypermedia computer-mediated environments: Conceptual foundations. *Journal of Marketing, 60*(3), 50–68. https://doi.org/10.2307/1251841.

Hollebeek, L.D., Srivastava, R.K., & Chen, T. (2019). S-D logic-informed customer engagement: Integrative framework, revised fundamental propositions, and application to CRM. *Journal of the Academy of Marketing Science, 47*(1), 161–185. http://doi.org/10.1007/s11747-016-0494-5.

Hossain, M. (2020). Sharing economy: A comprehensive literature review. *International Journal of Hospitality Management, 87*, 102470, 1–11. https://doi.org/10.1016/zj.ijhm.2020.102470.

Hu, S.J. (2013). Evolving paradigms of manufacturing: From mass production to mass customization and personalization. *Procedia CIRP, 7*, 3–8. https://doi.org/10.1016/j.procir.2013.05.002.

Iankova, S., Davies, I.A., Archer-Brown, C., Marder, B.L., & Yau, A. (2018). A comparison of social media marketing between B2B, B2C and mixed business models. *Industrial Marketing Management, 81*, 169–179. https://doi.org/10.1016/j.indmarman.2018.01.001.

Itani, O.S., Kassar, A.N., & Correia Loureiro, S.M. (2019). Value get, value give: The relationships among perceived value, relationship quality, customer engagement, and value consciousness. *International Journal of Hospitality Management, 80*, 78–90. https://doi.org/10.1016/j.ijhm.2019.01.014.

Jiang, B., & Tian, L. (2016). Collaborative consumption: Strategic and economic implications of product sharing. *Management Science, 64*(3), 1171–1188. https://doi.org/10.1287/mnsc.2016.2647.

Kaplan, A.M., & Haenlein, M. (2010). Users of the world, unite! The challenges and opportunities of social media. *Business Horizons, 53*(1), 59–68. https://doi.org/10.1016/j.bushor.2009.09.003.

Keller, K.L. (2001). Mastering the marketing communications mix: Micro and macro perspective on integrated marketing communication programs. *Journal of Marketing Management, 17*(7–8), 819–847. https://doi.org/10.1362/026725701323366836.

Kietzmann, J.H., Hermkens, K., McCarthy, I.P., & Silvestre, B.S. (2011). Social media? Get serious! Understanding the functional building blocks of social media. *Business Horizons, 54*, 241–251. https://doi.org/10.1016/j.bushor.2011.01.005.

Kim, N.L., & Jin, B.E. (2020). Why buy new when one can share? Exploring collaborative consumption motivations for consumer goods. *International Journal of Consumer Studies, 44*, 122–130. https://doi.org/10.1111/ijcs.12551.

Kitchen, P.J., & Burgmann, I. (2010). Integrated marketing communication. In J.N. Sheth & N.K. Malhotra (Eds.), *Wiley international encyclopedia of marketing*. John Wiley & Sons Ltd.

Klepek, M., & Starzyczna, H. (2018). Marketing communication model for social networks. *Journal of Business Economics and Management, 19*(3), 500–520. https://doi.org/10.3846/jbem.2018.6582.

Kliatchko, J. (2005). Towards a new definition of integrated marketing communications (IMC). *International Journal of Advertising, 24* (1), 7–33. https://doi.org/10.1080/02650487.2005.11072902.

Kliatchko, J., & Schultz, D.E. (2014). Twenty years of IMC: A study of CEO and CMO perspectives in the Asia-Pacific region. *International Journal of Advertising, 33*(2), 373–390. https://doi.org/10.2501/IJA-33-2-373-390.

Kull, K. (2007). The model of internet–based marketing communication. Tellin Technical University. http://www.mattimar.ee/publikatsioonid/ettevottemajandus/2004/06_Kull.pdf.

Maciaszczyk, M., & Kocot, M. (2021). Behavior of online prosumers in organic product market as determinant of sustainable consumption. *Sustainability, 13*(3), 1157. https://doi.org/10.3390/su13031157.

Morgan, R.M., & Hunt, S.D. (1994). The commitment-trust theory of relationship marketing. *Journal of Marketing, 58*(3), 20–38. https://doi.org/10.2307/1252308.

Nikodemska-Wołowik, A.M., & Bednarz, J. (2019). Family enterprises in the context of consumer ethnocentrism and relationship-building. *Management Issues, 17*(181), 77–92. https://doi.org/10.7172/1644-9584.81.4.

Park, H., & Armstrong, C.M.J. (2017). Collaborative apparel consumption in the digital sharing economy: An agenda for academic inquiry. *International Journal of Consumer Studies, 41*, 465–474. https://doi.org/10.1111/ijcs.12354.

Pędzik M., Bednarz, J., Kwidziński Z., Rogoziński T., & Smardzewski, J. (2020). The idea of mass customization in the door industry using the example of the company porta KMI Poland. *Sustainability, 12*(9), 3788. https://doi.org/10.3390/su12093788.

Piller, F. (2004). Mass customization: Reflections on the state of the concept. *International Journal of Flexible Manufacturing Systems, 16*, 313–334. https://doi.org/10.1007/s10696-005-5170-x.

Pluta-Olearnik, M. (2018). Integrated marketing communication – Concepts, practice, new challenges. *Marketing of Scientific and Research Organizations, 28*(2), 121–138. https://doi.org/10.14611/minib.28.06.2018.12.

Porcu, L., del Barrio-Garcia, S., & Kitchen, P. (2017). Measuring integrated marketing communication by taking a broad organisational approach the firm-wide IMC scale. *European Journal of Marketing, 51*(3), 692–718. https://doi.org/10.1108/EJM-08-2015-0587.

Ramaswamy, V. (2009). Leading the transformation to co creation of value. *Strategy & Leadership, 37*(2), 32–37. https://doi.org/10.1108/10878570910941208.

Sashi, C.M. (2012). Customer engagement, buyer-seller relationships, and social media. *Management Decision, 50*(2), 253–272. https://doi.org/10.1108/00251741211203551.

Schultz, D.E., Tannenbaum, S.I., & Lauterborn, R.F. (1993). *The new marketing paradigm: Integrated marketing communications.* NTC Business Books.

Steinhoff, L., Arli, D., Weaven, S., & Kozlenkova, I.V. (2019). Online relationship marketing. *Journal of the Academy of Marketing Science, 47*, 369–393. https://doi.org/10.1007/s11747-018-0621-6.

Sunikka, A., & Bragge, J. (2012). Applying text-mining to personalization and customization research literature – Who, what and where?. *Expert Systems with Applications, 39*(11), 10049–10058. https://doi.org/10.1016/j.eswa.2012.02.042.

Tapscott, D., & Williams, A.D. (2006). *Wikinomics: How mass collaboration changes everything.* Penguin.

Toffler, A. (1981). *The third wave.* Bantam Books.

Trainor, K.J., Andzulis, J.M., Rapp, A., & Agnihotri, R. (2014). Social media technology usage and customer relationship performance: A capabilities-based examination of social CRM. *Journal of Business Research, 67*(6), 1201–1208. https://doi.org/10.1016/j.jbusres.2013.05.002.

Tseng, M.M., Jiao, R.J., & Wang, C. (2010). Design for mass personalization. *CIRP Annals – Manufacturing Technology, 59*(1), 175–178. https://doi.org/10.1016/j.cirp.2010.03.097.

Vesanen, J. (2007). What is personalization? A conceptual framework. *European Journal of Marketing, 41*(5/6), 409–418. https://doi.org/10.1108/03090560710737534.

Zajc, M. (2015). Social media, prosumption, and dispositives: New mechanisms of the construction of subjectivity. *Journal of Consumer Culture, 15*(1), 28–47. https://doi.org/10.1177/1469540513493201.

Ziemba, E., Eisenbardt, M., Mullins, R., & Dettmer, S. (2019). Prosumers' engagement in business process innovation – The case of Poland and the UK. *Interdisciplinary Journal of Information, Knowledge and Management, 14*, 119–143. https://doi.org/10.28945/4320.

3 Technological innovations and consumer behaviour

Tomasz Grzegorczyk

Introduction

Innovations are particularly important for obtaining and sustaining a competitive advantage (Teece, 1998). Disruptive technology products generate discontinuous innovation change (Hopp et al., 2018), and dynamically influence the established technology, markets, as well as consumers (Kamolsook et al., 2019). Research confirms that technology's impact on consumer behaviour is increasing (Hoyer et al., 2020).

It is crucial for the high-tech companies' success to create products that meet the ever-increasing expectations of consumers and are accepted by them (Im & Workman, 2004; Kline & Rosenberg, 1986; Viardot, 2004). This is a demanding challenge, as technologically advanced products tend to evoke conflicting feelings (Mick & Fournier, 1998) because they often are characterized by especially positive (e.g. relative advantage) and negative features (e.g. multidimensional risk), which are the foundation of ambivalent attitudes. Frank et al. (2021) underline that for companies to convince consumers to adopt these technologically advanced products, they need to obtain marketing knowledge concerning the determinants of their adoption.

At the centre of the next phase of the digital revolution, there are three technology clusters: Internet of Things (IoT), Artificial Intelligence (AI, e.g. chatbots/robots), and Augmented Reality (AR) which can be intertwined in a single product (Hoyer et al., 2020; Kumar et al., 2021). The changes brought by these technologies are manifold and broad: they will impact companies, societies, and governments on many levels. They also evoke the most conflicting consumer attitudes and have the greatest potential to influence the customer experience. Moreover, due to the COVID-19 pandemic, consumers have become increasingly dependent on new technologies such as AR (Bartosik-Purgat et al., 2021). Consequently, lately, they concern researchers the most. This chapter aims to identify the key factors which determine the consumer acceptance of those technologies. The research method used is a scoping literature review.

DOI: 10.4324/9781003263685-5

Technology acceptance models and factors

Theories like the theory of reasoned action (TRA; Fishbein & Ajzen, 1975) and its successor – the theory of planned behaviour (TPB; Ajzen, 1991) use models to explain and predict user behaviour with only a few variables. Davis (1989), inspired by those theories, created the Technology Acceptance Model (TAM) aimed at explaining and predicting the acceptance (understood as the intention to use) of information systems (IS) in an organizational setting. In 2003 its successor was introduced – the Unified Theory of Acceptance and Use of Technology (UTAUT, Venkatesh et al., 2003). Those models were used in countless studies aimed at explaining consumer acceptance of various technological innovations. In 2012 Venkatesh et al. adapted UTAUT to consumer use creating UTAUT2. According to UTAUT2, technology acceptance is determined by performance expectancy, effort expectancy, social influence, facilitating conditions, hedonic motivation, price value and habit, and is moderated by age, gender, and experience. However, lately, many studies do not directly use TAM and its successors to study the acceptance of a particular technology, but they rather combine them with other theories and variables (both product- and consumer-oriented).

There are similarities between the concept of user acceptance and perceived consumer value. One of the main ideas behind the latter is that perceived value consists of both positive and negative elements (benefits and costs) (Zeithaml, 1988). In their choices consumers aim to gain more benefits than sacrifices made (Sheth et al., 1991). Among offered possibilities, they choose those for which they expect to obtain the highest value (benefits minus costs) (Sheth et al., 1991). These costs play a critical role when it comes to products and services novel to consumers (Babin & Harris, 2017), especially if they are based on new, disruptive technology (Frank et al., 2021). Consequently, many authors decide to study the factors negatively influencing user acceptance. To this aim, they often make use of the concept of perceived risk which is "the expectation of losses associated with the purchase and acts as an inhibitor to purchase behaviour" (Peter & Ryan, 1976, as cited in Featherman & Pavlou, 2003, p. 454). Kline and Rosenberg (1986) state that the more innovative the product is and the more significant changes it introduces, the greater the uncertainty associated with it.

Various facets of perceived risk are distinguished in literature: psychosocial risk (harm to identity or self-esteem), financial risk, time risk (loss of time because of late delivery, for example), social risk, physical risk, privacy loss risk, and product/service risk (when the expectations about the product or service are not met) (Grzegorczyk, 2020b). Research findings of acceptance models of various technological innovations showed that those dimensions of perceived risk have a negative effect on consumer acceptance (e.g. Yang et al., 2016).

A common point between UTAUT2 and the theory of perceived value is that many of the factors from UTAUT2 bear significant similarity to the four elements of value in accordance with the PERVAL model (Grzegorczyk, 2019). According to PERVAL consumer value consists of quality, emotional, social, and monetary (price) value (Sweeney & Soutar, 2001). Others include utilitarian, hedonic, and symbolic components (Babin & Harris, 2017; Sheth et al., 1991; Smith & Colgate, 2007). All in all, consumer value is often regarded as the main determinant of consumer intentions and behaviours (Babin & Harris, 2017; Frank et al., 2021).

Consumers and Artificial Intelligence

AI has the capability to perform tasks by intelligent, human-like behaviour (Du & Xie, 2021). This technology is regarded as crucial in terms of future success in the consumer market (Ameen et al., 2021). AI technology is embedded into tangible products and services. Among the former are autonomous vehicles (AVs), social robots, robotic lawnmowers, and vacuum cleaners (Rijsdijk et al., 2007), while among the latter – chatbots and digital assistants (Rese et al., 2020).

Among those, AVs draw the most attention of both consumers and researchers (e.g. Choi & Ji, 2015; Kaur & Rampersad, 2018). AVs are vehicles that can drive without the aid of a human operator (Kaur & Rampersad, 2018). Currently, vehicles are only partly autonomous, capable of, for instance, autonomous parking, but their level of autonomy increases. In the future, they will reach full autonomy, which allows for unsupervised steering. AVs surpass traditional cars in various ways. First, AVs may increase safety due to the elimination of human error (Fagnant & Kockelman, 2015). Second, thanks to superior route planning and better efficiency, AVs will reduce road congestion, fuel emission, and economy (Fagnant & Kockelman, 2015). Third, AVs allow consumers to save time and to engage in non-driving activities during their travel (Clark & Feng, 2017). Fourth, AVs enable travelling for people who are unable to drive on their own. However, the introduction of AVs is linked with multiple challenges, e.g. safety hazards, the question of legal liability for road accidents, ethical and regulatory issues, which result in consumers' fear of this tech (Penmetsa et al., 2019). AVs also are a challenge to the traditional role of drivers and driving pleasure. Even though the benefits of AVs seem to significantly outweigh the risks associated with them, consumer acceptance of this technology is still uncertain. While many studies concerning attitudes towards AVs were conducted, the results are mixed. Some found that the positive attitude prevails (e.g. Penmetsa et al., 2019), while others show the contrary (e.g. Hryniewicz & Grzegorczyk, 2020; Konig & Neumayr, 2017).

Many researchers focus on how demographic factors influence AVs' consumer acceptance. For example, younger male drivers have a more positive attitude towards AVs and were more likely to buy one (Bansal et al., 2016; Hohenberger et al., 2017). Furthermore, factors such as higher income (Bansal et al., 2016) and living in an urban area (Shabanpour et al., 2018) positively affect consumers' attitudes towards AVs. A meta-analysis of studies that are not based on behaviour theories found that the acceptance of AVs was determined by AVs' safety, performance-to-price value, mobility, travel time, symbolic value, as well as environmental friendliness (Jing et al., 2020). Other analysis established the significance of legal liability and regulation issues of AVs (Liu et al., 2019).

In accordance with a meta-analysis of AV acceptance studies (Jing et al., 2020), the most often cited behaviour theories were (respectively): TAM, TPB, UTAUT, Diffusion of Innovation Model (Rogers, 1983), TRA. The most often cited factors were (respectively): perceived ease of use, perceived usefulness, trust, attitude, social norm, perceived risk, and compatibility (Jing et al., 2020). As the number of studies increases, researchers concentrate on more detailed situations, technologies, and respondents, e.g. ridesharing (Gurumurthy & Kockelman, 2020) or autonomous delivery vehicles (Kapser & Abdelrahman, 2020). Some researchers combine different theories and perspectives. For example, Hryniewicz and Grzegorczyk (2021), combine TAM with the dual perspective model of agency and communion in the communication strategy context. They show that consumers prefer to know both whether AVs are communal (safe) and agentic (useful effective), but they are more prone to accept a communal AV than an agentic one (Hryniewicz & Grzegorczyk, 2021).

When it comes to AI services, chatbots bring the most attention to consumers and researchers. They are designed to conduct conversations with consumers through text (traditional chatbots) or audio (voicebots) (Hoyer et al., 2020). Their aim is to simulate human conversation, sometimes in the customer service context. Chatbots also work as personal assistants (e.g. Apple's Siri and Amazon's Alexa), supporting consumers in daily tasks such as seeking information or making orders via the Internet. Ashfaq et al. (2020) found that information and service quality positively influence consumers' satisfaction, and that perceived enjoyment, perceived usefulness, and perceived ease of use are significant predictors of chatbot acceptance. However, privacy issues and the immaturity of technology negatively influence consumer acceptance (Rese et al., 2020). Moreover, anthropomorphic chatbots may satisfy the need for human interaction (Sheehan et al., 2020) and the authenticity of conversation plays a role in their acceptance (Rese et al., 2020). While Ciechanowski et al. (2019) confirmed that consumers are eager to interact with chatbots, they also found that users experienced the uncanny valley effect in human-like chatbots. This effect manifests as a feeling of strong discomfort experienced in contact with artificial objects which can hardly be distinguished from humans.

Research on both (partly) AVs and chatbots shows the biggest issues for the adoption of AI products and services. The lack of control over AI and safety concerns requires a very high level of trust towards AI products or their manufacturer (Choi & Ji, 2015; Hengsler et al., 2016). Furthermore, designing the appropriate level of anthropomorphism of AI is also a challenge for companies.

Consumers and the Internet of Things

IoT technology helps to create a "smart world" where communication between various devices and people is ubiquitous (Lu et al., 2018). In 2025, the number of IoT devices is predicted to reach 75 billion (Oshana & Kraeling, 2019). IoT makes use of technological development of communication technology, sensing devices, AI (especially machine learning), and big data processing techniques (Atzori et al., 2014).

Van Deursen and Mossberger (2018) consider IoT as

> systems that (1) contain ubiquitous "everyday" objects that are accessible through the Internet and equipped with sensing, storing, and processing capabilities that allow these objects to understand their environments; (2) contain identifying and networking capabilities that allow them to communicate information about themselves; (3) involve object-object, object-person, and person-person communication; and (4) make autonomous decisions.

Touzani et al. (2018) state that there are four types of IoT devices: (1) devices that follow simple orders (e.g. connected coffeemakers); (2) objects that provide access to information (e.g. applications with QR codes); (3) objects that collect and analyse data and provide consumers with reports (e.g. smartwatches), and which can even set them challenges (e.g. connected forks); and (4) objects that can act autonomously (e.g. intelligent cars).

What is important from the consumer's point of view is that the communication between the user and IoT devices (as well as between IoT devices) is easy and effective (Kumar et al., 2021). Consequently, IoT devices can discreetly "embed themselves into the lives of users, automate routine activities, and improve functionality by reducing the need for human intervention" (Kumar et al., 2021, p. 867). Mani and Chouk (2019) describe a smart thermostat that, with time, can learn the habits of users and adjust the temperature by itself.

Researchers usually focus on specific IoT appliances. The most often researched are wearable and smart home devices. The former includes smartwatches, smart glasses, activity trackers (e.g. bracelets), smart clothing, or jewellery (e.g. smart rings). Smart thermostats, smart door locks, or voice assistants are examples of the latter. In a systematic literature review, Marikyan et al. (2019) gathered smart home user-perceived benefits and barriers. The main barriers are technological (security, usability, privacy intrusion, reliability, complexity), financial, ethical, and legal (price, costs, fear of misuse of private data, lack of legal conduct) and psychological nature (human barrier, resistance to innovation, lack of prior knowledge). The main perceived benefits are health-related (comfort, users' safety, reduction of medical errors), environmental (reduction of energy usage), financial (cheaper costs of virtual communication), and psychological (entertainment) (Marikyan et al., 2019).

According to a systematic literature review of wearable devices adoption (Ferreira et al., 2021) perceived utility and visibility are important factors driving adoption intent, suggesting that smartwatches represent a kind of "fashionology" (i.e., fashion and technology). Other factors are expected benefits, including utility, ease of use, and image. Moreover, device portability and resilience are essential for prolonged use. Consumer acceptance barriers of wearable devices include concerns linked to the privacy of collected data, sensor durability, and cost/benefit ratio of wearing devices (Ferreira et al., 2021).

Similarly, in a systematic literature review, Lu et al. (2018) show that one of the key drivers of consumer resistance to IoT is privacy concerns. Privacy in the marketing context is understood as the consumer's ability to control their personal information (Mani & Chouk, 2019). Firms gather vast datasets regarding consumer behaviour on the Internet. IoT not only allows to gather more data and of detailed and sensitive nature, but also IoT devices and services rely on this data to perform better. "Without data, IoT does not exist" (Weinberg et al., 2015).

Privacy paradox is a phenomenon according to which consumers are generally concerned over the loss of privacy, but they fail to keep their data safe (Bandara et al., 2020). While some studies negate the existence of the privacy paradox, others show the opposite (Aleisa et al., 2020). According to Weinberg et al. (2015), consumers compare the conveniences offered by IoT and the losses in privacy (privacy calculus). The privacy calculus has already been researched in the context of mobile devices (Barth et al., 2019; Keith et al., 2013) and location-based services (Sun et al., 2015). Touzani et al. (2018) found that consumers are sceptic towards the "good intentions" of IoT providers in terms of privacy and surveillance. Moreover, Kim et al. (2019) found that while the perceived benefit is positively related to willingness to provide private information, perceived privacy risk does not influence such willingness in the context of healthcare IoT services, smart transport, and smart home services.

Consumers and Augmented Reality

AR applications are usually installed on mobile (e.g. smartphones) or wearable (e.g. AR glasses) devices (Rauschnabel et al., 2018). AR allows superimposing digital content in a real-world environment (Flavián et al., 2019). For example, AR enables virtually trying on clothes or glasses, bringing stores and products to consumers' houses. Two AR characteristics (environmental embedding and simulated physical control) can decrease consumers' cognitive load, enhance their cognitive fluency, and consequently improve their product attitude (Fan et al., 2020). AR applications create more interactive, vivid, and richer experiences for consumers (Hilken et al., 2017) and improve consumer flow experience (Javornik et al., 2016). Other popular applications of AR are games (e.g. Pokemon Go) which thanks to this technology become more playful (Li & Fang, 2020). Consumers also find AR especially useful in the areas of education, medicine, and tourism (Grzegorczyk et al., 2019).

In a future-oriented study, Rauschnabel (2021) investigates consumer acceptance of holographic AR substitutes for real products. For example, instead of buying a TV one would buy a cheap application in app store. The findings demonstrate mixed acceptance rates: high for some product categories (e.g. post-it notes, navigation technology) and low for other ones (e.g. pets, memorabilia). Rauschnabel (2021) also identified product and consumer characteristics (e.g. utilitarian benefits, digitalized products, familiarity with AR) as drivers of consumer acceptance of AR's substitution function. If this vision comes true, AR might have an even more remarkable impact on businesses, companies, and societies than previously predicted.

While many studies found that the utilitarian value of AR was the most important determinant of AR acceptance in e-commerce (e.g. Hilken et al., 2017; Rese et al., 2017; Yim et al., 2017), Bonnin (2020) presented surprisingly different findings: AR's usefulness was of little significance. Similarly, Javornik (2016) claims that consumers' experience with AR is more hedonic (affective) than utilitarian (cognitive). Hedonic motivation and similar factors (e.g. enjoyment) have been shown to impact AR's acceptance in e-commerce (e.g. Hilken et al., 2017; Yim et al., 2017). However, Rese et al. (2017) found the relative importance of hedonic (enjoyment, pleasure, fun) and utilitarian (information) aspects varies for different kinds of AR apps. Hedonic factors may also play the biggest role during the first contact with this technology – which is crucial, as most consumers still have not yet used AR (Javornik, 2016). Moreover, consumers also value AR's ease of use (Huang & Liao, 2015; Rese et al., 2017) and novelty (Grzegorczyk et al., 2019).

There are some factors hampering the rate of AR adoption. These are higher demand for computing power and lack of usefulness in some application areas (Grzegorczyk et al., 2019). While AR is a tool aimed at reducing the risk of unwanted online purchase by allowing to get a better sense of product features (Kim & Forsythe, 2008), Bonnin (2020) showed that the risk of buying an unsatisfactory product decreases the attractiveness of AR store and its patronage intention. Playing AR games may also be connected with physical risk (Rauschnabel et al., 2017). Moreover, AR's use requires access to the device's camera which raises the question of data safety. Similarly to other IoT devices, consumers are also concerned about marketers collecting and using private data (Dacko, 2017).

The future of consumer and new technologies

"Prediction is very difficult, especially about the future" is a famous citation attributed to Niels Bohr. However, we still may be sure of further technological progress, especially in terms of AI, IoT, and AR. While each of those technologies has a different tempo and scope of development, they are probably headed in the same direction. The technological advancement will encompass miniaturization of devices, the refinement of governing algorithms, and the merging of those technologies. While AI, IoT, and AR already share many commonalities, AI algorithms will probably be embedded into every IoT and AR device, and almost all AI and AR devices will become a part of IoT.

These technologies will become ubiquitous, more unobtrusive, almost invisible, and seamlessly merged into our lives. For example, we will use AI voicebots to browse the Internet, control smartphone applications and other IoT devices. It will be also more and more difficult for consumers to avoid using those technologies as they become a part of our surroundings. Interestingly, while those technologies seem to be a natural habitat for generation Y and Z consumers, technological progress might paradoxically "restore" them for elder generations. The benefits offered by those technologies might become too difficult to ignore and the common barrier of difficulty of use will become non-existent.

When it comes to particular products, AVs will reach the next levels of autonomy, finally reaching full autonomy (level 5) allowing for unsupervised driving in all conditions. While some predict it might happen by 2030 (Skeete, 2018), it will probably happen later. This will change the pattern of consumption we are used to in the automotive industry. Consumers will not buy cars widely; due to costs, autonomous cars will be rented on sharing platforms for particular trips and journeys (Skeete, 2018). However, a significant challenge might constitute ethical and safety concerns (Haenlein & Kaplan, 2019). Consumers might be unwilling to trust the safety of unsupervised vehicles, although that might be a problem only at the early stages of diffusion. Some might also be discouraged by moral dilemmas: how should the car act in the face of an imminent accident, if it can "choose" who should suffer the most – the driver or the pedestrian? Does the number of victims matter? The Moral Machine experiment shows that people have varied opinions on this matter (Awad et al., 2018).

It seems that also the diffusion of the IoT is inevitable. Not only the amount of data gathered will rise, but also their type and quality (e.g. detailed health data). Data becomes increasingly valuable for companies, as it brings new light on consumer nature and preferences. While according to consumer *declarations* privacy is a crucial issue, actual consumer behaviour shows the opposite (Aleisa et al., 2020). Although the level of privacy invasion will increase with additional devices we will be surrounded by, so will the benefits of IoT. Consequently, consumer privacy trade-off calculation should not change significantly. For example, while AR will be at the forefront of potential privacy invasion due to the cameras it requires to function, the possibilities of "holografication" of our reality might seem to be too enticing for consumers. However, the lack of certain features, such as haptic experiences, may hamper its diffusion.

Practical implications

The market uncertainty of the high technology consumer sector is manifested as uncertainty about the product's value for the consumer, as well as the consumer's future needs. To meet these challenges, in line with the marketing orientation of the company, companies should study the determinants of consumers' decisions and cooperate with consumers from the early stages of developing an innovative product (Grzegorczyk, 2020a; Mohr et al., 2010). They should focus not only on the current needs of consumers but also on their future ones. However, consumers may have a hard time verbalizing those. They may also underestimate their need for innovative products (Rauschnabel, 2021). Consequently, companies willing to take over the markets of the future should not be afraid to strive for even more disruptive innovations which AI, IoT, and AR bring along. For example, "consumer value grows with higher AI product autonomy" (Frank et al., 2021, p. 12).

Managers should not hold back from entering the market with those novel technologies. Although their full potential is very far from being achieved, they already offer various benefits and consumers are willing to overlook minor flaws in the case of emerging technologies (Scholz & Duffy, 2018). Novelty and wow-effect should play an important role in the marketing of AI, AR, and IoT.

Researchers are increasingly focused on the hedonic and symbolic value of new technologies (Frank et al., 2021). Therefore, firms should highlight such features in product design, advertising, and selling activities. This is also valid for products previously not associated with entertainment, such as autonomous cars. The more autonomous cars become, the more leisure opportunities they should offer (e.g. multimedia tablets or comfortable sleeping seats) (Frank et al., 2021).

Findings are mixed whether companies should focus more on maximizing products' benefits or minimizing consumer sacrifices. Some authors claim that companies should focus more on the elimination of risks perceived by consumers (e.g. Ameen et al., 2021). Convenience and usefulness might not compensate for the loss of privacy or lack of human interaction. Furthermore, firms should aim for strengthening their brand reputation by implementing consumer data protection policies. This could be supported by promotional and educational campaigns.

Conclusions

There already is substantial research on acceptance determinants of emerging technologies which is confirmed by analysed empirical consumer studies and systematic literature reviews. As this analysis has shown, AI, IoT, and AR have the potential to disrupt existing markets and drastically change consumer habits. Most studies dwelling into the factors influencing consumer adoption of those novel technologies are based on TAM and UTAUT2 or – less often – on perceived value theory. However, those acceptance models are commonly modified and extended with additional (both positive and negative) factors.

Some factors play a significant role in all those technologies. For example, usefulness and perceived enjoyment (or utilitarian and emotional/hedonic value) are commonly found to influence acceptance. However, which of those seems to be pivotal depends on a particular implementation of technology (e.g. type of application; Rese et al., 2020). Similarly, consumers are concerned about safety when using certain AI, AR, and IoT products and services (e.g. AVs, AR games), but not in others. Furthermore, all those technologies may invade consumer privacy (especially IoT and AR). However, researchers have difficulty measuring the true impact of this threat, as consumer declarations seem to differ from their actions. This may be the result of the privacy calculus – consumer sacrifices are neglected due to significantly more important benefits. Some factors are more technology-specific. For example, AI products and services are prone to function independently from the user which may result in the fear of loss of autonomy.

There is no consensus if companies should focus on increasing the general benefit of their products or diminishing consumer sacrifices. Nevertheless, increasing trust towards the innovating company, their products and technology might help both.

The leading limitation of the literature review resides in its method because it does not have a systematic character. Because of the broad thematical scope of this chapter, it has a narrative character. Therefore, some studies have been overlooked and no quantitative analysis has been performed. This may result in the limited generalizability of the findings.

There is a plethora of possible future research directions. One of those might be introducing more experimental studies, focusing on actual consumer behaviour instead of depending on declarations. Researchers might also dwell on the emotional responses of consumers. Another research avenue might be focusing on different consumer segments (e.g. dependent on age or psychological variables) and comparing their attitudes towards technological innovations. Another important research direction is the study of the impact of cultural differences on technology acceptance. Those might differ significantly and most of the literature on technology acceptance concentrates on the Western population (Aleisa et al., 2020). Furthermore, consumer attitudes and their determinants will change along with technological development and the market offer. Consequently, researchers should follow those. The merging of AI, IoT, and AR technology should encourage researchers to broaden the scope of their studies.

Companies should not wait for those technologies to mature – AI, IoT, and AR already are attractive to consumers in multiple industries. Implementing those technologies into both existing and new products and services not only will increase consumer value but also improve the company's image.

However, it is crucial for companies to carefully manage the integration of those technologies with existing solutions to provide a seamless consumer experience. While chatbots are often used in customer service, they still have limited capabilities in resolving complex consumer issues or queries. Algorithms should be trained to recognize such cases and swiftly hand the conversation over to a human agent (Hoyer et al., 2020).

In order to reduce consumers' concerns companies should increase their trust, both towards the emerging technology and the company. It can be achieved by public transparency, data protection policy, gradual introduction of the technology, as well as proactive communication connected with benefit-oriented information.

Bibliography

Ajzen, I. (1991). The theory of planned behavior. *Organizational Behavior and Human Decision Processes, 50*, 179–211.

Aleisa, N., Renaud, K., & Bongiovanni, I. (2020). The privacy paradox applies to IoT devices too: A Saudi Arabian study. *Computers and Security, 96*, 101897. https://doi.org/10.1016/j.cose.2020.101897.

Ameen, N., Tarhini, A., Reppel, A., & Anand, A. (2021). Customer experiences in the age of artificial intelligence. *Computers in Human Behavior, 114*, 106548. https://doi.org/10.1016/j.chb.2020.106548.

Ashfaq, M., Yun, J., Yu, S., & Loureiro, S.M.C. (2020). I, Chatbot: Modeling the determinants of users' satisfaction and continuance intention of AI-powered service agents. *Telematics and Informatics, 54*(April), 101473. https://doi.org/10.1016/j.tele.2020.101473

Atzori, L., Iera, A., & Morabito, G. (2014). From "smart objects" to "social objects": The next evolutionary step of the Internet of Things. *IEEE Communication Magazine, 52*(1), 97–105.

Awad, E., Dsouza, S., Kim, R., Schulz, J., Henrich, J., Shariff, A., Bonnefon, J.F., & Rahwan, I. (2018). The moral machine experiment. *Nature, 563*(7729), 59–64. https://doi.org/10.1038/s41586-018-0637-6.

Babin, B.J., & Harris, E. (2017). *Consumer behavior* (8th ed.). Cengage.

Bandara, R., Fernando, M., & Akter, S. (2020). Explicating the privacy paradox: A qualitative inquiry of online shopping consumers. *Journal of Retailing and Consumer Services, 52*(August 2019), 101947. https://doi.org/10.1016/j.jretconser.2019.101947.

Bansal, G., Zahedi, F.M., & Gefen, D. (2016). Do context and personality matter? Trust and privacy concerns in disclosing private information online. *Information Management, 53*, 1–21. https://doi.org/10.1016/j.im.2015.08.001.

Barth, S., de Jong, M.D.T., Junger, M., Hartel, P.H., & Roppelt, J.C. (2019). Putting the privacy paradox to the test: Online privacy and security behaviors among users with technical knowledge, privacy awareness, and financial resources. *Telematics and Informatics, 41*(February 2019), 55–69. https://doi.org/10.1016/j.tele.2019.03.003.

Bartosik-Purgat, M., Grzegorczyk, T., & Rakowska, W. (2021). Consumer acceptance of AR technology in e-commerce in the light of the Covid-19 pandemic: A conceptual perspective. In E. Mińska-Struzik & B. Jankowska (Eds.),

Toward the "new normal" after Covid-19 – A post-transition economy perspective (pp. 186–195). Poznań University of Economics and Business Press. https://doi.org/10.18559/978-83-8211-061-6/II6.

Bélanger, F., & Crossler, R. (2011). Privacy in the digital age: A review of information privacy research in information systems. *MIS Quarterly,* 35(4), 1017–1041. doi:10.2307/41409971.

Bonnin, G. (2020). The roles of perceived risk, attractiveness of the online store and familiarity with AR in the influence of AR on patronage intention. *Journal of Retailing and Consumer Services, 52*(August 2019). https://doi.org/10.1016/j.jretconser.2019.101938.

Choi, J.K., & Ji, Y.G. (2015). Investigating the importance of trust on adopting an autonomous vehicle. *International Journal of Human–Computer Interaction, 31*(10), 692–702. https://doi.org/10.1080/10447318.2015.1070549.

Chouk, I., & Mani, Z. (2019). Factors for and against resistance to smart services: Role of consumer lifestyle and ecosystem related variables. *Journal of Services Marketing,* 33(4), 449–462. https://doi.org/10.1108/JSM-01-2018-0046.

Ciechanowski, L., Przegalinska, A., Magnuski, M., & Gloor, P. (2019). In the shades of the uncanny valley: An experimental study of human–chatbot interaction. *Future Generation Computer Systems, 92,* 539–548. https://doi.org/10.1016/j.future.2018.01.055.

Clark, H., & Feng, J. (2017). Age differences in the takeover of vehicle control and engagement in non-driving-related activities in simulated driving with conditional automation. *Accident Analysis & Prevention, 106,* 468–479. https://doi.org/10.1016/j.aap.2016.08.027. PMID: 27686942.

Dacko, S.G. (2017). Technological forecasting & social change enabling smart retail settings via mobile augmented reality shopping apps. *Technological Forecasting & Social Change, 124,* 243–256. https://doi.org/10.1016/j.techfore.2016.09.032.

Davis, F.D. (1989). Perceived usefulness, perceived ease of use, and user acceptance of information technology. *MIS Quarterly, 13*(3), 319–340.

Du, S., & Xie, C. (2021). Paradoxes of artificial intelligence in consumer markets: Ethical challenges and opportunities. *Journal of Business Research, 129*(February 2019), 961–974. https://doi.org/10.1016/j.jbusres.2020.08.024.

Fagnant, D.J., & Kockelman, K. (2015). Preparing a nation for autonomous vehicles: Opportunities, barriers and policy recommendations. *Transportation Research Part A Policy,* 77, 167–181. https://doi.org/10.1016/j.tra.2015.04.003.

Fan, X., Chai, Z., Deng, N., & Dong, X. (2020). Adoption of augmented reality in online retailing and consumers' product attitude: A cognitive perspective. *Journal of Retailing and Consumer Services, 53*(February 2019), 101986. https://doi.org/10.1016/j.jretconser.2019.101986.

Featherman, M.S., & Pavlou, P.A. (2003). Predicting e-services adoption: A perceived risk facets perspective. *International Journal of Human-Computer Studies, 59,* 451–474. https://doi.org/10.1016/S1071-5819(03)00111-3.

Ferreira, J.J., Fernandes, C.I., Rammal, H.G., & Veiga, P.M. (2021). Wearable technology and consumer interaction: A systematic review and research agenda. *Computers in Human Behavior, 118*(November 2020). https://doi.org/10.1016/j.chb.2021.106710.

Fishbein, M., & Azjen, I. (1975). *Belief, attitude, intention and behaviour: An introduction to theory and research.* Addison-Wesley.

Flavián, C., Ibáñez-Sánchez, S., & Orús, C. (2019). The impact of virtual, augmented and mixed reality technologies on the customer experience. *Journal of Business Research, 100*(November 2018), 547–560. https://doi.org/10.1016/j.jbusres.2018.10.050.

Frank, B., Herbas-Torrico, B., & Schvaneveldt, S.J. (2021). The AI-extended consumer: Technology, consumer, country differences in the formation of demand for AI-empowered consumer products. *Technological Forecasting and Social Change, 172*(June). https://doi.org/10.1016/j.techfore.2021.121018.

Grzegorczyk, T. (2019). Pomiar wartości postrzeganej przez konsumentów w badaniach akceptacji innowacji technologicznych, *Zeszyty Naukowe Uniwersytetu Ekonomicznego w Krakowie, 983*(5). https://doi.org/10.15678/ZNUEK.2019.0983.0503.

Grzegorczyk, T. (2020a). Company's proactive marketing orientation in the high-tech sector. *Scientific Quarterly "Organization and Management", 1*(49), 57–69. https://doi.org/10.29119/1899-6116.2020.49.4.

Grzegorczyk, T. (2020b). Istota i wymiary postrzeganego przez konsumentów ryzyka związanego z produktami zaawansowanymi technologicznie. *Zeszyty naukowe Politechniki Poznańskiej. Organizacja i Zarzadzanie, 81*, 47–59. https://doi.org/10.21008/j.0239-9415.2020.081.04.

Grzegorczyk, T., Sliwinski, R., & Kaczmarek, J. (2019). Attractiveness of augmented reality to consumers. *Technology Analysis and Strategic Management, 31*(11), 257–1269. https://doi.org/10.1080/09537325.2019.1603368.

Gurumurthy, K.M., & Kockelman, K.M. (2020). Modeling Americans' autonomous vehicle preferences: A focus on dynamic ride-sharing, privacy & long-distance mode choices. *Technological Forecasting Social Change, 150*, 119792. https://doi.org/10.1016/j.techfore.2019.119792.

Haenlein, M., & Kaplan, A. (2019). A brief history of artificial intelligence: On the past, present, and future of artificial intelligence. *California Management Review, 61*(4), 5–14. https://doi.org/10.1177/0008125619864925.

Hengstler, M., Enkel, E., & Duelli, S. (2016). Applied artificial intelligence and trust – The case of autonomous vehicles and medical assistance devices. *Technological Forecasting and Social Change, 105*, 105–120. https://doi.org/10.1016/j.techfore.2015.12.014.

Hilken, T., de Ruyter, K., Chylinski, M., Mahr, D., & Keeling, D.I. (2017). Augmenting the eye of the beholder: Exploring the strategic potential of augmented reality to enhance online service experiences. *Journal of the Academy of Marketing Science, 45*(6), 884–905. https://doi.org/10.1007/s11747-017-0541-x.

Hohenberger, C., Sporrle, M., & Welpe, I.M. (2017). How and why do men and women differ in their willingness to use automated cars? The influence of emotions across different age groups. *Transportation Research Part A: Policy and Practice, 94*, 374–385. https://doi.org/10.1016/j.tra.2016.09.022.

Hopp, C., Antons, D., Kaminski, J., & Oliver Salge, T. (2018). Disruptive innovation: Conceptual foundations, empirical evidence, and research opportunities in the digital age. *Journal of Product Innovation Management, 35*(3), 446–457. https://doi.org/10.1111/jpim.12448.

Hoyer, W.D., Kroschke, M., Schmitt, B., Kraume, K., & Shankar, V. (2020). Transforming the customer experience through new technologies. *Journal of Interactive Marketing, 51*, 57–71. https://doi.org/10.1016/j.intmar.2020.04.001.

Hryniewicz, K., & Grzegorczyk, T. (2020). How different autonomous vehicle presentation influences its acceptance: Is a communal car better than agentic one? *PLoS One, 15*(9 September). https://doi.org/10.1371/journal.pone.0238714

Huang, T.L., & Liao, S. (2015). A model of acceptance of augmented-reality interactive technology: The moderating role of cognitive innovativeness. *Electronic Commerce Research, 15*(2), 269–295. https://doi.org/10.1007/s10660-014-9163-2.

Im, S., & Workman, J.P. (2004). Market orientation, creativity, and new product performance in high-technology firms A. *Journal of Marketing, 68*, 114–132. http://doi.org/10.1509/jmkg.68.2.114.27788.

Javornik, A. (2016). 'It's an illusion, but it looks real!' Consumer affective, cognitive and behavioural responses to augmented reality applications. *Journal of Marketing Management, 32*(9–10), 987–1011. https://doi.org/10.1080/0267257X.2016.1174726.

Jing, P., Xu, G., Chen, Y., Shi, Y., & Zhan, F. (2020). The determinants behind the acceptance of autonomous vehicles: A systematic review. *Sustainability, 12*, 1719. https://doi.org/10.3390/su12051719.

Kamolsook, A., Badir, Y.F., & Frank, B. (2019). Consumers' switching to disruptive technology products: The roles of comparative economic value and technology type. *Technological Forecasting and Social Change, 140*(January), 328–340. https://doi.org/10.1016/j.techfore.2018.12.023.

Kapser, S., & Abdelrahman, M. (2020). Acceptance of autonomous delivery vehicles for last-mile delivery in Germany – extending UTAUT2 with risk perceptions. *Transportation Research: Part C Emerging Technologies, 111*, 210–225. https://doi.org/10.1016/j.trc.2019.12.016.

Kaur, K., & Rampersad, G. (2018). Trust in driverless cars: Investigating key factors influencing the adoption of driverless cars. *Journal of Engineering and Technology Management, 48*, 87–96. https://doi.org/10.1016/j. jengtecman.2018.04.006.

Keith, M.J., Thompson, S.C., Hale, J., Lowry, P.B., & Greer, C. (2013). Information disclosure on mobile devices: Re-examining privacy calculus with actual user behavior. *International Journal of Human-Computer Studies, 71*(12), 1163–1173. https://doi.org/10.1016/j.ijhcs.2013.08.016.

Kim, D., Park, K., Park, Y., & Ahn, J.H. (2019). Willingness to provide personal information: Perspective of privacy calculus in IoT services. *Computers in Human Behavior, 92*(October 2018), 273–281. https://doi.org/10.1016/j.chb.2018.11.022.

Kim, J., & Forsythe, S. (2008). Adoption of virtual try-on technology for online apparel shopping. *Journal of Interactive Marketing, 22*(2), 45–59.

Kline, S., & Rosenberg, N. (1986). An overview of innovation. In R. Landau & N. Rosenberg (Eds.), *The positive sum strategy. Harnessing technology for economic growth* (pp. 275–306). National Academy Press.

Konig, M., & Neumayr, L. (2017). Users' resistance towards radical innovations: The case of the self-driving car. *Transportation Research Part F: Traffic Psychology and Behaviour, 44*, 42–52. https://doi.org/10.1016/j.trf.2016.10.013.

Kumar, V., Ramachandran, D., & Kumar, B. (2021). Influence of new-age technologies on marketing: A research agenda. *Journal of Business Research, 125*(October 2019), 864–877. https://doi.org/10.1016/j.jbusres.2020.01.007.

Li, C.Y., & Fang, Y.H. (2020). I searched, I collected, I experienced: Exploring how mobile augmented reality makes the players go. *Journal of Retailing and Consumer Services, 54*(151), 102018. https://doi.org/10.1016/j.jretconser.2019.102018.

Liu, P., Guo, Q., Ren, F., Wang, L., & Xu, Z. (2019). Willingness to pay for self-driving vehicles: Influences of demo-graphic and psychological factors. *Transportation Research Part C: Emerging Technologies, 100*, 306–317. https:// doi.org/10.1016/j.trc.2019.01.022.

Lu, Y., Papagiannidis, S., & Alamanos, E. (2018). Internet of things: A systematic review of the business literature from the user and organisational perspectives. *Technological Forecasting and Social Change, 136*(2), 285–297. https://doi.org/10.1016/j.techfore.2018.01.022.

Marikyan, D., Papagiannidis, S., & Alamanos, E. (2019). A systematic review of the smart home literature: A user perspective. *Technological Forecasting and Social Change, 138*(September 2018), 139–154. https://doi.org/10.1016/j.techfore.2018.08.015.

Mick, D.G., & Fournier, S. (1998). Paradoxes of technology: Consumer cognizance, emotions, and coping strategies. *Journal of Consumer Research, 25*(2), 123–143. https://doi.org/10.1086/209531.

Mohr, J. Sengupta, S., & Slater, S. (2010). *Marketing of High—Technology Products and Innovations*. New Jersey.

Oshana, R., & Kraeling, M. (2019). *Software engineering for embedded systems: Methods, practical techniques, and applications*. Newnes.

Penmetsa, P., Adanu, E.K., Wood, D., Wang, T., & Jones, S.L. (2019). Perceptions and expectations of autonomous vehicles – A snapshot of vulnerable road user opinion. *Technological Forecasting & Social Change, 143*, 9–13. https://doi.org/10.1016/j.techfore.2019.02.010.

Peter, J., & Ryan, M. (1976). An investigation of perceived risk at the brand level. *Journal of Marketing Research, 13*, 184–188.

Rauschnabel, P.A. (2021). Augmented reality is eating the real-world! The substitution of physical products by holograms. *International Journal of Information Management, 57*(November), 102279. https://doi.org/10.1016/j.ijinfomgt.2020.102279.

Rauschnabel, P.A., He, J., & Ro, Y.K. (2018). Antecedents to the adoption of augmented reality smart glasses: A closer look at privacy risks. *Journal of Business Research, 92*(November), 374–384. https://doi.org/10.1016/j.jbusres.2018.08.008.

Rauschnabel, P.A., Rossmann, A., & tom Dieck, M.C. (2017). An adoption framework for mobile augmented reality games: The case of Pokémon Go. *Computers in Human Behavior, 76*(August), 276–286. https://doi.org/10.1016/j.chb.2017.07.030.

Rese, A., Baier, D., Geyer-Schulz, A., & Schreiber, S. (2017). How augmented reality apps are accepted by consumers: A comparative analysis using scales and opinions. *Technological Forecasting and Social Change, 124*, 306–319. https://doi.org/10.1016/j.techfore.2016.10.010

Rese, A., Ganster, L., & Baier, D. (2020). Chatbots in retailers' customer communication: How to measure their acceptance? *Journal of Retailing and Consumer Services, 56*(June), 102176. https://doi.org/10.1016/j.jretconser.2020.102176

Rijsdijk, S.A., Hultink, E.J., & Diamantopoulos, A. (2007). Product intelligence: Its conceptualization, measurement and impact on consumer satisfaction. *Journal of the Academy of Marketing Science, 35*(3), 340–356. http://doi.org/10.1007/s11747-007-0040-6.

Rogers, E.M. (1983). *Diffusion of innovations*. The Free Press.

Scholz, J., & Duffy, K. (2018). We ARe at home: How augmented reality reshapes mobile marketing and consumer-brand relationships. *Journal of Retailing and Consumer Services, 44*(May), 11–23. https://doi.org/10.1016/j.jretconser.2018.05.004.

Shabanpour, R., Golshani, N., Shamshiripour, A., & Mohammadian, A. (2018). Eliciting preferences for adoption of fully automated vehicles using best-worst analysis. *Transportation Research Part C: Emerging Technologies, 93*, 463–478. https://doi.org/10.1016/j.trc.2018.06.014.

Sheehan, B., Jin, H.S., & Gottlieb, U. (2020). Customer service chatbots: Anthropomorphism and adoption. *Journal of Business Research, 115*(February 2019), 14–24. https://doi.org/10.1016/j.jbusres.2020.04.030.

Sheth, J., Newman, B., & Gross, B. (1991). Why we buy what we buy: A theory of consumption values. *Journal of Business Research, 22*(2), 159–170.

Skeete, J.P. (2018). Level 5 autonomy: The new face of disruption in road transport. *Technological Forecasting and Social Change, 134*(May 2018), 22–34. https://doi.org/10.1016/j.techfore.2018.05.003.

Smith, J., & Colgate, M. (2007). Customer value creation: A practical framework. *The Journal of Marketing Theory and Practice, 15*(1), 7–23. http://doi.org/10.2753/MTP1069-6679150101.

Sun, Y., Wang, N., Shen, X.L., & Zhang, J.X. (2015). Location information disclosure in location-based social network services: Privacy calculus, benefit structure, and gender differences. *Computers in Human Behavior, 52*, 278–292.

Sweeney, J.C., & Soutar, G.N. (2001). Consumer perceived value: The development of a multiple item scale. *Journal of Retailing, 77*(2), 203–220. https://doi.org/10.1016/S0022-4359(01)00041-0.

Teece, D.J. (1998). Capturing value from knowledge assets: The new economy, markets for know-how, and intangible assets. *California Management Review, 40*(3), 55–79.

Touzani, M., Charfi, A.A., Boistel, P., & Niort, M.C. (2018). Connecto ergo sum! An exploratory study of the motivations behind the usage of connected objects. *Information and Management, 55*(4), 472–481. https://doi.org/10.1016/j.im.2017.11.002.

Van Deursen, A.J.A.M., & Mossberger, K. (2018). Any thing for anyone? A new digital divide in Internet-of-Things skills. *Policy & Internet, 10*(2), 122–140. https://doi.org/ 10.1002/poi3.171.

Venkatesh, V., Morris, M., Davis, G., & Davis, F. (2003). User acceptance of information technology: Toward a unified. *MIS Quarterly, 27*(3), 425–478.

Venkatesh, V., Thong, J., & Xu, X. (2016). Unified theory of acceptance and use of technology: A synthesis and the road ahead. *Journal of the Association for Information Systems, 17*(5), 328–376.

Viardot, E. (2004). *Successful marketing strategy for high-tech firms*. Artech House.

Weinberg, B.D., Milne, G.R., Andonova, Y.G., & Hajjat, F.M. (2015). Internet of Things: Convenience vs. privacy and secrecy. *Business Horizons, 58*(6), 615–624. https://doi.org/10.1016/j.bushor.2015.06.005.

Yang, H., Yu, J., Zo, H., & Choi, M. (2016). User acceptance of wearable devices: An extended perspective of perceived value. *Telematics and Informatics, 33*(2), 256–269. https://doi.org/10.1016/j.tele.2015.08.007.

Yim, M. Y. C., Chu, S. C., & Sauer, P. L. (2017). Is Augmented Reality Technology an Effective Tool for E-commerce? An Interactivity and Vividness Perspective. *Journal of Interactive Marketing, 39*, 89–103. https://doi.org/10.1016/j.intmar.2017.04.001

Zeithaml, V.A. (1988). Consumer perceptions of price, quality, and value: A means-end model and synthesis of evidence on JSTOR. *Journal of Marketing, 52*(3), 2–22.

4 E-commerce in light of digital technology development

A consumer perspective

Małgorzata Bartosik-Purgat and Barbara Jankowska

Introduction

The global development of information and communication technologies continues to contribute to changes in the functioning of societies around the world (Abumalloh et al., 2020; Zhu et al., 2020). The Internet offers people more and more opportunities to refine and accelerate all kinds of processes that take place in their daily lives. In the past, the commercial sector was characterised by, among others, direct contact between the seller and the buyer at the place where the transaction took place (e.g. in a store or at a market) (Ignat & Chankov, 2020; Ramírez-Correa et al., 2019). In the 1990s, entities from the commercial sector began to use the Internet for their activities. At that time, the first online platforms emerged (e.g. Amazon in the United States – 1994; e-bay in the United States – 1995; Rakuten in Japan – 1997; Allegro in Poland – 1999; Mercado Libre in Argentina – 1999; JD.com in China – 1998; Alibaba Group in China – 1999), which offered the possibility of ordering and buying goods in the form of adding products of various brands and categories to a virtual basket. This is how electronic commerce (e-commerce) was born. As a result of this situation, many individual producers began offering their products for online sale. The development of e-commerce became especially popular among individual Internet users (on *Business-to-Consumer* – B2C and *Consumer-to-Consumer* – C2C markets), but with time it also began to be used in *Business-to-Business* – B2B markets (Abumalloh et al., 2020; Peltier et al., 2020). E-commerce platforms offer not only selling possibilities, but also communication between companies and consumers (Sullivan & Kim, 2018).

A permanent increase in e-commerce can now be observed (Nogueira et al., 2021; Tokar et al., 2021), and since the COVID-19 pandemic broke out and national lockdowns have become a reality, the number of e-consumers shopping online has grown even faster than before (Tokar et al., 2021; Tran, 2021) and has become an integral part of lives of a majority of individual consumers (Zhu et al., 2020), in both developed and emerging economies (Akhlaq & Ahmed, 2016). People started buying products online that they would never have bought online before (Tran, 2021). In their newest report

DOI: 10.4324/9781003263685-6

entitled *60 percent of the world population is now online*, Kemp (2021) indicates that 92.2.% of Internet users aged 16–64 visited an online retail site or store, 78.6% purchased products online, and 40.1% sold products online. High percentages of consumers who had bought something online in the previous month were to be found in Asia, e.g.: Indonesia (88.1%), the Philippines (86.2%), Malaysia (85.7%), South Korea (84.1%), Singapore (82.5%), China (79%); European countries, e.g. United Kingdom (86.9%), Ireland (84.9%), Germany (84.9%), Italy (82.9%), Poland (82.9%), Austria (82.6%), Spain (81%), France (79.4%), Switzerland (79.2%); and the United States (81.4%). Nogueira et al. (2021) indicate that about 44.5% of the world's population purchased goods in e-commerce in 2020. The value of the e-commerce B2C market in 2020 has been valued at about US$ 2.44 trillion (Nogueira et al., 2021).

These high of e-commerce all over the world are caused by a number of factors, including increasing access to the Internet, the variety of offers available online (Abumalloh et al., 2020; Mangiaracina et al., 2015), the improvement of IT tools that allow for the efficient execution of transactions, the changing needs of buyers, a reduced amount of time buyers have for offline shopping, and limitations and concerns related to the COVID-19 pandemic, including lockdowns (Kissler et al., 2020; Tran, 2021). This, in turn, forced the creation and development of more and more modern, convenient, and safe forms of payment, fast methods of delivery, and the extension of consumer rights (Ignat & Chankov, 2020; Kolotylo-Kulkarni et al., 2021; Sullivan & Kim, 2018; Tokar et al., 2021). Indeed, consumer protection is one of the most important aspects of many online retailers nowadays (Bartosik-Purgat & Jankowska, 2020), but many customers still have doubts concerning information privacy and the use of their data shared during e-commerce transactions (Belwal et al., 2021; Zhu et al., 2020). That is why many producers explain fair practices and ensure confidentiality in the use of consumer data on their e-commerce platforms (Belwal et al., 2021).

The wide range of aspects related to e-commerce, as well as observations concerning the behaviour of both e-consumers and producers selling their products online, has contributed to the emergence of many, important research questions and we attempt to study the following in this chapter:

RQ1: Why do people decide to buy/sell online? Where do they look for information about online offers?
RQ2: Who are online consumers in terms of age and gender?
RQ3: What kind of products do consumers buy online?
RQ4: What kind of devices do consumers use for online shopping?
RQ5: What kind of payment and delivery do consumers choose in online shopping?

Based on the above RQs, the main objective of this chapter is to identify e-consumer behaviour in light of the development of digital technologies and solutions in e-commerce.

To achieve the main goal, we applied the SALSA method (*Search, Appraisal, Synthesis, and Analysis*) as the main research method (Grant & Booth, 2009). To conduct a literature analysis of published sources, the Emerald and Elsevier databases were used, and the time scope of the papers was 2015–2021, the period during which the highest level of growth in e-commerce and digital technologies has been observed (Nogueira et al., 2021; Tokar et al., 2021). The keywords used in the searching phase included: "e-commerce", "digital technologies", "consumer behaviour", "gender", and "age". In the appraisal phase, it became clear that the thematic scope presented in the selected papers was not enough to answer all research questions. As a result, we applied a snowball sampling method in the next step (Chromy, 2008), through which we reached additional papers (both scientific and popular science) and reports related to our research questions. These were evaluated based on inclusion and exclusion criteria associated with our overall research aims in order to obtain the final papers for analysis. In the two last stages of the SALSA procedure (Synthesis and Analysis), we concentrated on analysing and synthesising the chosen papers, concluding, and summing up the main findings (Grant & Booth, 2009).

Whilst the scientific literature provides interesting research results concerning e-commerce facilitators (e.g. Abumalloh et al., 2020; Bartosik-Purgat & Jankowska, 2020), the main contribution of this current chapter remains the complex description of trends related to digital technology development and consumer behaviour in e-commerce, especially in light of the COVID-19 pandemic (Kissler et al., 2020; Nogueira et al., 2021). The conducted analysis and its results have a number of business implications which can be used in e-commerce strategy creation (the main practical implications are presented at the end of this chapter). The chapter is structured as follows: First, the results of the literature review related to specific RQs are presented, after which conclusions are forwarded, including business implications and predictions for the future of e-commerce.

Literature review

The models and determinants of online shopping

The most recognised and most frequently used models of e-commerce are B2C and C2C. With the e-B2C model, a company decides to sell products or services to final consumers via online platforms (Wang et al., 2020). This is one of the most popular forms of e-commerce, and its advantages for companies include, among others, low start-up costs, a much shorter decision-making process on the part of the customer, and the ease of entering foreign markets and thus searching for customers globally. However, from a consumer perspective, the wide range of products, convenience, time for comparisons of products and services, and usually lower prices are underlined (Abumalloh et al., 2020; Akhlaq & Ahmed, 2016; Mangiaracina et al., 2015; Nogueira et al., 2021). The disadvantages of this model for companies may include the difficulty to acquire loyal customers, which translates into the need to increase spending on online marketing. In addition, as it is the most popular e-business model today, there is a problem of significant price competition, which is often referred to as "price wars", which only highlights the scale of the problem. In the B2C model, the quality of customer service is also important due to the fact that e-commerce consumers are becoming ever more demanding (Nogueira et al., 2021; Sullivan & Kim, 2018). Individual customers have high expectations regarding the quality of service, and each of them should be approached in a personalised manner (Jain & Sundström, 2021).

Consumers decide to buy products online for many reasons. The most commonly chosen motives indicated by Wang et al. (2020) are convenience, quality concern, and price. These elements are also emphasised by Mangiaracina et al. (2015), but these authors also add the possibility of the best delivery and payment system choice and the high level of service that online retailers provide. Based on the factors valued by online shoppers, Nguyen et al. (2019) identified three groups of e-consumers. First, there are consumers oriented towards price (e.g. price of products and delivery), second, there are those oriented towards convenience (speed of delivery, flexibility), and third, those oriented to value and money (both aspects associated with convenience and price) (Nguyen et al., 2019). Tokar et al. (2021) state that by doing more of their activities each day via online platforms (e.g. education, work, banking), people have become accustomed to online shopping and have accepted online realities. Nevertheless, the authors underline that probably the most influential stimulus for buying goods online the convenience – i.e. products are delivered directly to homes or other convenient pickup locations. Kemp (2021) presents the percentages of global Internet users (16–64 years old) who indicated the determinants influencing an increase in their online shopping. 52.6% of respondents answered that it would be free delivery, 40.3% coupons and discounts, 33.8% reviews from other customers, 32.6% easy return policy, 29.6% quick and easy online checkout processes, 28.2% next day delivery, 26.8% loyalty points, 22% lots of "Likes" or good comments on social media, 20.2% information that producer is eco-friendly, 18.9% ability to spread payments over time without interest, 18.2% ability to pay cash on delivery, 15.3% exclusive content or services, 14.9% "guest" check out, 14.5% live-chat to speak to the company, and 12.4% a "buy" button on social media (Kemp, 2021).

The development of new online tools and applications, as well as the skills of individual users, have led to rapid growth in the C2C market, in which there is a direct relationship between consumers, including the sale, purchase, and exchange of goods or services on auction portals or barter platforms, e.g. on the Vinted app or social media services such as Facebook (Saarijärvi et al., 2018). The advantages of using the C2C model include the chance to reach a huge group of recipients due to the high popularity of auction sites and social platforms, as well as the relatively low cost of selling, compared to B2B or B2C models (Saarijärvi et al., 2018). The main disadvantage of this model is the lack of control over the sales process, as there are often problems with non-receipt of payments or lost parcels.

The development of C2C platforms in recent years (Saarijärvi et al., 2018) has in part been driven by environmental issues (Awwad et al., 2018; Guo et al., 2019; Nogueira et al., 2021; Yrjölä et al., 2017). In contrast to consumers who continue to buy new products, platforms such as Vinted – where people sell products they no longer use (e.g. clothes, shoes, toys, accessories, etc.) – allow consumers to give products "a second life" and contribute to the protection of the environment (Yrjölä et al., 2017). But, it should be also underlined that the high growth of online retail of any sort contributes to "packaging and waste, traffic and emissions, and energy and resource consumption" (Tokar et al., 2021, p. 323).

There are many sources where people look for information about producers, their offers, and services, and in the digital era people also now use online tools to gather such information. There has been a growth observed in the importance of informal channels and sources. Online shoppers try to find out more about a particular offer not only directly from the producer's website, but also from other clients. That is why e-Word-of-Mouth (e-WoM) and social commerce (SC) are becoming more and more important in gathering information about sellers and products available online (Bartosik-Purgat, 2018b; Grange et al., 2020; Kim & Kim, 2018; Mou & Benyoucef, 2021; Saarijärvi et al., 2018). People ask other Internet users about their opinions and experiences of particular brands or producers and use a diverse range of Internet forums, blogs, or social media platforms. The findings of some research showed that consumers trust more such opinions than producers and marketers (Fu et al., 2018). Sullivan and Kim (2018) also indicate that the trust and credibility of online sellers may guarantee repurchase. Social platforms are used not only for searching and sharing information but also, as mentioned above, as platforms for offering/selling goods (new or already used) (Grange et al., 2020; Kim & Kim, 2018). Social media may also be employed by so-called influencers who sometimes work on behalf of particular producers. Sometimes, influencers underline that the content they present is not sponsored. Findings of the research conducted by Stubb and Colliander (2019) indicate that such posts are perceived by consumers as more credible, and generate higher source and message credibility. In related research, Abumalloh et al. (2020) underline the importance of recommender agents while online shopping among female Arab consumers.

Personal characteristics of online consumers in terms of age and gender

The personal characteristics of potential consumers may impact the adoption of the products and services by companies. Indeed, personal characteristics are perceived as the most significant determinants that help to understand the needs, preferences, and behaviour of consumers (Akhlaq & Ahmed, 2016;

Panda & Swar, 2016; Ramírez-Correa et al., 2019). Nevertheless, Peral-Peral et al. (2015) indicate that psychological aspects are also very important in understanding consumers' motivation towards the adoption and use of new technologies.

The scientific literature in the analysed period time (2016–2021) does not clearly indicate the differences between women and men towards online shopping (Dewi et al., 2020), despite the fact that before this period, researchers had underlined an important gender gap in consumer's online shopping (e.g. Akhlaq & Ahmed, 2016). Nevertheless, there have been some attempts to identify any differences. Bartosik-Purgat et al. (2017) distinguished gender as a significant variable in consumer activities via social media in different countries. Gender influences the recommendation of products to other social media users. In China, women recommend products via social media more than men, whilst in Germany and the United States, such activities are mostly done by men. Dewi et al. (2020) underlined that anxiety towards online purchase intentions is a more often recognisable determinant among Indonesian women than it is men. Other interesting and applicable results were presented by Akhlaq and Ahmed (2016), who researched Pakistani consumers. There was no significant difference noticed between men and women concerning the numbers of online buyers and the frequency. However, the authors identified differences in other elements consumers take into account. For example, they indicated that women are more sensitive towards the online environment for shopping, pay more attention to security, and like shopping in a safe online environment. In addition, women prefer online stores that emphasise the possibility of submitting claims (e.g. problems with bought products) and operating legally (Akhlaq & Ahmed, 2016).

The data presented by Kemp (2021) in their newest report *60 percent of the world population is now online* presents e-commerce adoption by age and gender (percentage of global Internet users who bought something online through any device in the previous month). It indicates a slight dominance of women buying online over men in each age group. The highest percentage of women who had bought something online in the previous month was observed in the 25–34 age group, whilst the 55–64 group was the lowest. The results of measurements conducted by Eurostat do not identify a difference between the number of women and men who are active online buyers (Eurostat.eu, 2021).

Dhanapal et al. (2015) researched online shoppers in Malaysia based on age. They concluded that representatives of generation X and Y are more eager to do online shopping and are more frequent online consumers than baby boomers. Similar results have been found by Eurostat.eu (2021), which found that about 80% of consumers aged 16–24 and 25–54 had bought online in 2020, in comparison to just 57% of 55–74-year-olds. It should also be noted that there was a large real term increase in the number of young online buyers between 2010 and 2020 (Eurostat.eu, 2021). Almost the same conclusions can be drawn from the database presented by Statista.com. (2021, August 23), i.e.: Millennials (24–35) are the largest group of online and the smallest are baby boomers (Statista.com, 2021, August 23).

Categories of products bought online

The number of product types purchased online has certainly increased since the COVID-19 pandemic started and lockdowns in many countries influenced an increase in online sales volumes. This was due to, first, the limited movement of people, and second, their fear of being infected with the coronavirus (Kissler et al., 2020). However, our literature analysis has not indicated the particular product categories purchased by online customers and so much data needs to be gathered from international statistical sources like Statista.com or Eurostat.eu.

Data presented by Statista.com (2021, August 20) indicates the e-commerce share of total retail revenue in the United States as of May 2020, sorted by product category. They indicate that books, music, and video accounted for 62.7% of retail revenues for that category. Next, there were computers and consumer electronics (49.5%), toys and hobbies (47.8%), office equipment and supplies (39.3%), apparel and accessories (36.7%), furniture and home furnishings (29.9%), health, personal care and beauty (13%), auto and parts (5.2%), food and beverage (3.7%), and other categories. Wang et al. (2020) indicate that food also belongs to a list of product categories that are quite often sold via online platforms, with consumers usually choosing packaged food, in particular dairy products, snacks, and baby food (Wang et al., 2020).

The Eurostat.eu database (2021, June) shows the percentages of individuals from European countries who bought or ordered goods or services over the Internet for private use in the previous three months. The most frequently purchased were clothes (including sports clothing) and shoes or accessories (63% of a total number of purchases), the second category of products within online purchases were furniture, home accessories, or gardening products (29%). Next, probably because of lockdowns and the closure of restaurants were deliveries from restaurants, fast-food chains, and catering services (28%). This was followed by cosmetics, beauty or wellness products (27%), printed books, magazines or newspapers at the same level (27%), and computers, tablets, mobile phones, or accessories (both 26%). European consumers also bought medicine and dietary products (23%), food and beverages (19%), consumer electronics (18%), children's toys (17%), and other products. CDs, DVDs, vinyl were bought less often than in the United States (Eurostat, 2021, June; Statista.com, 2021, August 20).

Devices used by consumers for online shopping

The development of digital technologies offers a broad range of devices that can be used by buyers during online shopping (Wagner et al., 2020). Individual consumers have many possibilities to access online shops, e.g. computers, smartphones, tablets, or even Internet-enabled TV (Wagner et al., 2020). All these devices offer unique facets that should be analysed by retailers to be able to adapt their offers and e-channels for the needs of particular groups of consumers (McLean et al., 2018). In addition, the diversification of devices used by customers may differentiate and adapt touchpoints on the journey map of an e-consumer.

In the case of mobile devices such as smartphones and tablets, people not only use the sellers' websites but also specific applications that allow for convenient and quick online transactions (Omar et al., 2021). E-channel apps for mobile devices are suitable touchpoints for customers, which allow them to interact with firms (Lemon & Verhoef, 2016; Wagner et al., 2020). Some companies meet the needs and preferences of consumers and try different e-channel touchpoints, e.g. Amazon offers three different touchpoints for tablets: a website adapted for tablets, a shopping app for tablets, and a "window" shopping app (Wagner et al., 2020).

Research conducted by Bartosik-Purgat (2018a) indicated the importance of mobile devices (e.g. smartphones, tablets) in e-consumer behaviour with regard to gathering and sharing information via social media platforms. The conclusions of a project conducted by Wagner et al. (2020) among German online shoppers show that the highest percentage of online shopping is handled by laptops/notebooks (87.3%), followed by personal computers (PC) (75.3%), smartphones (66.7%), tablets (30.7%), netbooks (18.9%), classic mobile phones (14.1.%), and Internet-enabled TV (via game console) (8.8%). Likewise, Kemp (2021) indicates that 63.8% of world e-commerce traffic originates from mobile devices like smartphones, 33.4% from laptops and desktops, and 2.8% from tablet devices. The same research emphasises that e-consumers in 2020 using mobiles most often bought luxury products, beauty products, clothes, and consumer electronics. By contrast, computers were used for financial services and energy payments (Kemp, 2021). The highest transaction values of online purchases made via mobile devices (as a percentage of all e-commerce transactions) were found in many Asian countries – South Korea (65%), China (63%), Indonesia (61%), Philippines (61%), Thailand (60%), Vietnam (60%), Malaysia (59%), Hong Kong (57%), Singapore (55%); some African countries – Nigeria (65%), South Africa (53%); and Middle Eastern countries – Saudi Arabia (59%) and UAE (57%). Transaction values were somewhat lower in Europe – Belgium (25%), Poland (26%), Canada (26%), France (31%), and the Netherlands (32%) (Kemp, 2021).

Payment and delivery methods used by consumers in online shopping

Bartosik-Purgat and Jankowska (2020) introduce the 3P (*Payment, Place, Price*) concept within consumer activities in e-commerce. On the one hand, cybercrime and fraud mean that people are distrustful. But, on the other hand, the enormous amount of information that reaches us from various websites and the ever-increasing number of our activities carried out on the Internet means that our vigilance may have weakened. This is why cyber-security plays a more significant role than ever (Haney & Lutters, 2021) and the same security problems pertain to e-purchases. E-consumers are offered a great range of payment methods to be used in e-commerce; not only credit cards and bank transfers, but also payment systems as prepaid card payments, e-wallets, mobile payments, cryptocurrencies, e-checks, and app-payment (Grüschow et al., 2016; Williams, 2021). In many countries (e.g. India) cash is still the most useful payment method, with customers usually choosing a cash-on-delivery option. Moreover, e-commerce shops usually offer more than one payment method and this choice offers more comfortable conditions for customers, which may, in turn, increase online purchases.

Kemp (2021) outlines the payment methods used in online global shopping in 2020 (share of global e-commerce transactions by payment methods): digital or mobile wallet (44.5%) was the most frequent option, followed by credit or debit card (35.1%), bank transfer (7.7%), charge and deferred debit card (3.3%), cash on delivery (3.3.%), buy now and pay later (2.1.%), post-pay (0.8%), and other payment methods (3.1%). E-wallet was the most popular in China (72%) with the worldwide average (45%), and credit cards in Japan (58%), South Korea (57%), Canada (55%), and Turkey (52%). Debit cards were used the most in Ireland (36%), Denmark (31%), Belgium (30%), and the United Kingdom (29%). E-consumers from the Netherlands (60%) and Poland (53%) mainly used bank transfers. Cash on delivery as a method of payment in e-commerce was used the most in Vietnam (28%), the Philippines (24%), Nigeria (23%), Thailand (22%), Indonesia (15%), and Peru (14%).

The next issue in the 3P concept in e-commerce is *placing*, which means the delivery methods of purchased products or services. Delivery possibilities are very important issues in consumers' decisions during online shopping and attention is paid to this factor (Kemp, 2021) because it concerns at least two key aspects: the time (speed) and place (way) of delivery (Nguyen et al., 2019). That is why online retailers offer different "last-mile delivery" (movements of goods from a transportation hub to the end-user) options to satisfy their customers (Ignat & Chankov, 2020).

The most frequent delivery solutions presented in the literature include home delivery (AHD), collection & delivery points (CDPs), controlled access systems, reception boxes, and parcel lockers (Kandula et al., 2021; Mangiaracina et al., 2019). Generally, e-consumers prefer the fastest, cheapest, most convenient, and flexible form of delivery. On the one hand, consumers prefer free shipping the most, but on the other hand, they are often willing to pay more for fast delivery (Mangiaracina et al., 2019). Kandula et al. (2021) indicate that the most preferred option is home delivery, and the "offering delivery time windows in advance is difficult". However, proposing an estimated delivery time during a purchase may improve e-customer satisfaction (Kandula et al., 2021).

Conclusions, implications, and directions of future research

The significance of e-commerce continues to increase in the era of mass digitalisation of our lives. The determinants of this situation are multifaceted. First, they are related to the macroeconomic conditions (e.g. IT infrastructure, access to the Internet, etc.); second, they concern companies' profiles and capacities (e.g. category of products offered online, the channel of distribution, IT capabilities, etc.); and third, they are connected with the needs, features and behaviour of consumers (e.g. traits, IT capabilities, lifestyle, etc.). Moreover, the growth of online shopping has been greatly influenced by the sudden and unexpected COVID-19 pandemic (Kissler et al., 2020), which has almost forced consumers into online shopping and the online selling of many groups of products.

The research method used in this paper allowed us to answer our initial research questions and identify research gaps that should be developed in the future. With regard to RQ1 (the determinants of online shopping) the findings of the literature review indicated many stimuli influencing this consumer behaviour; convenience, a wide range of products, and competitive prices were all underlined, but there were also many "new" stimuli identified associated with the development of social platforms (Abumalloh et al., 2020; Kumar & Ayodeji, 2021; Mangiaracina et al., 2015; Nguyen et al., 2019; Nogueira et al., 2021). For example, the amount of "Likes" on social media platforms, the opinions of other clients who bought the products, attractive website content, or the possibility to chat with producers while shopping. These results have a very applicable character because they show the producers what kind of elements should be taken into account when devising e-commerce platforms. For example, the implementation of chatbots or virtual assistants could be a good solution to increase sales (Adamopoulou & Moussiades, 2020; Hsieh & Lee, 2021). Other matters of concern for online sellers include credibility and building trust with clients (Sullivan & Kim, 2018).

In answering RQ2, it has been found that personal characteristics such as age and gender help to describe differences in online consumer behaviour. This can contribute directly to the adaptation of products and services, and indirectly to the satisfaction of particular consumers. The findings of the analyses conducted in the study show that generations X, Y, and Z are more frequent online buyers than older generations. Taking into account the high level of adoption of innovation by younger consumers (Calvo-Porral et al., 2020), the use of the newest technologies could be fruitful when devising offers for this group, e.g. technologically advanced payment methods, product personalisation, augmented reality, chatbots, or virtual assistants (Adamopoulou & Moussiades, 2020; Hsieh & Lee, 2021), all of which are welcomed by young consumers (McGinnis, 2019). By contrast, e-commerce retailers offering products for older people should place attention on traditional online customer services, whilst also emphasising purchase safety and credibility.

When it comes to gender, the results of analyses have not shown a difference in the number of women and men buying online. However, there are other differences between the two groups. For example, women pay more attention to security when shopping online and seem to be more prudent clients. Women also pay attention to the general online environment while shopping (Akhlaq & Ahmed, 2016). Thus, online platforms dedicated to women should not only be safe but also visually attractive. Gender issues constitute a significant knowledge gap in the literature on the use of new technologies in consumer behaviour, including online shopping and these aspects should be developed in future research projects.

This notwithstanding, age and gender remain important determinants that should be considered while preparing e-commerce offers and platforms. Different generations and genders have differentiated needs, preferences, and behaviour patterns and so adapting e-commerce services to these needs may increase the volume of sales among particular consumer segments.

Our research has also found a gap in the literature concerning the categories of products sold online (RQ3). Statistical data indicates that clothes, shoes, accessories, furniture, home accessories, and gardening products are among the most commonly bought (Eurostat.eu, 2021, June; Statista.com, 2021, August 20). The increase in online shopping for certain product categories is related to the coronavirus pandemic and temporary lockdowns in many countries. The online sales growth of furniture and gardening products is strictly associated with people staying at home for a large proportion of 2020 and 2021 and have not been able to partake in their normal recreational activities, including holidays. Instead, many have decided to renovate, redecorate or repair their immediate environment. Results of the analysis show that despite the pandemic, food was bought much less online comparatively. This is due, first, to the specificity of these products (e.g. short expiry date or special transport requirements), and second, because grocery stores and pharmacies remained open throughout the pandemic.

The volumes of online sales of particular product categories will continue to depend on the global situation and the changes in people's lifestyles. Online retailers should use digital technologies to attract their offers and service. For example, augmented reality may be used to a greater extent by online sellers of furniture, clothes, accessories, or cosmetics as it allows consumers to see how the products fit their requirements.

With regard to RQ4, the results of the literature review indicate the significance of mobile devices (smartphones and tablets) for e-commerce activities. Nevertheless, laptops and PCs are also often used for these purposes. Mobile devices "accompany" people in their daily life anytime and almost everywhere (Omar et al., 2021; Wang et al., 2015). They are useful and convenient devices, satisfying many of their users' needs. Mahapatra (2017) also emphasised convenience as the main determinant influencing the growth of mobiles for online shopping. Such findings may lead to the conclusion that the companies should develop adequate applications and mobile-friendly websites that will be useful and comfortable for users. These technological solutions will increase the availability of the shop and its offer and may increase sales and subsequent visits (Tseng et al., 2021).

With reference to RQ5, the payment methods offered by e-commerce platforms and used by consumers are varied. They usually depend on many factors, concerning both e-sellers and e-buyers). On the one hand, the IT capabilities of e-commerce shops are important in this case, but so too are e-commerce consumers' attitudes, individual possibilities, and trust, as well as more macroeconomic factors such as infrastructure, Internet access, payment costs, general economic development, etc. (Grüschow et al., 2016; Williams, 2021).

The literature analysis conducted for this study tallies with the above claims about the economic and infrastructural development of particular countries. E-consumers from developed countries use more advanced payment methods while people in less developed economies still prefer cash on delivery. However, one important conclusion is that there is again a limited amount of scientific research on consumer attitudes towards e-commerce purchases and preferred payment methods.

Delivery options for e-commerce likewise depend on many factors, including the logistics system the company offers (e.g. automatisation systems), the distance between the e-store or warehouse and the final destination, type of product, and consumer preferences (including demographic variables) (Mangiaracina et al., 2019). Online retailers should always ascertain the payments and logistics preferences of their potential buyers and adapt their systems accordingly.

This chapter has contributed to a better understanding of the existing body of knowledge and data related to many aspects of the development of e-commerce. The future of e-commerce will undoubtedly be linked to the application of new technologies and instruments of Industry 4.0, such as augmented reality, chatbots, virtual assistants, and the Internet of Things (IoT) (Hsieh & Lee, 2021; Masood & Egger, 2020; Mozafari et al., 2021; Oke & Arowoiya, 2021). These instruments may be also used in the internationalisation of e-commerce platforms to attract customers from all over the world. If this is the case, then will be necessary to adjust both the offer and the service to cultural, geographical, infrastructural, and temporal distances. If travel restrictions are extended (or there are concerns about longer-distance travel), people might also increasingly buy online products from many corners of the world. On the other hand, environmental awareness and the increase of environmental pollution caused by transport in connection with the increase in e-commerce may contribute to the need for the invention of other, pro-environmental forms of delivery, and indeed markets.

Next, the upward trend in the development of e-commerce will continue to be associated with the stable increase in the number of social media users (Kemp, 2021) and the development of new social instruments, e.g. TikTok. There is likely to be stable growth in SC (online sales with the usage of social media) during the coming months and years. On top of this, Livestream shopping (live commerce) may become a significant form of e-commerce in the future (In Livestream shopping online retailers organise short Internet sessions during which they present selected products from their offer. Then, Internet users can interact with the presenters, ask them questions and, of course, make purchases). Such a method will ensure direct communication between retailer and customer, which is very important, especially for younger generations of buyers. Livestream sessions also allow anyone to exhibit absolutely anything for selling and it offers the additional advantage that there is no need for special premises, studios, operators, photographers, or even in the case of C2C, your own e-shop, and no sales commission needs to be paid to platforms. However, Facebook and Instagram do charge "hidden" commissions from advertising and promotions.

Mobile platforms and mobile payment systems will also continue to develop and there will be an emphasis on increased concern for personal data protection and securing e-commerce platforms against cybercrime. Different payment methods, such as "buy now - pay later" options, may develop in the future. This method allows postponement of the payment date by up to 45 days for free. Thanks to this, customers can order and test the products before they decide to pay for them. Payment for products after receipt of the package reduces the fear of buying some products remotely, and quite high deferred payment limits enable consumers to make larger purchases.

The last, but by no means least important trend which will be developed in the future concerns artificial intelligence (AI) which helps companies automate sentiment analysis and monitor social moods related to a particular brand or a specific product or service on an ongoing basis (Park et al., 2021). Sentiment analysis is likely to become key to understanding customer opinions about many different aspects of a company's operations, from product functionality, through price, to after-sales service. It also allows companies to quickly detect and react to changes in consumer behaviour caused by local or international events (Karthik & Ganapathy, 2021). A detailed analysis of thousands of customer statements posted online may, in the future lay, the foundation for many businesses that will then use this data to create new products.

Acknowledgments

The study was conducted within the *Economics in the face of the New Economy* research project financed by the Regional Initiative for Excellence programme of the Minister of Science and Higher Education of Poland, years 2019–2022, grant no. 004/RID/2018/19, financing 3,000,000 PLN.

Bibliography

Abumalloh, R.A., Ibrahim, O., & Nilashi, M. (2020). Loyalty of young female Arabic customers towards recommendation agents: A new model for B2C E-commerce. *Technology in Society, 61*, 101253. https://doi.org/10.1016/j.techsoc.2020.101253.

Adamopoulou, E., & Moussiades, L. (2020). Chatbots: History, technology, and applications. *Machine Learning with Applications, 2*, 100006. https://doi.org/10.1016/j.mlwa.2020.100006.

Akhlaq, A., & Ahmed, E. (2016). Gender differences among online shopping factors in Pakistan. *Organizations and Markets in Emerging Economies,* 7(1), 74–89. https://doi.org/10.15388/omee.2016.7.1.14216.

Awwad, M., Shekhar, A., & Iyer, A.S. (2018, September 27–29). Sustainable last-mile logistics operation in the era of E-commerce. *Proceedings of the International Conference on Industrial Engineering and Operations Management*, Washington, DC. http://ieomsociety.org/dc2018/papers/179.pdf.

Bartosik-Purgat, M. (2018a). M-communication in product information exchange – An international comparison. *Folia Oeconomica. Acta Universitatis Lodziensis, 2*(334), 97–113. http://dx.doi.org/10.18778/0208-6018.334.07.

Bartosik-Purgat, M. (2018b). Social media and e-WoM communication in the customer decision-making process – An international context. *Journal of Management and Business Administration. Central Europe, 26(2), 16–33. https://doi.org/10.7206/jmba.ce.2450-7814.226.*

Bartosik-Purgat, M., Filimon, N., & Hinner, M. (2017). Determinants of social media's use in consumer behaviour: An international comparison. *Economics and Business Review, 3*(2), 79–100. https://doi.org/10.18559/ebr.2017.2.5.

Bartosik-Purgat, M., & Jankowska, B. (2020). Exploiting e-commerce trends for international market expansion: The perspective of Polish fashion firms. *European Journal of International Management, 14*(6), 1049–1069. http://dx.doi.org/10.1504/EJIM.2020.10019859.

Belwal, R., Al Shibli, R., & Belwal, S. (2021). Consumer protection and electronic commerce in the Sultanate of Oman. *Journal of Information, Communication and Ethics in Society, 19*(1), 38–60. https://doi.org/10.1108/JICES-09-2019-0110.

Calvo-Porral, C., & Pesqueira-Sanchez, R. (2020). Generational differences in technology behaviour: Comparing millennials and generation X. *Kybernetes, 49*(11), 2755–2772. https://doi.org/10.1108/K-09-2019-0598.

Chromy, J.R. (2008). Snowball sampling. *Encyclopedia of Social Science Research Methods, 10*(2), 824–825.

Dewi, C.K., Mohaidin, Z., & Murshid, M.A. (2020). Determinants of online purchase intention: A PLS-SEM approach: Evidence from Indonesia. *Journal of Asia Business Studies, 14*(3), 281–306. https://doi.org/10.1108/JABS-03-2019-0086.

Dhanapal, S., Vashu, D., & Subramaniam, T. (2015). Perceptions on the challenges of online purchasing: A study from 'baby boomers', generation 'X' and generation 'Y' point of views. *Contaduría y Administración, 60*(1), 107–132.

Eurostat.eu (2021, June). *E-commerce statistics for individuals.* https://ec.europa.eu/eurostat/statistics-explained/index.php?title=E-commerce_statistics_for_individuals#General_overview.

Fu, S., Yan, Q., & Feng, G.C. (2018). Who will attract you? Similarity effect among users on online purchase intention of movie tickets in the social shopping context. *International Journal of Information Management, 40*, 88–102. https://doi.org/10.1016/j.ijinfomgt.2018.01.013.

Grange, G., Benbasat, I., & Burton-Jones, A. (2020). A network-based conceptualization of social commerce and social commerce value. *Computers in Human Behavior, 108*, 105855. https://doi.org/10.1016/j.chb.2018.12.033

Grant, M.J., & Booth, A. (2009). A typology of reviews: An analysis of 14 review types and associated methodologies. *Health Information & Libraries Journal, 26*, 91–108. doi.org/10.1111/j.1471–1842.2009.00848.x.

Grüschow, R.M., Kemper, J., & Brettel, M. (2016). How do different payment methods deliver cost and credit efficiency in electronic commerce? *Electronic Commerce Research and Applications, 18*, 27–36. https://doi.org/10.1016/j.elerap.2016.06.001.

Guo, X., Jaramillo, Y.J.L., Bloemhof-Ruwaard, J., & Claassen, G.D.H. (2019). On integrating crowdsourced delivery in last-mile logistics: A simulation study to quantify its feasibility. *Journal of Cleaner Production, 241*, 118365. https://doi.org/10.1016/j.jclepro.2019.118365.

Haney, J.M., & Lutters, W.G. (2021). Cybersecurity advocates: Discovering the characteristics and skills of an emergent role. *Information and Computer Security*, Vol. ahead-of-print No. ahead-of-print. https://doi.org/10.1108/ICS-08-2020-0131.

Hsieh, S.H., & Lee, C.T. (2021). Hey Alexa: Examining the effect of perceived socialness in usage intentions of AI assistant-enabled smart speaker. *Journal of Research in Interactive Marketing, 15*(2), 267–294. https://doi.org/10.1108/JRIM-11-2019-0179.

Ignat, B., & Chankov, S. (2020). Do e-commerce customers change their preferred last-mile delivery based on its sustainability impact? *The International Journal of Logistics Management, 31*(3), 521–548. https://doi.org/10.1108/IJLM-11-2019-0305.

Jain, S., & Sundström, M. (2021). Toward a conceptualization of personalized services in apparel e-commerce fulfillment. *Research Journal of Textile and Apparel*, Vol. ahead-of-print No. ahead-of-print. https://doi.org/10.1108/RJTA-06-2020-0066.

Kandula, S., Krishnamoorthy, S., & Roy, D. (2021). A prescriptive analytics framework for efficient E-commerce order delivery. *Decision Support Systems, 147*, 113584. https://doi.org/10.1016/j.dss.2021.113584.

Karthik, R.V., & Ganapathy, S. (2021). A fuzzy recommendation system for predicting the customers interests using sentiment analysis and ontology in e-commerce. *Applied Soft Computing, 108*, 107396. https://doi.org/10.1016/j.asoc.2021.107396

Kemp, S. (2021, April 22), *60 percent of the world population is now online*. https://wearesocial.com/blog/2021/04/60-percent-of-the-worlds-population-is-now-online.

Kim, N., & Kim, W. (2018). Do your social media lead you to make social deal purchases? Consumer-generated social referrals for sales via social commerce. *International Journal of Information Management, 39*, 38–48.

Kissler, S.M., Tedijanto, C., Goldstein, E., Grad, Y.H., & Lipsitch, M. (2020). Projecting the transmission dynamics of SARS-CoV-2 through the postpandemic period. *Science, 368*(6493), 860–868. https://doi.org/10.1126/science.abb5793.

Kolotylo-Kulkarni, M., Xia, W., & Dhillon, G. (2021). Information disclosure in e-commerce: A systematic review and agenda for future research. *Journal of Business Research, 126*, 221–238. https://doi.org/10.1016/j.jbusres.2020.12.006.

Kumar, V., & Ayodeji, O.G. (2021). E-retail factors for customer activation and retention: An empirical study from Indian e-commerce customers. *Journal of Retailing and Consumer Services, 59*, 102399. https://doi.org/10.1016/j.jretconser.2020.102399.

Lemon, K.N., & Verhoef, P.C. (2016). Understanding customer experience throughout the customer journey. *Journal of Marketing, 80*(6), 69–96. https://doi.org/10.1509/jm.15.0420.

Mahapatra, S. (2017). Mobile shopping among young consumers: An empirical study in an emerging market. *International Journal of Retail and Distribution Management, 45*(9), 930–949.

Mangiaracina, R., Marchet, G., Perotti, S., & Tumino, A. (2015). A review of the environmental implications of B2C e-commerce: A logistics perspective. *International Journal of Physical Distribution & Logistics Management, 45*(6), 565–591. https://doi.org/10.1108/IJPDLM-06-2014-0133.

Mangiaracina, R., Perego, A., Seghezzi, A., & Tumino, A. (2019). Innovative solutions to increase last-mile delivery efficiency in B2C e-commerce: A literature review. *International Journal of Physical Distribution & Logistics Management, 49*(9), 901–920. https://doi.org/10.1108/IJPDLM-02-2019-0048.

Masood, T., & Egger, J. (2020). Adopting augmented reality in the age of industrial digitalization. *Computers in Industry, 115*, 103112.

McGinnis, D. (2019, March 13). *How do different generations use voice assistants?* https://www.salesforce.com/blog/voice-assistant-generations-research/.

McLean, G., Al-Nabhani, K., & Wilson, A. (2018). Developing a mobile applications customer experience model (MACE) – Implications for retailers. *Journal of Business Research, 85*, 325–336. https://doi.org/10.1016/j.jbusres.2018.01.018.

Mou, J., & Benyoucef, M. (2021). Consumer behavior in social commerce: Results from a meta-analysis. *Technological Forecasting and Social Change, 167*, 120734. https://doi.org/10.1016/j.techfore.2021.120734.

Mozafari, N., Weiger, W.H., & Hammerschmidt, M. (2021). Trust me, I'm a bot – Repercussions of chatbot disclosure in different service frontline settings. *Journal of Service Management*, Vol. ahead-of-print No. ahead-of-print. https://doi.org/10.1108/JOSM-10-2020-0380.

Nguyen, D.H., Leeuw, S., Dullaert, W., & Foubert, B.P.J. (2019). What is the right delivery option for you? *Consumer Preferences for Delivery Attributes in Online Retailing, 40*(4), 99–321. https://doi-org.ez81.periodicos.capes.gov.br/10.1111/jbl.12210.

Nogueira, G.P.M., Rangel, J.J.A., & Shimod, E. (2021). Sustainable last-mile distribution in B2C e-commerce: Do consumers really care? *Cleaner and Responsible Consumption, 3*, 100021. https://doi.org/10.1016/j.clrc.2021.100021.

Oke, A.E., & Arowoiya, V.A. (2021). An analysis of the application areas of augmented reality technology in the construction industry. *Smart and Sustainable Built Environment*, Vol. ahead-of-print No. ahead-of-print. https://doi.org/10.1108/SASBE-11-2020-0162.

Omar, S., Mohsen, K., Tsimonis, G., Oozeerally, A., & Hsu, J.H. (2021). M-commerce: The nexus between mobile shopping service quality and loyalty. *Journal of Retailing and Consumer Services, 60*, 102468. https://doi.org/10.1016/j.jretconser.2021.102468.

Panda, R., & Swar, B.N. (2016). Electronic retailing: A review of determinants of 'online shopping intentions' in India. *Indian Journal of Science and Technology, 9*(15), 1–6.

Park, S., Cho, J., Park, K., & Shin, K. (2021). Customer sentiment analysis with more sensibility. *Engineering Applications of Artificial Intelligence, 104,* 104356. https://doi.org/10.1016/j.engappai.2021.104356.

Peltier, J.W., Dahl, A.J., & Swan, E.L. (2020). Digital information flows across a B2C/C2C continuum and technological innovations in service ecosystems:

A service-dominant logic perspective. *Journal of Business Research, 121*, 724–734. https://doi.org/10.1016/j.jbusres.2020.03.020.

Peral-Peral, B., Arenas-Gaitán, J., & Villarejo-Ramos, Á.F. (2015). From digital divide to psycho-digital divide: Elders and online social networks. *Comunicar, 23*(45), 57–64. https://doi.org/10.3916/C45-2015-06.

Ramírez-Correa, P.E., Grandón, E.E., & Arenas-Gaitán, J. (2019). Assessing differences in customers' personal disposition to e-commerce. *Industrial Management & Data Systems, 119*(4), 792–820. https://doi.org/10.1108/IMDS-07-2018-0280.

Saarijärvi, H., Joensuu, J., Rintamaki, T., & Yrjölä, M. (2018). One person's trash is another person's treasure: Profiling consumer-to-consumer e-commerce in Facebook. *International Journal of Retail & Distribution Management, 46*(11/12), 1092–1107. https://doi.org/10.1108/IJRDM-04-2017-0091.

Statista.com (2021, August 23). *Distribution of digital buyers in the United States as of February 2020, by age group.* https://www.statista.com/statistics/469184/us-digital-buyer-share-age-group/.

Statista.com (2021, August 20). *E-commerce share of total retail revenue in the United States as of May 2020, by product category.* https://www.statista.com/statistics/203043/online-share-of-total-us-retail-revenue-projection/.

Stubb, C., & Colliander, J. (2019). "This is not sponsored content" – The effects of impartiality disclosure and e-commerce landing pages on consumer responses to social media influencer posts. *Computers in Human Behavior, 98*, 210–222. https://doi.org/10.1016/j.chb.2019.04.024.

Sullivan, Y.W., & Kim, D.J. (2018). Assessing the effects of consumers' product evaluations and trust on repurchase intention in e-commerce environments. *International Journal of Information Management, 39*, 199–219. https://doi.org/10.1016/j.ijinfomgt.2017.12.008.

Tokar, T., Jensen, R., & Williams, B.D. (2021). A guide to the seen costs and unseen benefits of e-commerce. *Business Horizons, 64*(3), 323–332.

Tran, L.T.T. (2021). Managing the effectiveness of e-commerce platforms in a pandemic. *Journal of Retailing and Consumer Services, 58*, 102287. https://doi.org/10.1016/j.jretconser.2020.102287.

Tseng, T.H., Lee, C.T., Huang, H.T., & Yang, W.H. (2021). Success factors driving consumer reuse intention of mobile shopping application channel. *International Journal of Retail & Distribution Management*, Vol. ahead-of-print No. ahead-of-print. https://doi.org/10.1108/IJRDM-08-2020-0309.

Wagner, G., Schramm-Klein, H., & Steinmann, S. (2020). Online retailing across e-channels and e-channel touchpoints: Empirical studies of consumer behavior in the multichannel e-commerce environment. *Journal of Business Research, 107*, 256–270. https://doi.org/10.1016/j.jbusres.2018.10.048.

Wang, O., Somogyi, S., & Charlebois, S. (2020). Food choice in the e-commerce era: A comparison between business-to-consumer (B2C), online-to-offline (O2O) and new retail. *British Food Journal, 122*(4), 1215–1237. https://doi.org/10.1108/BFJ-09-2019-0682.

Wang, R.J., Malthouse, E.C., & Krishnamurthi, L. (2015). On the go: How mobile shopping affects customer purchase behavior. *Journal of Retailing, 91*(2), 217–234.

Williams, M.D. (2021). Social commerce and the mobile platform: Payment and security perceptions of potential users. *Computers in Human Behavior, 115*, 105557. https://doi.org/10.1016/j.chb.2018.06.005.

Yrjölä, M., Rintamäki, T., Saarijärvi, H., & Joensuu, J. (2017). Consumer-to-consumer e-commerce – Outcomes and implications. *The International Review of Retail, Distribution and Consumer Research, 27*(3), 300–315.

Zhu, R., Srivastava, A., & Sutanto, J. (2020). Privacy-deprived e-commerce: The efficacy of consumer privacy policies on China's e-commerce websites from a legal perspective. *Information Technology & People, 33*(6), 1601–1626. https://doi.org/10.1108/ITP-03-2019-0117.

Part II

Digital consumers in Europe

5 Digital consumers' scenes in Finland

Jaana Kivivuori and Monica Tamminen

Introduction

COVID-19 has radically changed the way we work, how we consume entertainment, and where we take part in our hobbies. During the pandemic, the ability to use digital services improved, and many things changed. Finland has been a leading country in the use of mobile devices, thanks to the ecosystem of actors and the fact how the market has been shaped in cooperation with various participants. Enthusiasm and a strong need for innovativeness increased the monetary value of enterprises. At the beginning of building the infrastructure, the focus was on data transfer. From that starting point, there has been a big leap into a multichannel system.

Digital business, e-government, recreational, and cultural activities happen online, increasingly in a wireless environment with mobile devices such as smartphones and tablets (Chopdar et al., 2018; Zhang et al., 2012). M-commerce can provide enhanced and engaging user experience, personalisation, convenience, localisation, and ubiquity (anytime and anywhere); ease of use and usefulness which appeal to consumers who are accustomed to a society operating 24/7/365 (Ashraff et al., 2017; Chopdar et al., 2018).

Among under 25-year-old people, a major shift in technology has taken place from e-commerce to m-commerce (see also Ashraff et al., 2017, p. 29). Mobile devices enable ubiquitous consumption defined as the ability to access the web and consume goods and services anytime and anyplace (Cox, 2004). In this chapter, we concentrate mainly on the shopping of goods but also discuss the use of services such as m-banking, e-government, and cultural entertainment among different age groups to show how Finns have adopted digital services and how habitual it has become. Consumers have become even more demanding and impatient, because they have multiple channels at their disposal, in addition to networks, friends, and influencers.

Generation Z (born 1998–2010) takes an indulgent view to spend money as it wishes. It places a higher degree of importance on leisure time, contrary to Generation X (born 1961–1980), which was still slightly characterised by the large baby-boomer generation (born 1945–1960). Generation Z also influences the consumption of their parents. Although Generation Z is marked

DOI: 10.4324/9781003263685-8

by social relationships, members of this generation tend to feel lonely. The Finnish culture can be classified as normative and with reason. People can also ask for advice from their Ōura device (Asikainen, 2021; Ōura, 2021). Generation Z has grown up surrounded by technology and does not know life without a smartphone or Internet. Generation Y (Millennials, born 1981–1997), is accustomed to changes because it has experienced a time without smartphones.

Technology acceptance, high-speed data networks, advanced devices, and applications catering to ultimate, ubiquitous, and omnichannel digital ecosystems form the backbone of a modern, digitally interconnected society. The technology and the applications have developed rapidly, the service offering has broadened, and the content services are more user-friendly. Due to the lockdown, the digital competence of users has been enhanced, and the reliable operation of online services has been improved. Information security is especially topical because it is known that consumers are actively seeking a suitable market. The learning curve in using various remote i.e., digital services has been steep in all age groups, especially in the older age groups.

In this chapter, we discuss the technical abilities and user experience trends in different age groups based on statistical data. We observe how the consumer's journey is shaped by the community and what is the brand awareness among Finns, and what are the values the brands should stand for. Especially the young generations demand responsibility from businesses. Lastly, we offer business ideas which the entrepreneurs should seize in the following years. Institutions become less important, as the individuals sell services or goods peer to peer and second hand on various platforms. The fact how skillful the consumer can use devices and applications determines how interesting the product is global.

Technical connections and usage

With the change in digital consumer behaviour in Finland, the pandemic year has had the following impacts: First of all, it has increased democracy, because older generations have begun to use digital devices to compensate for the lack of communication. To protect their own health, the elderly have switched to online grocery shopping, a new favourite way to buy food, which is probably here to stay. Finnish online shops have taken development steps. Shopping events brought changes in physical shops because consumers want to touch the products or hold them before making a decision, but they might purchase them elsewhere. Especially for young people, sustainability and online second-hand shops are important. Both for younger and elderly generations, culture and leisure-time activities were provided in digital format. As 82% of young people use a mobile phone, m-commerce has become to stay.

Finnish households have and use several broadband solutions simultaneously. Companies and the Finnish government are building and developing communication networks and services, adding features that are needed for secure and user-friendly e-commerce, m-commerce, e-banking, and e-government services. Consumers relax by watching streaming movies or series, and e-events (theatre, concerts, art exhibitions, museum tours) or by engaging in e-exercise.

Sixty-percent of the world's population, and 90% of Finns, use the Internet (OSF, 2019). High-speed data networks, advanced devices, and applications catering to ultimate digital ecosystems form the backbone of a modern, digitally interconnected society. The Finnish government has stipulated in the Information Society Code that everyone must have the possibility to access communication networks and use communication services that are affordable, technologically reliable, of high quality, and secure (Information Society Code 917/2014, Article 1). Finland can be seen as a welfare state, a feminine culture, that values equality and solidarity (see Hofstede et al., 2010, pp. 170–171). The focus is on working to make a living, and managers strive for consensus (Hofstede Insights, 2021). A small power distance is connected to a higher education level that is available for every person who is keen on getting oneself educated (see Hofstede et al., 2010, pp. 67–69). The European Union has recognised Finland as the leading digital economy in Europe in terms of connectivity, human capital, use of Internet services, integration of digital technology, and public services (European Commission, 2020, p. 14).

People in more individualistic European countries, like in Finland, were more likely to have access to the Internet and e-mail, and they used the computer for shopping, banking, and providing information to public authorities more often (Hofstede et al., 2010, p. 123). Consumers have several broadband options from which to choose, and many people use different network connections device-specifically. The 4G mobile broadband, and increasingly the 5G broadband, is available for every mobile phone and tablet, fixed networks for TV and computers, and Wi-Fi. Even some smartwatches have a built-in mobile connection (DNA, 2021). Moreover, employers offer an Internet connection to telecommuters. Finland's backbone network is built with optical fibre. The last kilometre, i.e., connection to homes and businesses, has several technical options. Cable TV operators also offer fast bandwidth with coaxial cable connections. Fixed Wi-Fi broadband connections, popular in Europe, are practically non-existent in Finland. Instead, the 4G and 5G mobile broadbands are extremely popular (BCO Finland, 2021). As of September 2021, the 4G 30 Mbit/s mobile network covers 99.9% of Finnish households and the 5G 300 Mbit/s 87.2%. The latest 5G mobile broadband covers 5% of Finland's territory and about 80% of the households (Traficom, 2021).

Smartphones are in practically every pocket. Mobile operator DNA reported in May 2020 that 96% of Finns between 16 and 74 use smartphones (DNA, 2020a). A total of 99% of the people aged 16–24, 59% aged 65–74, and 24% aged 75–89 have a smartphone. Mobile operator Telia reported in September 2021 that 60% of the sales in new phones are 5G phones, meaning 5G subscriptions have gained momentum. Owners of 5G phones use data

40% more than customers using 4G for streaming services. Social media use is growing steadily, and data usage is estimated to grow even more (Telia, 2021).

Mobile broadband subscriptions are reasonably priced; 85.3% of mobile phone owners have had an unlimited data transmission subscription in 2020/21 (FiCom, 2020). This affordability lowers the threshold to use Internet services and access networks many times per day – usually, the Internet connection is always on. For younger generations, it makes it possible to live online, at home, and on the go. In June 2021, DNA reported that 81% of 7-year-olds and 99% of 8-year-olds have mobile phones. This helps them to become digitally savvy at an early age (DNA, 2021).

Brand appreciation

The lockdown highlighted the importance of domestic food production: food products were available, even despite the hoarding of some products, e.g. fat products, eggs, and frozen goods. The increased demand for daily consumer goods led to challenges, e.g. in the toilet paper and soap availability. Remote working and layoffs freed more time for leisure, so people wanted to do things on their own, renovate and do handicrafts. In a country at the feminine pole, like Finland, home-related products were purchased (Hofstede et al., 2010, p. 164). "Hügge" activities are also characteristic of an individualistic culture, including baking, gardening, and decorating. These activities became so popular that the flour shelves were emptied and plants were sold out in gardening stores. When all basic needs are fulfilled, the demand for luxury services increases. People lived a simple life during the lockdown – it was all about surviving the difficult times. They spent more time with their family, doing their things together. In a way, this was like a return to the agrarian society where everyone was occupied with their chores while sitting together in the main room (Cf. Hofstede et al., 2010, pp. 86, 131).

Online grocery shopping increased the most during COVID-19. In 2019, 24% of Finns shopped for food and groceries online (Tikkanen et al., 2019). Reportedly, one-fourth increased online grocery shopping (Borgström et al., 2020; PostNord, 2020). The amount of Finns shopping for groceries online increased by 50% due to COVID-19: it was particularly popular in the Helsinki metropolitan area (Borgström et al., 2020). Also, PostNord (2020) stated that groceries and pharmacy goods are two notable newcomers to the online market. Finnish Commerce Federation reported that in 2021 groceries accounted for 2% of online shopping, compared to 0.6% in 2020. According to Statistics Finland (OSF 2020a), buying groceries online has finally made a breakthrough.

Market Research Company surveys the brand attitudes among consumers annually. Out of 559 brands, 79 were included in the 2021 survey. The respondents were 15–79 years old. The most popular brands are characterised by signs of their origin, production method, and nutritional quality, and daily products, such as porridge flakes, flours, cheeses, toilet and kitchen papers, and napkins. Instead of using an international standard in their classification, Market Research Company uses Finland-specific metrics based on experience: the critics percentage is subtracted from the promoter percentage, resulting in the Net Promoter Score (NPS). The score of 40 stands for excellent brand popularity. 20–39 is good, and 0–19 is low. A score below 0 stands for low brand appreciation (Market Research Company, 2021).

Fazer, a Finnish sweets company, has been listening to its customers in the past years and asking for consumer wishes on social media. However, Fazer's score was below 40 in this survey, even though the company has previously been one of the top 10 brands. The best price-to-value experience was among the consumers using the S bonus card of the S Group retail and service network and the users of Yle Areena (the streaming platform of the Finnish Broadcasting Company). The insurance company customers feel that they get no value for their money, and the discount stores have become more popular. The following brands are seen as the most responsible ones: Valio as the producer of milk and cheese (among the elderly), the textile company Marimekko and the sweets company Fazer (among women and under 25-year-olds), and the fuel company Neste (among men and people with income over €80,000) (Market Research Company, 2021).

The Nordic Swan sustainability mark is one of the 10 most popular brands. The Finnish streaming platform for radio and television content, Yle Areena, was included in the survey for the first time, and it debuted as the second most popular brand. The Finnish Broadcasting Company (Yle, the parent company of Yle Areena) was in fifth place (Market Research Company, 2021). The popularity of Yle was probably affected by online trolling and the spreading of disinformation. In a small-power-distance society, such as Finland, people trust the authorities and follow the news a lot (Hofstede et al., 2010, pp. 77, 79).

The most appreciated brand is Fiskars, known for its scissors and gardening tools, now for the third time in a row. The appreciation of Google has dropped: now, it is in the top 50. The consumer appreciates Finnishness and responsibility. However, the brands that improved their rating the most show how appreciation can vary: Samsung was the favourite of the young, and Stockmann the favourite of the elderly. Women show more appreciation for brands than men. The most appreciated brands among women were Fiskars, the Nordic Swan, the domestic raw material mark "Hyvää Suomesta", Yle, and Fazer. Men's top brands were Fiskars, S bonus card, the lock company Abloy, ceramic ware company Arabia, and Yle Areena. The 15–24-year-olds like to express their likes and dislikes strongly. The brand has to be meaningful for their own lives. For the young, these brands are Fazer, the domestic mark "Hyvää Suomesta", the Key Flag Symbol for products and services produced in Finland, the Nordic Swan, and Fiskars. The elderly respondents' (60–79-year-olds) top brands were Fiskars, Yle, Yle Areena, Fazer, and Abloy.

According to the survey results, there is a potential target group that appreciated a specific brand but does not use it: the group of highly educated men with high income who are under 50 years old and live in a one-family house in southern Finland or the metropolitan area, with children. If the brand would engage especially this target group, the company would probably gain more consumers. A non-committed brand target group is women over 60 years old, living in apartment flats in Southwestern Finland – they choose the brand based on their habits but do not particularly appreciate the brand. Their households consist of one person only.

Generally, status purchases are more frequent in masculine cultures. People in masculine cultures buy more expensive watches and more genuine jewellery (Hofstede et al., 2010, pp. 163–164). According to the Market Research Company's survey (2021), Finns will consume less money in jewellery, toys, sweets, and beverages during the following year. More money will be spent on plant protein and plant milk products, and hotel and caring industry services. However, there are significant differences between consumer groups (Market Research Company, 2021). Jewellery is considered a foreign good which might be seen as more attractive than local products, but the tendency is for national products (Hofstede et al., 2010, p. 164). Then, the Finnish company, named after the national epos, Kalevala, might rise on the brand rating list. It depends on whether the Finns act as ethnic or cosmopolitan consumers in the future.

Topical social trends

It seems that the change in consumption affects the use of money. In the following, we discuss the topical trends, Finnish online behaviour, and exchange of experiences. The pandemic has resulted in the biggest boom in social media use since Facebook. The amount of social network service users has risen by 8% and is now 69% (Pönkä, 2020). In general, consumption of news and the use of different messaging applications have increased due to the COVID-19 situation (DNA, 2020b).

The young are ever more aware of the changes in the environment and lifestyles. The question is whether we return to the previous way of life after the crisis. Sitra, a fund subject to the Finnish Parliament, paves the way for the following four trends (Dufva, 2020):

1 excessive consumption and variable availability of resources
   - growing consumption means that many resources will become more and more scarce or the cost of acquiring them will increase. Challenges may arise with respect to the availability of critical materials for the industry. Construction sand is also at risk of running out, as is fresh water in many regions. There is a growing need to increase the use of alternative materials as well as the circulation of materials;

2 AI applications permeate society
   - self-driving cars, voice-controlled machines, personalised recommendations, and other AI applications are becoming increasingly commonplace. More and more decision-making power is assigned to algorithms, underscoring questions of transparency, liability, and distortions in the used data;

3 the next wave of digitisation
   - digitisation, or the use of digital technology in services and human interaction, is already part of daily life. In the short term, the interesting future trends in this area include virtual reality, augmented reality, voice control, gesture control, the Internet of Things or the Internet of Everything, as well as an emphasis on energy efficiency. Also, of interest in the longer term are blockchain-driven services and the emergence of quantum computing;

4 the growth of health technology
   - portable devices to monitor health have become increasingly common, and they are still being developed further. More data enables more personalised and preventive care. At the same time, new treatments are being developed based on genome editing and modifying the microbiome, for example.

What is true regarding Finns, they might come across as emotionally aggressive. Customers in higher uncertainty-avoidance cultures tended to be hesitant towards information and new products. They were slower in introducing electronic communication tools (mobile phones, e-mail, the Internet) (Hofstede et al., 2010, pp. 191–198). Despite this, the Finns believe that their use of digital services will increase further in the future, which goes hand in hand with a weak uncertainty-avoidance culture. For example, online authentication is thought to become more common, as 75% predict that they will use mobile ID as a substitute for online logins in the next two years. Also, 65% predict that they will pay using online banking, such as Apple Pay or MobilePay, in the next two years (DNA, 2020a).

People aged 15–34 years use an average of four social media services. The youngest age group, 10–14, and those aged 35–54 years use an average of three services. People aged 55–64 years use an average of two services, and those who are aged 65–74 years use one social media service. Respondents aged 75+ years reported they do not use social media services. As regards gender differences, men reported using an average of two social media services and women reported using three such services. In total, an average of three social media services was used by the respondents (OSF, 2017).

In 2020, 92% of Finns between the ages of 16 and 89 years used the Internet – 86% of them daily. Eighty-two percent accessed the Internet or Internet services several times a day (OSF, 2020c). Most people accessed the Internet for communication purposes (social network services 69%), news and amusement (news 85%, Internet TV 74%, and video-on-demand 49%), e-services (88%), such as online shopping, online banking, and e-government (88%, healthcare, taxation) (OSF, 2020c). DNA's survey indicates that a staggering 97% of the respondents use e-services (DNA, 2020b).

Facebook, WhatsApp, and Instagram, respectively, are the most popular social network services and are used weekly. People aged 6–24 years use Instagram and WhatsApp, while people aged 25–89 years use Facebook and WhatsApp (OSF, 2020d). A large portion of Finn's (77%) uses YouTube weekly (Pönkä, 2020). YouTube has been the second most popular network service, after Google, for ten years in a row. People use social media more on mobile phones than on portable computers (Pönkä, 2020).

Proportionally, the biggest increase in social network service use occurred in the older age groups, i.e., those aged 65–74 and 75–89 years. It is notable that, due to COVID-19, communication between family members has moved to the Internet. The older generations have become motivated to learn and use advanced skills to communicate (OSF, 2020a).

During the last decade, banks and service providers have eagerly promoted e-invoicing and m-banking. Finland, Sweden, and China lead the way in becoming a cashless society (Festipay, 2018). In Europe, the extensive "Study on the payment attitudes of consumers in the euro area" (SPACE), commissioned by central banks, found that Finland has the most comprehensive point-of-sales network that accepts card payments. Of these payment terminals, 92% accepted contactless payments (card payment, mobile phone, or QR code) (Takala, 2020).

According to the SPACE study, many consumers in the euro area have paid regular and recurring payments through direct debiting (41%). In Finland, consumers usually pay invoices using e-invoicing, where payments are sent directly to an e-bank account or using bank transfers. Paying invoices in cash has become a rarity in Finland: about 1% of the invoices were paid in cash in 2020 (Takala, 2020).

Online banking was one of the most popular e-services in 2020 (OSF, 2020a). Direct debit is extremely popular in Finland. The e-invoice is one form of direct debiting where the service provider sends the invoice information directly to the consumer's bank account and on the due date, the money is automatically transferred to the service provider's bank account. People who do not use online banking also have the opportunity to use direct debiting (Takala, 2020). All banks, and the majority of service providers operating in Finland, offer this type of service. Therefore, Finns do not have to access their online banking accounts to pay recurring payments such as mobile phone, gym, electricity, rent, or insurance payments. In the case of occasional payments, e.g. when ordering from online shops, consumers only need the recipient's account number and amount of the purchase. Eighty-seven percent of the respondents aged 16–89 years answered affirmatively to the question: "Have you used online banking during the last three months". The most active users were respondents aged 25–44 years, of which 98% had used online banking during the last month. A total of 45% of senior citizens aged 75–89 years used e-banking. Due to COVID-19, the use of e-banking increased nine percentage points compared to 2019 (OSF, 2020a). In addition to online banking, controlling household appliances and equipment is becoming increasingly popular. For example, in 2020, security systems (10%) and heating systems (7%) were the most common types of household systems that Finns aged 16–89-years controlled remotely (OSF, 2020a).

Mobile phone as an integral part of life

Social network services, online shopping, and digital services offered by banks, insurance companies, and the government are increasingly accessed through mobile phones or tablets. Already in 2016, mobile devices were used more for bank services than desktop computers (Karjaluoto et al., 2019, 252). In 2018 46%, in 2019 52%, and in 2020 53% embraced mobility (Borgström et al., 2020). The most active m-consumers (70%) are people under 30, but 32% of people over 60 years also make purchases with their mobile phones.

In 2020, senior citizens markedly increased their daily use of different Internet services, compared to 2019. Those aged 65–74 years increased their Internet use by six percentage points, and those in the 75–89 age group by seven percentage points (OSF, 2020a). The reasons for the increase were shopping, social distancing, social network services, communicating with friends and family when the face-to-face meeting was not possible. Further, the pandemic was one reason for the growth in the use of online banking services.

Finnish online shopping has also seen changes in payment methods. Payment through online banking has been and still is the most common method of payment, regardless of gender. A total of 72% of women and 65% of men use online banking to pay for online shopping (Borgström et al., 2020). Mobile payment is also becoming popular. In 2018, 46% of consumers shopped with their mobile phone or tablet; in 2019, it increased to 52%. In 2019, 63% of the people aged 25–34 years m-shopped, the proportion of women being more than men. In 2019, 29% of consumers in the 66–74 age group paid purchases with a mobile phone (Tikkanen et al., 2019). In 2020, 57% of women and 49% of men paid with a mobile phone when shopping online. Women shop for clothes online, and many online clothing stores offer mobile shopping applications for easy shopping (Borgström et al., 2020).

Sixty-three percent of Finns buy online because it is handy (27%) (Tikkanen et al., 2019, p. 14). Online shopping is easy: it is convenient and saves time; it is open 24/7 (20%), and it offers a wide range of goods (20%) (PostNord, 2021; Tikkanen et al., 2019, p. 14). Also, the goods are often different than the ones in the brick-and-mortar shops. Fifteen percent of consumers want to save money (Tikkanen et al., 2019, p. 14). Women shop in their favourite online shop, and men seek bargains (Posti, 2021; Tikkanen et al., 2019). Senior citizens appreciate security/health, and they want to avoid crowds due to the pandemic (Borgström et al., 2020).

Young Finns, especially, stop using an online shop if they face technical difficulties, the freight/delivery costs are too expensive, and if the shop does not have an easy payment method (Borgström et al., 2020). Customers want to have several payment methods from which to choose (PostNord, 2020). Quick delivery (24%) and the possibility to choose the place to pick up the delivery (52%) are key features in online shopping (PostNord, 2020, p. 22), i.e., customers want to decide how, when, and where their goods are delivered. They also want to have the option to change the delivery destination after the delivery has been dispatched (PostNord, 2020).

The environment is one of the reasons why Finns purchase goods in Finnish online shops (PostNord, 2020). Fifty percent of consumers under the age of 30 choose eco-friendly delivery if it is available (Borgström et al., 2020), and compensation on carbon emission is also important (PostNord, 2020). Security and reliability are also important (von Zansen et al., 2017, 19, 49) when they are deciding where to shop. Finnish online shops are now offering better user experiences and a wider selection of products. The number of Finnish online shops has increased. Still, when Finns shop online, they often buy from international online shops. Finns make most cross-border online purchases in Europe (PostNord, 2020). The trend to shop more in Finnish online shops began in 2019 and has increased during the pandemic (Borgström et al., 2020; PostNord, 2020).

Online shopping is an integral part of Finns' daily life, as 73% of Finns all together, and 84% of people under 50 years, reported in 2020 that they shopped online during the past 28 days (Borgström et al., 2020). A quarter of Finns has increased online shopping due to COVID-19 (PostNord, 2020). Also, the older age groups have increased online shopping for security reasons, i.e., to avoid physical contact to decrease the contamination risks (Borgström et al., 2020).

Online shopping behaviour can be examined through categorisation based on user experiences: pioneers, i.e., active users (20%), basic users (38%) and experimenters, or sceptics (41%). Consumers typically at the ages between 18 and 34 years are pioneers in online shopping, and they believe they will buy only online by 2025. This group forms 20% of all consumers. The sceptical experimenters, 41% of the consumers, are mostly over 50 years. Buying online increased rapidly in the first three months of the pandemic, from March 2020 to June 2020. Recently, as much as 60% of the consumers have shopped online during the last month, making half of the pioneers and a third of the basic users. Thirty percent of the consumers felt the COVID-19 pandemic prompted their intentions to purchase goods online. Half of the pioneer online shoppers (50%) reported the same (Posti, 2021).

Borgström et al. (2020) divide online shopping into three main categories: physical goods, services, and tourism/travel. For years, travel was, by far, the most popular category, but due to COVID-19, it decreased to 16% of the online shopping turnover in 2020. Travel tickets for destinations abroad and within Finland, as well as for parking, were the most popular purchase items (Borgström et al., 2020). Due to restrictions, sports events, gym, theatre, and concert tickets were not sold, but items that could be consumed sitting on the couch at home became popular. As regards leisure-time services, subscription and streaming services, such as Netflix, Spotify, HBO, BookBeat, and Storytell, accounted for 34% of sales while digital media, news, and e-books accounted for 11% of sales. The demand for physical goods exploded to a staggering 58% of online shopping turnover (Borgström et al., 2020, p. 6). The most popular items are still clothing, footwear, and accessories (54%), home electronics (48%), books and audiobooks (34%), and cosmetics and skincare (31%) (PostNord, 2020).

The most popular shopping items during the pandemic have been physical goods and groceries (Borgström et al., 2020). People bought more interior design items, household appliances, daily articles, cosmetics, and items for pets. Some of these purchases were first-time online purchases. Because of the increase in sales of these goods and online shopping becoming more common, the media has created the impression that the total increase in online shopping has skyrocketed. When considering the sales volume of online shopping, the skyrocketing increase is, in fact, misinformation, as the volume has actually declined by €2 billion (Borgström et al., 2020, pp. 3, 5).

Because no tickets could be sold, cultural service providers experienced a sharp decline in sales during the pandemic. However, a repositioning of the camera onto the virtual stage served as a theatre. There were weekly Facebook broadcasts of play rehearsals and life behind the scenes – all taking place in the comfort of one's home on the laptop or mobile phone. Some museums offered new services, such as 360-degree virtual tours with augmented reality technologies and video tours, complete with a guide (Digital Museum, 2021).

Professional artists could take a breather and gather up vital energy, or they could shoot a film (keeping in mind the use of masks and distance between colleagues). The artists began to create a new culture and interactivity. Surprisingly, most of the companies that filed for bankruptcy in 2021 were not cultural service providers. Rather, they were restaurants, construction engineering companies, IT and logistics companies (PRH, 2021). Theatres were able to survive due to the public financial support they were granted. Cinemas and individual artists did not usually get any support. In 2020, Business Finland offered small and medium-sized companies (SMEs) support, amounting to €1 billion in total. Half of the companies that received the support planned to go digital. However, a year later almost half of the companies had to give the support back because they did not carry out their plans (Muilu, 2021). Once COVID-19 subsides, Business Finland (2021) will give financial support to Finnish innovations in sustainability and resilience.

There are also success stories of how sales increased during the pandemic. Real-estate agents offered virtual 3D viewings of the properties on sale; potential buyers could visit the properties from the comfort of their living room. Sales in summer cottages picked up again, as people got used to the idea of working remotely. Indeed, summer cottages and boats were snapped up quickly by buyers. Those who already owned summer cottages spent more time there. After the first shock of being in a pandemic was over, people began to renovate their houses or flats or create outside green spaces (see Hofstede et al., 2010, p. 164). The construction industry heated up, and the prices of Finnish gold, timber, and other materials also increased significantly.

Seamless user experience – purchase path

The purchasing experience has moved from the stores to the sofa with the friends who are usually virtually present on Instagram, for example. The more consumers shop online, the pickier they become. This is especially true for Generation Z, 18–24-years-olds (born 1997–2015). However, this is also true for Generation Y, or Millennials, who are aged 25–40 years (born 1981–1996). They choose the online shop that offers the best consumer experience, catering to their individual needs (PostNord, 2020). Before making a purchase decision, a consumer may visit several online shops, physical shops, shopping centres, look up information in social media, listen to what influencers have to say, and they may ask their friends' opinions. The touchpoints are, therefore, in both the physical and virtual worlds. When making a purchase decision, according to Philip Kotler (2000), customers proceed through the following steps: problem recognition; information search; evaluation of alternatives; purchase; e-couponing; post-purchase.

In omnichannel shopping, early studies on m-commerce suggest that mobile devices could be the starting point for a conversation with other channels (Chopdar et al., 2018). Companies need to plan a seamless omnichannel customer experience. Flexible and operational supply chains are competitive factors (von Zansen et al., 2017, p. 72).

Consumers find out about new products from friends, search engines, online shops, brick-and-mortar shops, and brand webpages (Kurjenoja, 2020). Search engines have shifted from Google towards online marketplaces and the products they offer. The brands have a story, and they are either trusted or not. People tend to seek information directly from the brand homepage and not via an intermediate platform, such as Google. In the brand appreciation survey by Market Research Company (2021), Google has dropped from the top 10 into the top 50 categories. The increased amount of banking scams and information security threats might have decreased Google's brand rating.

Consumers follow companies and brands with Instagram (40%), Twitter (35%), LinkedIn (29%), and Facebook (27%) (AudienceProject, 2019). Consumers' demands have become more fastidious while at the same time they have become more impatient as they focus on multiple things at a time. Companies use augmented reality to create unforgettable experiences: customers can see on their mobile phone how a new piece of furniture, e.g. a sofa, would look in their living room. This is a way to create an emotional connection between the brand and the customer (Dagmar, 2020, 2021).

Generation Z is fond of using Zalando and Amazon for their online shopping (PostNord, 2021). Some big Finnish companies could answer this demand. Finlayson is a 200-year-old company that improved its sales by discussing the values of the company. Home linen has to be beautiful, but quality and responsibility for recycling are also important factors. The trends of the 1970s have re-emerged and responded to the wishes of Generation Z (Finlayson, 2021). The customers' stories are important to the company: the, what, how, and why people buy have changed. As noted by Simon Sinek, the stories create meaning. Finlayson's customer stories mention:

- social proof is a common phenomenon in the generation;
- friend requests merit affiliation;
- scarcity of special bed linen, also Finlayson's limited editions;
- fairness and safety as attributes in reciprocity.

Finlayson organises social shopping situations where consumers interact with others during the shopping event. In these cases, the customers influence the decisions of others.

Mobile shopping calls for diverse ways of mobile payment that the customers can easily pay using their mobile device. The willingness of people under 30 to pay by MobilePay partly explains the popularity of mobile payment. Online retailers should ensure their online shop works well on mobile devices. Companies in the B-to-C business market via Facebook, Instagram, and Twitter, whereas B-to-B companies use LinkedIn, Facebook, and Instagram. The primary aim of marketing is to increase awareness of the company's products and offerings by generating traffic on the webpage and binding the customer to the brand (Meltwater, 2020). Will it be true in 2025 that every fifth consumer will buy almost everything on the web, as the inquiry of the Finnish mail and logistical company suggests (Posti, 2021)?

Earlier the brand told the story; now, it is the customer that tells the story of the brand. Companies need their own channels to get into contact with the consumers. The digital purchase path resembles a roller coaster (Seppänen, 2019). When customers search for a solution for their problem, they encounter an impulse in an advertisement or a social media feed. Generation Z is interested in the opinions of influencers. They also expect easy-going payment. A complaint is a chance for a company to end the selling process well, i.e., it should be dealt with immediately and so well that the client is happy with the service and/or product.

Summary

The global pandemic reflects a meta-crisis: when the structures change, commerce should also cast new light on the transformation from squirrel skins to money, from money to plastic cards, from plastic cards to cryptocurrency. What we need it for is the welfare that is navigated by ecological sustainability, recycling, and equality. Because goods will not be needed as much as before, we will shift to services. When working remotely, employees value the independence and control they have of their work (see Dufva et al., 2020, pp. 50, 55). Finns cannot always tolerate uncertainty. They work hard to find the substance of their work, they have an emotional need for rules and expect to get a consultation, at least by the role models.

If we take a closer look at the six dimensions of Hofstede's insights, the power distance in Finland is small, communication is direct and engaging, which can be seen in how customers interact with companies. They collaborate with companies through their stories and by influencing the brand this way. The companies compensate the customers' encumbrances, for example, by offering a discount, in exchange for loyalty. Although the Finnish culture is more individualistic than collective, Generation Z wants to belong to a group and shows it (Hofstede Insights, 2021).

In this chapter, we stated that competition has turned to the quality of life with regard to Generation Z's success. Generation Z admires group membership. When competitive success is defined by masculinity, group activities turn the operation into femininity. Generation Z cherishes their free time which is dominated by being connected to similar-minded people. Status is not shown but can be seen as following the example of idols in social media or as searching for help in making decisions. Their concern is the motivation that promotes a sense of community. Moreover, they will form a society that promotes acceptance of differences in attitudes and true nature.

Although online shopping doubled at the beginning of the year 2021, the Finnish 150-year-old Lafayette-style department store, Stockmann, must undergo an organisational reform by the end of the year. When shopping, customers will be entertained and be inspired by the store's products. Apple has done this many years, i.e., customers can see the products and they order them to their home. Online shops and products are compared. Telephone subscriptions are made for a year or two, but why must a faithful consumer pay more than double the price for a longer subscription period?

When we examine Hall's high context and low context cultures, low context cultures favour written communication. This skill shows to be very valuable when communicating about the brands in social media. According to Hofstede et al. (2010, p. 275), Finns exhibit respect for traditions and are normative in their thinking. Especially Generation X values genuineness. Generation Z is however seen as focusing on achieving quick results, and being impatient, whereas Generation X values critical thinking (Hofstede Insights, 2021). The need for wide personal space for young people can lead to loneliness. The Millennials have not shown much interest in marriage, but according to Statistics Finland's data (OSF 2021) on population changes, the number of new marriages was decreased by 214 in 2020, while the number went down by 1,503 in the previous year.

The followers of Generation Z, the Alpha Generation, the eldest at the age of 11, represent the future. They will be a wealthy and technologically oriented generation. They do not know the world without smartphones, virtual reality, or mobile pay. They have settled down in the middle of the digital world and social media. That is why using technology, for them is the easiest and the most unaffected way to do things. Receiving purchase offers is not important for the Alpha Generation. This generation is interested in the content, i.e., they want to get to know the brand and its values for themselves.

Business ideas

In this chapter, we discussed Finnish online behaviour. Even though Finns have previously been cosmopolitan customers, they are moving over to Finnish online shops, because the buying experience and the offering have improved. Consumers feel that Finnish service providers are more reliable and information security is dealt with professionalism. Information security demands attention so that the perceived risk is minimised and the trust in digital channels remains (Chopdar et al., 2018, p. 110). Finland is categorised as an individualistic country. With weaker uncertainty avoidance, there is less of a prevailing sense of urgency (Hofstede et al., 2010, p. 198). If the tolerance for uncertainty is low, new things may be seen as risks and, therefore, they will not be utilised. There are different stages of m-commerce readiness, like searchability and immediacy, ubiquity and omnipresence (Ashraf et al., 2017, pp. 26, 33). The decision-making does not question the use of the product, but climate change might affect the choices. The temperature of the Baltic Sea is estimated to rise, which will lead to a thinner ice cover. The toxic blue-green algae inhibit the recreational use of the sea, as it makes the water unsuitable for swimming. However, the most sensitive region is Lapland.

Peer-to-peer sales open up countless opportunities. As consumers become more aware, the responsibility of companies for their actions grows. Occupational wellbeing, taking care of the employees, and the environmental aspects require a change in thinking all the way from driving profit to profit distribution. Wellbeing can be improved with multisectorality and, for example, the combination of various arts and work. Work has become more complicated, and people are using a tendering-like process in their job search. The new ecosystem calls for both broad and horizontal understanding and deep vertical competence in the whole issue. There is work, but not enough competent employees. As an employee, a Millennial appreciates togetherness, which makes the building of trust challenging during temporary jobs. Second, Millennials appreciate the balance between work and free time. In the third place, there is the personal growth that the job should offer (Mellanen & Mellanen, 2020, pp. 112, 119).

A well-functioning circular economy attracts customers from all over the globe, but is it reasonable to ship raw materials for long distances? The demands for sustainability will require new business models and processes for clothing and other materials, an ecological packaging, and short shipping routes. The suitability of recycled stone material has already been tested in construction, and geopolymers are being developed as a replacement for concrete (University of Oulu, 2021). Smart houses include technology for the control of lighting, heating, and ventilation.

In Finland, 10% of all disposed textiles are utilised. The pilot project of Waste Management of Southwestern Finland has kicked off with the recycling of clean and dry ragged clothing. Also, many companies accept second-hand clothing, such as Finlayson which makes rag rugs, towels, and new bedsheets out of used sheets and jeans. This concept change has proved to be profitable, as people are fond of memories: with the revival of the rag rugs and the "hügge" trend, people long after the tradition or security in the midst of rapid changes.

Bibliography

Ashraf, A.R., Thongpapanl, N.T., Menguc, B., & Northey, G. (2017). The role of m-commerce readiness in emerging and developed markets. *Journal of International Marketing, 25*(2), 25–51. https://doi.org/10.1509/jim.16.0033.

Asikainen, S. (2021). Maailma ilman brändejä [A world without brands]. Blog posting 09.03.2021. Kupli. https://www.kupli.fi/maailma-ilman-brandeja/.

AudienceProject. (2019). Insights. App & social media usage. https://www.audienceproject.com/wp-content/uploads/audienceproject_study_apps._social_media.pdf.

BCO Finland – Broadband Competence Office Finland. (2021). Why fibre? https://www.maaseutu.fi/en/bco/why-fibre.

Borgström, S., Majaniemi, P., Oksanen, M., Tikkanen, S., & Laurio, M. (2020). Verkkokauppa Suomessa 2020 [Online store in Finland 2020]. Report. Paytrail.

Business Finland. (2021). Innovaatiotutkimus hakee ratkaisuja Suomen talouden haasteisiin [Innovation research seeks solutions to Finnish economy challenges]. https://www.businessfinland.fi/suomalaisille-asiakkaille/tietoa-meista/tulokset-ja-vaikutukset/innovaatiotutkimus.

Chopdar, P.K., & Balakrishnan, J. (2020). Consumers response towards mobile commerce applications: S-O-R approach. *International Journal of Information Management, 53*, 1–16. https://doi.org/10.1016/j.ijinfomgt.2020.102106.

Chopdar, P.K., Korfiatis, N., Sivakumar, V.J., & Lytras, M.D. (2018). Mobile shopping apps adoption and perceived risks: A cross-country perspective utilizing the united theory of acceptance and use of technology. *Computers in Human Behavior, 86*, 109–128. https://doi.org/10.1016/j.chb.2018.04.017.

Cox, J. (2004). Ubiquitous consumption and the marketing mix. *Journal of Internet Commerce, 3*(2), 21–32. https://doi.org/10.1300/J179v03n02_02.

Dagmar. (2020). Sosiaalisen median trendit 2021 [Social media trends]. https://www.dagmar.fi/trendit/sosiaalisen-median-trendit-2021/.

Dagmar. (2021). Markkinoi kuluttajalle, jolla on kultakalan keskittymiskyky ja kuninkaan vaatimukset [Market to a consumer with the concentration of a goldfish and the requirements of the king.] https://www.dagmar.fi/asiakasymmarrys/markkinoi-kuluttajalle-jolla-on-kultakalan-keskittymiskyky-ja-kuninkaan-vaatimukset/.

Digimuseo [Digital Museum]. (2021). Entrance anywhere. https://digimuseo.fi/en/.

DNA. (2020a). Digitaaliset elämäntavat [Digital lifestyles – Using a smartphone & digital transaction]. Survey. https://www.sttinfo.fi/data/attachments/00432/8fc38167-b8d4-443f-be36-716dce51a4e8.pdf.

DNA. (2020b). Digitaaliset elämäntavat [Digital lifestyles – Watching TV content]. Survey. https://www.sttinfo.fi/data/attachments/00520/fc19227b-ef08-452e-9c33-0ed70294f355.pdf.

DNA. (2021). DNA:n heinäkuun 2021 myydyimmät puhelimet ja älykellot – koulujen alku kiihdytti puhelinten myyntiä [DNA's best-selling phones and smartwatches in July 2021 – The beginning of schools accelerated phone sales]. https://www.sttinfo.fi/tiedote/dnan-heinakuun-2021-myydyimmat-puhelimet-ja-alykellot-koulujen-alku-kiihdytti-puhelinten-myyntia?publisherId=1881&releaseId=69915194.

Dufva, M. (2020). Technology provides a lot of opportunities for – And a few threats to – The post-coronavirus times. Sitra 10.9.2020. https://www.sitra.fi/en/articles/technology-provides-a-lot-of-opportunities-for-and-a-few-threats-to-the-post-coronavirus-times/.

Dufva, M., Hellström, E., Hietaniemi, T., Hämäläinen, T., Ikäheimo, H.-P., Lähdemäki-Pekkinen, J., Poussa, L., Solovjew-Wartiovaara, A., Vataja, K., & Wäyrynen, A. (2020, November). Megatrendit koronan valossa. Sitran selvityksiä 171. Sitra. https://www.sitra.fi/julkaisut/megatrendit-koronan-valossa/.

European Commission. (2020). The digital economy and society index 2020 (DESI). Thematic chapters. https://innogrowth.org/wp-content/uploads/2020/07/DESI-2020.pdf.

Festipay. (2018). Top six cashless society countries: Finland, Sweden and China lead the way. Data by GlobalData. https://www.festipay.com/top-six-cashless-societies-finland-sweden-and-china-lead-way/.

FiCom. (2020). FiComin ICT-alaa koskeva lausunto hallitusneuvotteluiden käyttöön [FiCom's statement on the ICT sector for use in government negotiations].

Finlayson. (2021). Vastuullisemmat materiaalit [More responsible materials]. https://www.finlayson.fi/blogs/finlayson/vastuullisemmat-materiaalit?gclid=Cj0KCQjw5JSLBhCxARIsAHgO2Se_-4VbgOxSrdq5paz5o7pWEbVZ2SCXlzdod39uafZmHSxMC1EO08MaAgwJEALw_wcB.

Finnish Patent and Registration Office [PRH]. (2021). Konkurssit. Avoin data. https://konkurssit.com/.

Hofstede, G., Hofstede, G.J., & Minkov, M. (2010). *Cultures and organizations. Software of the mind. Intercultural cooperation and its importance for survival.* McGrawHill.

Hofstede Insights. (2021). What about Finland? Design a culture that will support your strategy. https://www.hofstede-insights.com/country/finland/.

Information Society Code (917/2014). Ministry of transport and communications, Finland.

Karjaluoto, H., Shaikh, A. A., Saarijärvi, H., & Saraniemi, S. (2019). How perceived value drives the use of mobile financial services apps. *International Journal of Information Management*, 47, 252–261. https://doi.org/10.1016/j.ijinfomgt.2018.08.014.

Kotler, P. (2000). *Marketing management: The millenium edition* (10th ed.). Prentice Hall.

Kurjenoja, J. (2020). Digikuluttajan ostopolku muutoksessa [The digital consumer's purchase path is changing]. Finnish Commerce Federation. https://kauppa.fi/uutishuone/2020/10/22/laadun-merkitys-kasvamassa-korona-muokkaa-kuluttajan-ostopolkua-mutta-kuinka-pitkaksi-aikaa/.

Lounais-Suomen Jätehuolto [Waste Management of Southwestern Finland]. (2021). End-of-life textiles. https://www.lsjh.fi/en/jatelaji/end-of-life-textiles/.

Mellanen, A., & Mellanen, K. (2020). Hyvät, pahat ja milleniaalit. Miten meitä tulisi johtaa. [The good, the bad and the Millennials. How we should be led.] Atena.

Meltwater. (2020). State of social media – miten sosiaalisen median markkinointi kehittyy vuonna 2021 [How social media marketing will develop in 2021]? https://www.meltwater.com/fi/blog/miten-sosiaalisen-median-markkinointi-kehittyy-tutkimus.

Muilu, H. (2021). Business Finland jakoi viime vuonna ennätysmäärän tukia – korona-apuun kului liki miljardi euroa. Yle. https://yle.fi/uutiset/3-11834979.

Official Statistics of Finland [OSF]. (2017). Average number of social media services used by Finns 2017. Leisure Surveys. Statistics Finland.

Official Statistics of Finland [OSF]. (2019). Väestön tieto-ja viestintätekniikan käyttö. 1. Suomalaisten internetin käyttö 2019. [Use of information and communication technologies by the population. 1. Finns' use of the Internet.] Statistics Finland. https://www.stat.fi/til/sutivi/2019/sutivi_2019_2019-11-07_kat_001_fi.html.

Official Statistics of Finland [OSF]. (2020a). Use of the Internet for following the media and for communication has increased. https://www.stat.fi/til/sutivi/2020/sutivi_2020_2020-11-10_tie_001_en.html.

Official Statistics of Finland [OSF]. (2020b). Väestön tieto- ja viestintätekniikan käyttö [Use of information and communication technologies by the population]. https://www.stat.fi/til/sutivi/2020/sutivi_2020_2020-11-10_fi.pdf.

Official Statistics of Finland [OSF]. (2020c). Väestön tieto- ja viestintätekniikan käyttö. Liitetaulukko 11. Internetin käyttö ja käytön useus 2020, %-osuus väestöstä. [Use of information and communication technologies by the population. Appendix table 11. Internet use and frequency of use 2020, % of population.] http://www.stat.fi/til/sutivi/2020/sutivi_2020_2020-11-10_tau_011_fi.html.

Official Statistics of Finland [OSF]. (2020d). Väestön tieto- ja viestintätekniikan käyttö. Liitetaulukko 25. Seuratut yhteisöpalvelut 2020, %-osuus väestöstä. [Use of information and communication technologies by the population. Appendix table 25. Community services monitored 2020, % of population.].

Official Statistics of Finland [OSF]. (2021). Decrease in the number of marriages contracted slowed down. https://www.stat.fi/til/ssaaty/2020/ssaaty_2020_2021-06-18_tie_001_en.html.

Ōura. (2021). Know why you feel how you feel. Ōura Health. https://ouraring.com/.

Pönkä, H. (2020). Sosiaalisen median katsaus 02/2020 [Social Media Review 02/2020]. Innowise. https://www.slideshare.net/hponka/sosiaalisen-median-katsaus-022020.

Posti. (2021). Suuri kansainvälinen verkkokauppatutkimus 2021 [Large international e-commerce survey 2021]. https://www.posti.fi/fi/yrityksille/vinkit-ja-caset/verkkokauppa/lataa-kansainvalinen-verkkokauppatutkimus.

PostNord. (2020). E-commerce in Europe 2020. How the pandemic is changing e-commerce in Europe. https://www.postnord.se/siteassets/pdf/rapporter/e-commerce-in-europe-2020.pdf.

PostNord. (2021). Zetat shoppaavat vaatteita, milleniaalit sisustavat [Zetas shop for clothes, millennials decorate]. https://www.postnord.fi/ratkaisumme/verkkokauppa/nuorten-ostokayttaytyminen.

Seppänen, N. (2019). Näin viitoitat asiakkaasi ostopolun [This is how you outline the purchase path of your customer]. Kupli. https://www.kupli.fi/nain-viitoitat-asiakkaasi-ostopolun/.

Takala, K. (2020). Tuoreen SPACE-tutkimuksen mukaan käteinen yhä suosituin maksutapa euroalueella – korona muuttanut maksukäyttäytymistä [According to a recent SPACE study, cash is still the most popular payment method in the euro area – Korona has changed payment behavior]. Bank of Finland. https://www.eurojatalous.fi/fi/blogit/2020/tuoreen-space-tutkimuksen-mukaan-kateinen-yha-suosituin-maksutapa-euroalueella-korona-muuttanut-maksukayttaytymista/.

Taloustutkimus [Market Research Company]. (2021). Brandtalk. Brändien arvostus [Brand valuation] 2021. YouTube 24.8.2021. https://www.youtube.com/watch?v=rICbQ8HxFeo&t=194s.

Telia. (2021). 5G-aikaan siirtyneet kuluttajat ovat ennätysahkeria netin käyttäjiä [The consumers switched to 5G are web's heavy users]. Press releases. https://www.epressi.com/tiedotteet/telekommunikaatio/5g-aikaan-siirtyneet-kuluttajat-ovat-ennatysahkeria-netin-kayttajia.html.

Tikkanen, S., Borgström, S., Majaniemi, P., Oksanen, M., Laurio, M., Melender, K., & Earl, K. (2019). Verkkokauppa Suomessa [Electronic commerce in Finland]. Paytrail. https://www.paytrail.com/hubfs/Verkkokauppa-Suomessa-2019.pdf?hsLang=fi.

Traficom. (2021). Half of the internet usage by Finns travels through the mobile network, 5G networks are being built at a rapid pace in the most densely populated areas. Finnish Transport and Communications Agency. https://www.traficom.fi/en/news/half-internet-usage-finns-travels-through-mobile-network-5g-networks-are-being-built-rapid#:~:text=The%205G%20network%20that%20can,5%25%20of%20the%20land%20area.

University of Oulu. (2021). Geopolymers are changing the world. https://www.oulu.fi/yliopisto/node/41024.

von Zansen, J., Haapanen, M., & Syrjänen, T. (2017). Digilogistiikka [Digital logistics]. Futugene. https://www.logistiikanmaailma.fi/wp-content/uploads/2017/10/Digilogistiikka.pdf.

Yle. (2021). Stockmann aloittaa yt-neuvottelut – vähennystarve enintään 60 työpaikkaa [Stockmann starts co-operation negotiations – Need to reduce a maximum of 60 jobs]. https://yle.fi/uutiset/3-12138064.

Zhang, L., Zhu, J., & Liu, Q. (2012). A meta-analysis of mobile commerce adoption and the moderating effect of culture. *Computers in Human Behavior, 28*(5), 1902–1911. https://doi.org/10.1016/j.chb.2012.05.008.

6 Digital consumers in Germany

Michael B. Hinner

Introduction

German consumers have not used digital media to the same extent that other European consumers have done (*Deutschland fällt in Digital-Ranking*, 2021; Europäische Kommission Deutschland, 2021; McKinsey, 2021). However, the recent COVID-19 pandemic, in part due to governmental measures and in part due to fear of infection, did change consumer behaviour in Germany (Birkner, 2020; Bitkom, 2021, March 10; Rabe, 2021). The question, though, is whether the changes will have a lasting impact on consumer behaviour or whether consumers will return to their old habits. Time will tell. But why are German consumers a bit more hesitant in using digital media than their EU neighbours? It seems that the infrastructure is partially to blame, but German culture seems to play a role as well. This chapter takes a closer look at consumer behaviour in Germany to ascertain the causes and reasons for this reluctance.

In order to better understand what role digital media plays in the shopping behaviour of German consumers, it is necessary to familiarise oneself with some statistical data because these data will help explain the purchasing behaviour. After all, the necessary infrastructure has to be available so that consumers can use the digital channels. It also helps if the consumers prefer cashless forms of payment for their purchases because cashless payment methods tend to make online purchases generally easier than trying to pay for the purchases in cash prior to or upon delivery; although that option is actually available in Germany. But generally speaking, the more cashless a society is, the easier it probably is to shop online or via other digital media. In both of these factors, Germany has not been among the frontrunners in Europe as noted above. This, in turn, may explain why German consumers are not among the top digital shoppers in Europe. It is also necessary to take a look at the measures the German government undertook to curb the COVID-19 pandemic to understand some of the recent changes in the behaviour of German consumers. These measures had a considerable impact on people's buying behaviour in Germany. As it is not yet clear whether these measures will have a lasting impact on consumer behaviour, it is also necessary to examine German culture because cultural norms influence people's behaviour.

DOI: 10.4324/9781003263685-9

Consequently, this chapter examines those factors which provide an insight into the current buying behaviour of German consumers and offers a brief outlook as to how German consumer behaviour might evolve in the future. The chapter is structured as follows: first, the relevant statistical data on digital media use will be presented which examines both the Internet and other digital media use in Germany and compares them with other European countries so that these data are put into a European context. Next follows a look at the use of cash and credit cards in the retail business. Here as well, the statistical data will also include a comparison with other European countries to put the data into perspective. A look is also taken at the governmental measures undertaken by the federal and state governments in an effort to curb the spread of COVID-19 in Germany. This information can be helpful in better understanding some of the changes in German consumer behaviour during the pandemic. Because it is not clear whether these perceived changes will have a lasting impact on shopping behaviour in Germany, it is also necessary to briefly examine some specific aspects of German culture to see how these characteristics might explain consumer behaviour in the country. This background information will help understand why it is not certain how the pandemic will influence the future behaviour of German consumers – whether the changes during the pandemic will have a lasting impact or only represent a temporary shift in behaviour necessitated by the pandemic and the resultant governmental countermeasures.

Statistical data

General facts and figures

Germany is an important market in Europe because it has the largest population in the EU with 83.1 million inhabitants. This number can be broken down as follows: 42.1 million are women and 41 million are men while 21.2 million people have a migration background and 11.4 million people do not hold German citizenship. The breakdown of the age groups in Germany are as follows: under 20 years, 18.4%; between 20 and 40 years, 24.5%; between 40 and 60 years, 28.1%; 60–80 years, 21.8%; 80 years and older, 7.1% (Statistisches Bundesamt, 2021a). These demographic factors will be explained further below. While age does play an important role, it is not discussed separately because age has an impact on all the categories discussed below.

Gender differences

As a number of studies indicate, gender seems to have an impact on shopping behaviour. Men tend to have a clear idea of what to buy without being too much influenced by the general ambience of the shopping environment, whereas women often desire a nice overall shopping environment (*Erlebnis vs. Aufgabe*, 2018). While every second female shopper in Germany buys what appears to be pleasing, only 39% of all male shoppers do so. In fact, men tend to buy new clothing typically when clothes no longer fit or are worn out while women tend to buy new clothes on impulse or as a reward for themselves (*Weibliche Konsumlust*, 2020). These gender differences are also reflected in online shopping behaviour. While 74.1% of all women under age 56 purchase books and magazines online, it is only 55.8% of all men who do so. The figures are similar when it comes to online purchases of toys. 75% of all women aged 46 and younger buy toys online, but only 40.7% of men in the same age category use the Internet to purchase toys (*Unterschiede zwischen Frauen und Männern*, n.d.). Women on average require more time to reach a decision than men also when it comes to online purchases. It seems that men and women follow a similar shopping behaviour online as they do offline. For women, the purchasing decision is based on the general context and environment as well as recommendations while men tend to focus on facts and figures as well as personal experiences (Henkel, 2016).

Ethnic background

As was noted above, 21.2 million people in Germany have diverse ethnic backgrounds. Studies indicate, for example, that consumers with Turkish roots are more brand conscious than the average German consumer, consume more sweets, and buy more baby food than other consumer groups in Germany (Druck, 2013). When it comes to Internet use, research indicates that people with a migration background tend to use the Internet more than ethnic Germans. Not surprisingly, younger people with a background in migration tend to use the Internet more than older people. The study also revealed that only a small minority (3%) of people of diverse ethnic backgrounds living in Germany access solely websites that are exclusively in their native language. In other words, the majority of Internet users who have a background in migration also access German websites (Worbs, 2010).

Digital media access

When it comes to Internet use, 88% of the German population as a whole uses the Internet whereas nearly 100% of those who are between 14 and 49 years old use the Internet on a regular basis (*Anteil der Internetnutzer in Deutschland*, 2021). Not surprisingly, the percentage of Internet users decreases as the age group gets older; for example, more than 42% of those who are 60 years old and older never use the Internet (*Anteil der Internetnutzer in Deutschland*, 2021). It seems the COVID-19 pandemic has boosted Internet use among Germans. According to a study by Bitkom e.V. (2021, March 10), Germans have spent more time in front of a computer during the pandemic than prior to it. For example, 55% of all respondents said they used digital technologies for shopping. In fact, 78% of all respondents said they used digital technologies more often than prior to the pandemic. Here as well, age seems to be a factor because up to 88% of the respondents under 65 said they increased the use of digital technologies while 52% of those aged 65 and older gave the same response. These numbers might seem sizeable, but Germany actually assumes the second to last place in Europe (Switzerland is in last place) when it comes to the use of digital media among those who are between 18 and 85 years old (McKinsey.de, 2021). 65% of that age group have used digital media in 2021 in Germany while 82% of the same group have used digital media in France and 80% of that age group have done so in The Netherlands. According to a McKinsey survey (2021), though, it seems while Internet use increased during the pandemic in Germany, this trend might be reversed once we enter a post-pandemic society. Apparently, many German consumers yearn for physical contact and wish to return to analog interaction with retailers. This could explain the general reluctance to use digital media among German consumers in a European comparison (Europäische Kommission Deutschland, 2021; McKinsey.de, 2021).

Income

Income is another factor that ought to be considered because the more one has to spend, the more one might be motivated to buy. In 2019, the adjusted gross disposable income of households per capita in Germany was 30,142 euros while it was 23,003 euros in Italy, 15,904 euros in Greece, or 14,969 euros in Croatia, for example (Eurostat, 2021). Germany has, thus, as far as the disposable income is concerned considerable potential within Europe. These numbers clearly indicate that Germany could be an attractive market, but there is room for development with regard to the use of digital media in the consumer sector as pointed out above.

Preferred payment methods

Germans have traditionally a preference for cash (Deutsch Bundesbank, 2021). While cashless payment methods typically result in fewer obstacles when it comes to online purchases, some retailers and service providers in Germany have actually undertaken the effort to permit cash payments for online purchases. Some vendors permit customers to pay in cash when the product or service is delivered at the doorstep, e.g. Lieferando, an online food delivery service (Lieferando, 2021). Others allow their customers to pay in cash at traditional stationary retail businesses, e.g. Barzahlen, where the online customer either prints out a barcode or gets an SMS text message on their mobile phones which they then take to a local dm-drogerie markt, a national drugstore chain, where they make the payment in cash in the shops (Schneider, 2013). Studies have shown that German consumers consider cash payments to be safer than online payment methods (Schneiders, 2015).

When it comes to credit card use, it is not surprising that German consumers prefer cash payments over credit card payments (Deutsche Bundesbank,

2021). In a European comparison of credit card use, Germany ranks near the bottom of the list as data from 2019 indicates. While in Germany the average consumer used a credit card 75.7 times in 2019, the average Danish consumer used a credit card 386.2 times, or the average Polish consumer 149 times during the same period of time (*Kartenzahlungen je Einwohner in der EU*, 2020).

So while in the past German consumers generally tended not to use digital media as a payment option in a European comparison, there is evidence that the use of digital media and cashless payment options has increased in Germany during the COVID-19 pandemic (Deutsche Bundesbank, 2021). With the advent of the pandemic in early 2020, data indicate that contactless payments with credit and/or debit cards began to increase. In 2020, 30% of all payments in Germany were made with a card. While this may not seem like a lot, three years earlier in 2017 only 9% of all payments had been by card. Cash payments still accounted for 60% of all payments in 2020. But in 2017, nearly three-quarters of all payments (74%) had been in cash. The COVID-19 pandemic changed the payment behaviour because 32% of all respondents said that they used a contactless payment method for the first time during the pandemic. Among respondents under 55 years and among women, the proportion of those using contactless payment methods was even higher (Bitkom, 2021, May 31; Bitkom, 2021, September 6).

However, payment by smartphone remains an option only among a small proportion of the population. Only 13% of the respondents said they had used their smartphone to pay at the cash register. But here as well, younger people tended to use their smartphones more often than older people (Deutsche Bundesbank, 2021). In fact, 87% of those between 18 and 19 years would like to see all retail shops and restaurants offer at least one digital payment option to their customers. This number decreases as the respondents get older; while 75% of those between 30 and 49 years would prefer to have such a digital payment option, 64% of seniors aged 65 years and older would prefer a digital payment option in retail shops and restaurants. On average, 74% of all German consumers prefer to have a digital payment option available at all points of sale (Bitkom, 2021, May 31; Bitkom, 2021, September 6). This clearly indicates that the pandemic seems to have changed the payment preferences among German consumers because 32% of all respondents said they had used contactless payment methods for the first time during the pandemic as noted above. 55% of those respondents said that hygiene was the primary motivator which is why 69% said they reduced cash payments for that reason during the pandemic (Bitkom, 2021, May 31; Bitkom, 2021, September 6). On the other hand, 59% of all Germans said that they prefer cash payments because this allows them to ensure that they will actually be able to pay for their purchases as they can see how much money they actually have left in their wallets. Another reason for using cash is a situation where a technical defect at the point of sale might prevent cashless payments (Bahr, 2020).

According to Bahr (2020), the main reasons for not using cash are as follows:

46% listed security reasons because cash could be stolen;
46% said they can save time because they do not need to go to an ATM;
41% said it is easier to keep track of payments;
39% listed health reasons because it reduces the risk of getting infected;
19% wanted to benefit from bonus programmes often associated with cashless
payment methods.

Nonetheless, researchers also point out that the transition from cash to cashless payment methods will probably take some time in Germany despite COVID-19. Many retailers and restaurant operators do not wish to switch to a cashless payment method because they are worried about the costs of installing such a system. They are also concerned that finding the right software can take time, and they are apprehensive about possible technical problems (Bahr, 2020).

The preference for cash over cashless payments can, in part, also be explained by the preference of savings accounts among Germans. While 47% use their current account to save their money and 43% a classic savings account, only 17% invest their money in stocks. The reason for this is the fear of losing the investment (*Genutzte Geldanlagen*, 2021). The financial crisis of 2008 reinforced the aversion of stocks among German consumers. Savings accounts and the like are preferred because it is believed that money in a bank is safer and more concrete than stocks because the stock market and stock prices can be very volatile. So savings accounts remain popular even though current interest rates are very low. This explains why some German politicians have called for higher interest rates so that the money Germans have in their bank accounts does not lose its value to inflation (*Neue EZB-Stratgegie gefordert*, 2020).

Increased package deliveries

Another worthwhile statistic to consider is the number of packages delivered from retailers to customers in Germany during the COVID-19 pandemic. According to the *Bundesverband Paket und Expresslogistiks e.V.* (BIEK) [Federal Association of Parcel and Express Logistics], about four billion parcels had been delivered in 2020 which are 400 million more than the previous year. This was an all-time high. As a result, the branch had to hire more staff to handle the extra volume. The Association sees the pandemic as the cause for this increase. This trend is expected to continue in the future as well which means that the branch expects consumers to order more products online and have them delivered to their homes (*Paketsendungen*, 2021). Deutsche Post also recorded a substantial increase in the number of parcels shipped via DHL in

2020 and also sees the pandemic as the primary cause for this upswing. The trend is expected to continue in 2021 as well (Kerler, 2020). The increase in parcels shipped and delivered to customers indicates that German consumers had probably placed these orders with the help of digital media because most of these parcels came from online vendors or mail order retailers who offered online services. This inference is supported by the fact that online vendors like Amazon, Zalando, DocMorris, and even eBay as well as the traditional mail-order retailers like Otto all registered considerable growth during the pandemic (Birkner, 2020; *Umfrage zur Nutzung von Online-Anbietern*, 2021; *Wer profitiert vom Online-Boom*?, 2020). The question, of course, is whether this trend will continue after the pandemic.

Governmental factors

It seems that measures are undertaken by the German government to curb the COVID-19 pandemic also had an impact on the use of digital media amongst German consumers. Germany is a federal state which means the political power is split between the federal government and the individual federal states. Certain rights are delegated to the individual states which can interpret and implement these rights individually (*Facts about Germany*, 2018). The states are, for example, responsible for implementing many health-related issues. The *Infektionsschutzgesetz* (IfSG) [Infection Protection Act] assigns the right to control pandemics and undertake effective countermeasures to the federal states. That explains, in part, why different federal states undertook different protective measures at different times during the COVID-19 pandemic (Saurer, 2020). As this created a very heterogeneous situation, the federal parliament amended the Infection Protection Act to give the federal government some more influence. For example, the federal government can now prohibit border crossings or track persons who have contracted the virus (Geinitz, 2020).

German Chancellor Angela Merkel and the heads of the 16 German federal states met virtually at regular intervals to determine what measures to undertake. In line with the German constitution, Chancellor Merkel could only recommend measures which the individual states could then adopt, adjust, or ignore (Oltermann, 2020). As the number of COVID-19 patients increased, the federal and state governments decided to impose a lockdown on March 22, 2020. This included, amongst other measures, also the closure of many retail and service businesses in Germany. All federal states kept only essential retailers open and closed all other businesses. Essential meant above all food retailers like supermarkets, produce stores, bakeries, butcher shops, etc.; it did not include restaurants or non-food retailers. This lockdown lasted until May 6, 2020 (*Covid-19-Pandemie*, 2021). This unusual situation initially led to panic purchases which resulted in a temporary shortage of toilet paper, noodles, canned goods, and other necessities and brief rationing of these items in many supermarkets. On November 2, 2020, a lockdown "light" became effective. It forced restaurants to close again along with a number of other service industries. Wholesale and retail businesses, though, were permitted to stay open (*Covid-19-Pandemie*, 2021). Because the number of COVID-19 patients did not decrease, the federal and state governments decided to tighten the restrictions which became effective on December 16, 2020, and closed again most retail businesses and service providers. These restrictions stayed in force until March 3, 2021, when the federal and state governments decided to ease the restrictions. Between April 23, 2021, and June 30, 2021, further amendments to the Infection Protection Act permitted individual states the right to impose curfews between 10:00 PM and 5:00 AM in those counties which had an incidence rate of 100 or higher over seven days (*Covid-19-Pandemie*, 2021).

These various restrictions which had been enacted by the federal and state governments in Germany during the pandemic had a direct impact on consumer behaviour as some of the above studies have shown. After all, when consumers are not permitted to shop in certain retail businesses or avail themselves of specific services, this leads to changes as to where consumers turn to in an effort to procure the goods or services they need or which they usually purchase. And shortages of specific items in shops forced consumers to turn to alternative venues as well. So it is not surprising that during these lockdown phases, German consumers were essentially forced to use the Internet to make their purchases. Not surprisingly, this is reflected in the online sales and package deliveries in Germany during the pandemic. Even after the restrictions associated with the lockdowns imposed by the state governments in 2020 and 2021 had been removed, online sales of necessities remained high (Bangemann, 2020; BEVH, 2021; Gassmann, 2020; Hahn, 2021; *Online-Handel wächst*, 2020; *Onlineshopping*, 2020; Rainsberger, 2020).

But it has to be remembered that these sales figures were all reached during the ongoing COVID-19 pandemic. Even though the lockdown restrictions and shop closures had been lifted, many consumers were still fearful of getting infected with the virus in face-to-face shopping or service venues (Bitkom, 2021, May 31; Gassmann, 2020; *Onlineshopping*, 2020). So it is not clear whether this shopping behaviour will continue after the pandemic is over because there are also signs that German consumers might return to their old shopping behaviour (*Kaufverhalten nach Corona*, 2021; Köhler, 2021). Interestingly, there are also indications that local stores have received a boost due to the pandemic (*Deutsche kaufen im Laden*, 2021) because German consumers believe food is fresher and safer if it is sold in local stores than if it is purchased online where it is not clear where the food comes from and who handled it (Gassmann, 2020; *Onlineshopping*, 2020; Wulff, 2019).

Cultural factors

To understand why German consumers might revert to their old shopping behaviour after the pandemic, it is necessary to briefly examine some aspects of German culture. After all, human behaviour, and thus also consumer behaviour, is influenced by the culture one grows up in. For many centuries, Germany had been the site of many battles and wars and the accompanying destruction of life and property which explains the yearning for safety, security, and stability. Economic hardships during the 20th century after both world wars reinforced the need for safety, security, and stability; e.g. hyperinflation in the Weimar Republic, the 1948 currency and economic reform in West Germany as well as the German monetary unification in 1990 (*History of Germany*, 2021). These past turbulences often serve as an explanation as to why German culture is considered to be high in uncertainty avoidance (Hofstede Insights, 2021). According to Hofstede Insights (2021), this means ambiguous situations are generally avoided because people do not like situations where they do not know what will happen. Instead, people prefer stability and predictability. Germany is also classified as a Long Term Orientation culture which means Germans tend to be thrifty and are more inclined to save (Hofstede Insights, 2021). This would explain, in part, the German preference for cash and savings accounts over credit cards and risky investment options as noted above.

This desire for stability and predictability is also reflected in German politics. For example, the first Chancellor of West Germany, Konrad Adenauer, was elected for four consecutive terms of office – albeit, he resigned halfway through the fourth term of office. Adenauer was 73 years old when he was elected and 87 years old when he resigned from office. Between 1917 and 1933, he had been the mayor of Cologne which made him a guarantor of stability and continuity. Helmut Kohl served four terms of office as Chancellor from 1982 to 1998. And Angela Merkel also served four terms in office, starting in 2005 (*Facts about Germany*, 2018). This aversion of change and instability is compounded by a general mistrust of technology (Theil, 2009) which is, not surprisingly, also reflected in the use of digital media. As pointed out above, Germans are not in the top league when it comes to digital use or cashless payment methods. Cultural values and norms can and do change, but not necessarily quickly – unless there are factors which force essentially a complete change in behaviour (Lustig & Koester, 2013; Oetzel, 2009; Samovar et al., 2017) such as the COVID-19 pandemic seems to have triggered.

The impact of the pandemic on consumer behaviour

During the recent COVID-19 pandemic, the behaviour changed, in part, due to the governmental measures as noted above. Online sales, for example, increased by 16.5% and the sales figures for food sales nearly doubled during the second quarter of 2020 when compared to the same period in 2019 (*Online-Handel wächst*, 2020). An increase in online purchases was registered in convenience goods, household appliances, and fashion; e.g. online sales for convenience goods increased by 51.2%. Those retailers who were only active online increased on average their sales by 20%. Amazon, for example, increased its sales by 37% in the third quarter of 2020. During the same period, the traditional stationary trade with its local stores exhibited only an increase of 4.7% (BEVH, 2021; *Online-Handel wächst*, 2020). This trend continued also in the fourth quarter of 2020. The *Bundesverband E-Commerce und Versandhandel* (BEVH) [German E-Commerce and Distance Selling Trade Association] announced that online sales for food increased substantially by 83% during the fourth quarter of 2020 when compared to the same period of 2019. The supermarket chains Edeka and Rewe seem to have profited the most from this development because they had also offered food delivery services to their customers (the so-called click and collect service) (*Wer profitiert vom Online-Boom*?, 2021).

The forced closure of many retail businesses and service providers during the lockdowns compelled a number of these enterprises and proprietors to use the Internet to generate at least some turnover. This led to the introduction of the so-called click and collect service in the retail and service sectors as noted above. "Click and collect" allowed retailers and service providers to present their products or service on the Internet or social media. Customers would then access these digital media, make their selection, place an order, and pick it up at a predetermined time and location (Brentnall, 2021; Edwards, 2021; *Einkaufen in Corona-Zeiten*, 2021). This service, though, has been reduced as the restrictions were lifted and people could once again go directly to the retail business or service provider. Research shows that while 23.4% of Germans used click and collect in 2020, this figure will increase only to 27.7% in 2024. The pandemic did not seem to increase the use of click and collect in Germany because in November 2020. only 7% of adults in Germany stated they have used click and collect more since the advent of the pandemic. In France, it had been 14% and in the UK 11%. Another explanation for this relatively low rate in Germany is the availability of this service. Most retailers only introduced the click and collect service during the pandemic (Brentnall, 2021; Edwards, 2021). It seems that age is once again a determining factor. The older the consumer, the less likely it is for that consumer to use this service in Germany. It seems that older consumers only used such digital options because other alternatives were not available (Kästner, 2021; KPMG, 2021). It is, thus, very likely that they will return to their old habits when that opportunity arises again in the post-pandemic era.

Who then seems to have profited from the lockdowns? Online drugstores increased their sales by about 47% and online pharmacies exhibited a growth of 53.5%. The online sales of clothing increased by 26%, and Otto [originally a mail-order retailer] saw its online sales increase by almost 60%. It was in particular the online sale of mobile phones, TVs, sofas, notebooks, and shoes that had been responsible for most of the sales at Otto. Online food delivery services like, for example, HelloFresh tripled its sales while Delivery Hero increased its sales by 99% during the third quarter of 2020. All told, the trade association BEVH notes that online sales increased by nearly 24% when compared to the previous year (*Wer profitiert vom Online-Boom?*, 2021). It should be noted, though, that overall consumer spending decreased by 4.6% in Germany in 2020. This was actually the largest decrease since 1970. However, German consumers had spent 6.3% more on food and beverages in 2020 than the previous year. This was due to the fact that restaurants were closed for a long time during the pandemic which explains why the restaurant and hotel industry in Germany had exhibited a drop of 33.2% in turnover in 2020 compared to 2019 (Statisches Bundesamt, 2021b).

A KMPG study shows that more than two-thirds of German consumers changed at least in part their shopping behaviour from stationary sales points to online services. The survey also revealed that almost every second, German had changed their shopping behaviour in favour of online sales during the pandemic. Many consumers purchased food for the first time online during the pandemic (KPMG, 2021). 85% of the surveyed online consumers reported that they buy clothing on a regular basis or occasionally online and about two-thirds buy furniture occasionally online (Kästner, 2021). A closer look at the online consumers revealed that it is primarily younger consumers who prefer to have the goods delivered to them instead of them going to the point of sales. And the younger the consumers, the more likely they are to use apps for their online purchases. 48% of German millennials said that they had used the "click and collect" service of food retailers (Kästner, 2021; KPMG, 2021). At the same time, another study shows that 19% of retailers reduced their online product range due to the pandemic while 11% of online retailers had experienced no change in their sales during the pandemic in 2020 (*Veränderungen im Online-Handel*, 2021).

While many studies indicate a change in consumer behaviour during the pandemic (*Anteil der Internetnutzer in Deutschland*, 2021; Bitkom, 2021, March 10; Gassmann, 2020; Rainsberger, 2020), some other studies seem to indicate a different trend (*Kaufverhalten nach Corona*, 2021; Köhler, 2021; *Umfrage zur Änderung des Einkaufsverhalten*, 2021). A study conducted during the pandemic in 2020 indicated that 30% of the respondents said they would most likely change their behaviour in favour of online purchases and 54% said it is probably likely that they would change their behaviour. Only 13% of the respondents said they probably would not change their behaviour in favour of online purchases (*Mögliche Veränderungen im Online-Einkaufsverhalte*, 2020). In July 2021, this seemed to have changed because during that month only 33% of respondents said they were purchasing products online which they had previously bought in traditional stationary stores. This represents a decrease of 10% when compared to mid-March, 2021 (*Umfrage zur Änderung des Einkaufsverhalten*, 2021). It seems hygiene had been a motivator as to why German consumers switched, even for the first time, to online purchases (Bangemann, 2020). This would explain why a number of German consumers no longer saw a need to continue their online purchases as the number of COVID-19 cases decreased in the country.

Discussion

So what do the above data and information tell us about German consumers and their use of digital media? It was seen that German consumers are, not surprisingly, influenced by their native culture which explains why they had been and to some extent continue to rely on cash as their preferred method of payment. It should, though, also be noted that for a long time, German retailers and service providers like restaurants refused and continue to refuse to accept credit cards because they do not like the high service fees typically associated with credit cards use (Bahr, 2020; *Kartenzahlung: Kosten für Händler*, 2021). That is why it would be interesting to discover if the cashless payment measures, which had to be implemented in most federal states during the lockdown by retailers and service providers, resulted in using debit or giro cards or whether it also meant more retailers and service providers began to accept credit cards. Here, the yearning for stability and predictability, which are characteristic features of German culture as noted above, seem to be the primary reason why Germans prefer cash. It has been proposed that German consumers prefer cash because they want to know how much money they have left in their pockets so as to avoid spending more than they actually have. Consumers had also stated they wanted to ensure they could still pay the bill if the business establishment has a technical defect that prevents the use of cashless payment methods (Bahr, 2020), i.e. predictability and Long Term Orientation. It would be interesting to discover if ethnicity plays a role in the preference for the method of payment in Germany, i.e. do inhabitants with a background in migration exhibit the same preference for cash ethnic Germans do?

Another major issue is privacy which plays a major role in why some German consumers are reluctant to use the Internet because the Internet permits the tracing of one's visits and habits. Here, though, there seems to be a difference due to age. Older people are more hesitant and concerned than younger people (Bitkom, 2011, 2021; *Jugendliche im Internet*, n.d.; *Zu sorgloser Umgang mit persönlichen Daten*, 2020). In fact, a number of studies have shown that younger people are more willing to share personal data. For example, 78% of young people between the age of 14 and 29 post personal data online while only 23% of those who are 65 and older do so (Bitkom, 2011).

Inner cities might suffer as a result of the pandemic as some studies indicate (*Kaufverhalten in der Krise*, 2021). However, other studies show that German consumers prefer to use local shops to online food vendors because it is assumed local shops are more likely to sell fresher products. It is also assumed, local shops are more likely to sell products from local producers than online vendors (*Deutsche kaufen im Laden*, 2021; McKinsey, 2021). And German consumers like the personal contact that is possible in local shops, but missing with online vendors (Wulff, 2019).

So it seems that the pandemic did have at least a momentary impact on the use of digital media. Health concerns and governmental measures essentially forced consumers to change their behaviour. And most consumers did change their behaviour as the above figures indicate. The big question, though, is whether this temporary change will turn into a permanent behavioural change. Most likely, older people will revert back to their old habits because people generally do not change their habits once they have become established unless they are forced to do so (Harris et al., 2016; Keltikangas-Järvinen, 1990; Terracciano et al., 2008). This is different with younger consumers who grew up with digital media, and as digital natives, they have different attitudes and are less concerned about possible security issues than their elders as noted above. But this should not come as a surprise because cultures can and do change. Technological advances and natural catastrophes are often a driving force in this change (Lustig & Koester, 2013; Oetzel, 2009; Samovar et al., 2017).

Implications

It seems retailers and service providers in Germany can expect younger consumers to use digital media also in the future. As these digital natives have more disposable income, they will be spending that income on products and services with the help of digital media. In order to address their needs, it is necessary to use various social media, making the ordering of goods or services via these media easy and convenient. This includes cashless payment methods and a delivery service because younger consumers want the product to come to them and not the other way around. They also prefer cashless payment methods (Kästner, 2021). With older consumers, it seems that options for cash payments ought to be available for online purchases because older German consumers prefer cash over card payments. And when it comes to food, it seems German consumers prefer to buy local – whether it is the origin of the food or the retail business where it is sold (Edwards, 2021). But here as well, it is mostly younger people who purchase food online.

References

Anteil der Internetnutzer in Deutschland bis 2020. (2021). Statista. https://de.statista.com/statistik/daten/studie/3101/umfrage/internetnutzung-in-deutschland-nach-altersgruppen/.

Bahr, I. (2020, August 24). *Nutzerstudie 2020: Wie die Krise bargeldloses Bezahlen in Deutschland ankurbelt.* Capterra. https://www.capterra.com.de/blog/1688/bargeldlos-bezahlen-nutzerstudie-2020.

Bangemann, E. (2020, June 23). *Wie Covid-19 das Konsumverhalten in Deutschland verändert.* EY Deutschland. https://www.ey.com/de_de/covid-19/wie-covid-19-das-konsumentenverhalten-in-deutschland-veraendert.

BEVH. (2021, July 2). *Onlinehandel mit Waren wächst im ersten Halbjahr 2021 deutlich um 23,2 Prozent.* https://www.bevh.org/fileadmin/content/05_presse/Pressemitteilungen_2021/02072021_PM_Halbjahreszahlen_2021_01.pdf.

Birkner, H. (2020, June 12). Online-Handel bekommt Auftrieb – trotz schlechter customer experience. *Horizont.* https://www.horizont.net/marketing/nachrichten/studie-zu-corona-auswirkungen-online-handel-bekommt-auftrieb-trotz-schlechter-customer-experience-183559.

Bitkom. (2011). *Datenschutz im Internet: Eine repräsentative Untersuchung zum Thema Daten im Internet aus Nutzersicht.* https://www.bitkom.org/sites/default/files/file/import/BITKOM-Publikation-Datenschutz-im-Internet.pdf.

Bitkom. (2021, March 10). *Corona sorgt für Digitaliserungsschub in deutschen Haushalten.* https://www.bitkom.org/Presse/Presseinformation/Corona-sorgt-fuer-Digitalisierungsschub-in-deutschen-Haushalten.

Bitkom. (2021, May 31). *Kontaktloses Bezahlen wird durch Corona zum Standard.* https://www.bitkom.org/Presse/Presseinformation/Kontaktloses-Bezahlen-wird-durch-Corona-zum-Standard.

Bitkom. (2021, September 6). *Drei Viertel wollen überall bargeldlos bezahlen können.* https://www.bitkom.org/Presse/Presseinformation/Drei-Viertel-wollen-ueberall-bargeldlos-bezahlen-koennen.

Brentnall, A. (2021, March 24). *Click-and-collect adoption in Germany remains low, but glimpses of growth are emerging.* E Marketer. https://www.emarketer.com/content/click-and-collect-adoption-germany-remains-low-glimpses-of-growth-emerging.

Covid-19-Pandemie in Deutschland. (2021, October 3). Wikipedia. https://de.wikipedia.org/wiki/COVID-19-Pandemie_in_Deutschland.

Deutsche Bundesbank. (2021, January 14). *Bezahlen in Deutschland im Corona-Jahr 2020: Karte und kontaktlos im Trend.* https://www.bundesbank.de/de/presse/pressenotizen/bezahlen-in-deutschland-im-corona-jahr-2020-karte-und-kontaktlos-im-trend-855058.

Deutsche kaufen im Laden um die Ecke. (2021, May 18). Tagesschau. https://www.tagesschau.de/wirtschaft/verbraucher/verbraucher-corona-laeden-101.html.

Deutschland fällt in Digital-Ranking auf vorletzten Platz Europas. (2021, September 2). Manager Magazin. https://www.manager-magazin.de/politik/digitalisierung-deutschland-in-ranking-auf-vorletztem-platz-in-europa-a-f0a7ef16-8903-4d9a-90c8-f72d732b8b9c.

Druck, D. (2013, September 17). *Der Ethno-Kunde – was er will und wie er kauft.* https://lebensmittelpraxis.de/zentrale-management/9285-der-ethno-kunde-was-er-will-und-wie-er-kauft.html.

Edwards, K. (2021, September 19). *Click & collect in Germany: Germany 2020 ecommerce country report.* E Commerce Germany News. https://ecommercegermany.com/blog/ click-collect-in-germany-germany-2020-ecommerce-country-report.

Einkaufen in Corona-Zeiten: Wie funktioniert click & collect in den einzelnen Bundesländern?. (2021, January 11). MDR. https://www.mdr.de/brisant/click-and-collect-100.html.

Erlebnis vs. Aufgabe: So unterschiedlich kaufen Frauen und Männer ein. (2018, May 14). *Hoseonline Magazin.* https://www.hoseonline.de/blog/kaufverhalten-frau-mann/.

Europäische Kommission Deutschland. (2021). Deutschland im digitalen Vergleich in der EU an Platz zwölf. https://ec.europa.eu/germany/news/20200611-digitalisierung_de.

Eurostat. (2021). *Verfügbares Pro-Kopf Einkommen der Haushalte.* https://ec.europa.eu/eurostat/de/web/products-datasets/product?code=sdg_10_20.

Facts about Germany. (2018). https://www.tatsachen-ueber-deutschland.de/files/2020-11/tatsachen_2018_eng.pdf.

Gassmann, M. (2020, April 29). Wie die Pandemie den deutschen Verbraucher für immer verändert. *Welt*. https://www.welt.de/wirtschaft/article207581085/Corona-veraendert-dauerhaft-Konsumentenverhalten-der-deutschen-Verbraucher.html.

Geinitz, C. (2020, March 21). Bund will Länder in der Corona-Bekämpfung entmachten. *Frankfurter Allgemeine Zeitung*. https://www.faz.net/aktuell/wirtschaft/bundesregierung-will-laender-in-der-corona-bekaempfung-entmachten-16689784.html.

Genutzte Geldanlagen der Deutschen in 2021. (2021, August 9). Statista. https://de.statista.com/statistik/daten/studie/13314/umfrage/aktuell-genutzte-geldanlagen-der-deutschen/.

Hahn, I. (2021, July 9). E-Commerce: 23 Prozent mehr Umsatz im 1. Halbjahr 2021. *stores+shop*. https://www.stores-shops.de/konzept/handelsstruktur/e-commerce-23-prozent-mehr-umsatz-im-1-halbjahr-2021/.

Harris, M.A., Brett, C.E., Johnon, W., & Deary, I.J. (2016). Personality stability from age 14 to age 77 years. *Psychology and Aging, 31*(8), 862–874. https://doi.org/10.1037/pag0000133.

Henkel, R. (2016, December 23). *Gender Marketing: Wieso Frauen auch im Internet anders shoppen als Männer*. IPSO. https://www.ispo.com/trends/id_79692538/wieso-frauen-auch-im-internet-anders-shoppen-als-maenner.html.

History of Germany. (2021, October 1). Wikipedia. https://en.wikipedia.org/wiki/History_of_Germany.

Hofstede Insights. (2021). Compare countries. Germany. https://www.hofstede-insights.com/product/compare-countries/.

Jugendliche im Internet – die neue 'Generation Sorglos'?. (n.d.). Klicksafe. https://www.klicksafe.de/themen/datenschutz/privatsphaere/datenschutz-broschuere-fuer-eltern-und-paedagogen/jugendliche-im-internet-die-neue-generation-sorglos/.

Kartenzahlungen je Einwohner in der EU nach Ländern 2019. (2020, September 15). Statista. https://de.statista.com/statistik/daten/studie/324905/umfrage/kartenzahlungen-je-einwohner-in-der-eu-nach-laendern/.

Kartenzahlung: Kosten für Händler 2021. (2021). https://www.ratgeber-kartenzahlung.de/kosten-fuer-haendler/.

Kästner, A. (2021, 29 April). *Wie sich Kaufverhalten und Warenkörbe durch Corona verändern*. https://www.sazbike.de/handel/corona-krise/kaufverhalten-warenkoerbe-corona-veraendern-2658747.html.

Kaufverhalten in der Krise: Online-Boom gefährdet Innenstädte. (2021, April 23). ARD-aktuell/Tagesschau.de. https://www.tagesschau.de/wirtschaft/verbraucher/corona-ifo-innenstaedte-sterben-konsum-online-handel-101.html

Kaufverhalten nach Corona: 'Wir treten in keine radikal neue Konsumwelt ein'. (2021, May 20). Deutschlandfunk Kultur. https://www.deutschlandfunkkultur.de/kaufverhalten-nach-corona-wir-treten-in-keine-radikal-neue.1008.de.html?dram:article_id=497528.

Keltikangas-Järvinen, L. (1990). The stability of self-concept during adolescence and early adulthood: A six year follow-up study. *The Journal of General Psychology, 117*(4), 361–368. https://doi.org/10.1080/00221309.1990.9921142.

Kerler, M. (2020, December 8). Deutsche Post verbucht wegen Corona historische Paket-Rekorde. *Augsburger Allgemeine*. https://www.augsburger-allgemeine.de/wirtschaft/Paketlieferung-Deutsche-Post-verbucht-wegen-Corona-historische-Paket-Rekorde-id58685511.html.

Köhler, M. (2021, July 12). Veränderungen durch Corona: Das andere Leben. *Frankfurter Allgemeine.* https://www.faz.net/aktuell/rhein-main/corona-hat-das-konsumverhalten-nicht-so-sehr-veraendert-17433081.html.

KPMG. (2021). *Online-Shopping: Kaufverhalten und Warenkörbe verändern sich.* https://home.kpmg/de/de/home/themen/2021/04/online-shopping-studie.html.

Lieferando. (2021). *Welche Zahlungsmethoden kann ich nutzen?* https://www.lieferando.de/kundenservice/artikel/welche-zahlungsmethoden-kann-ich-nutzen?topicSlug=zahlungsoptionen.

Lustig, M.W., & Koester, J. (2013). *Intercultural competence: Interpersonal communication across cultures.* Pearson.

McKinsey & Company Deutschland. (2021, May 24). *Trotz Pandemie: Deutsche Verbraucher bleiben Europas Online-Muffel.* https://www.mckinsey.de/~/media/mckinsey/locations/europeandmiddleeast/deutschland/news/presse/2021/2021-05-24digital sentiment survey2021/2021-05-24_de_pressemeldung_digital_sentiment_survey_vf.pdf.

Mögliche Veränderungen im Online-Einkaufsverhalten nach der Corona-Krise 2020. (2020). Statista. https://de.statista.com/statistik/daten/studie/1188762/umfrage/moegliche-veraenderungen-im-online-einkaufsverhalten-nach-der-corona-krise/.

Neue EZB-Stratgegie gefordert: Streinbrück und Stoiber wollen höhrere Zinsen. (2020, March 15). ntv. https://www.n-tv.de/wirtschaft/Steinbrueck-und-Stoiber-wollen-hoehere-Zinsen-article 21642650.html.

Oetzel, J.G. (2009). *Intercultural communication: A layered approach.* Vango Books.

Oltermann, P. (2020, November 16). Merkel forced to postpone plans to tighten lockdown rules. *The Guardian.* https://www.theguardian.com/world/2020/nov/16/merkel-germany-soft-covid-lockdown-chancellor-social-interaction.

Online-Handel wächst während Coronakrise kräftig. (2020, July 5). *Handelsblatt.* https://www.handelsblatt.com/unternehmen/handel-konsumgueter/e-commerce-online-handel-waechst-waehrend-coronakrise-kraeftig/25977628.html.

Onlineshopping: Wie sich das Einkaufsverhalten durch die Corona-Pandemie verändert hat. (2020, October 7). *eCommerce.* https://www.e-commerce-magazin.de/ onlineshopping-wie-sich-das-einkaufsverhalten-durch-die-corona-pandemie-veraendert-hat/.

Paketsendungen legen im Corona-Jahr 2020 sprunghaft zu. (2021, June 16). https://de.style.yahoo.com/paketsendungen-legen-corona-jahr-2020-131326073.html.

Rabe, L. (2021, August 4). *Umfrage zur Nutzung von Online-Anbietern während der Corona-Krise bis Juli 2021.* https://de.statista.com/statistik/daten/studie/1113973/umfrage/ verstaerkt-genutzte-online-anbieter-waehrend-der-corona-krise/.

Rainsberger, L. (2020, November 23). *Wie die Pandemie das Kaufverhalten nachhaltig verändert. Springer Professional.* https://www.springerprofessional.de/en/corona-krise/vertriebsstrategie/wie-die-pandemie-kundenbeduerfnisse-und-kaufverhalten-nachhaltig/18606742.

Samovar, L.A., & Porter, R.E., McDaniel, E.R., & Roy, C.S. (2017). *Communication between cultures* (9th ed.). Cengage Learning.

Saurer, J. (2020, May 13). COVID-19 and Cooperative Administrative Federalism in Germany. *The Regulatory Review.* https://www.theregreview.org/2020/05/13/saurer-covid-19-cooperative-administrative-federalism-germany/.

Schneider, K. (2013, March 13). Im Internet einkaufen, mit Bargeld zahlen. *Handelsblatt.* https://www.handelsblatt.com/finanzen/steuern-recht/recht/neues-bezahlsystem-im-internet-einkaufen-mit-bargeld-zahlen/7894882.html.

Schneiders, P. (2015, May 4). Online einkaufen, bar zahlen – das geht. *Frankfurter Allgemeine Zeitung.* https://www.faz.net/aktuell/finanzen/digital-bezahlen/bezahlweisen-online-einkaufen-bar-zahlen-das-geht-13571009.html.

Statistisches Bundesamt. (2021a). *Bevölkerungsstand: Amtliche Einwohnerzahl Deutschlands 2021.* https://www.destatis.de/DE/Themen/Gesellschaft-Umwelt/Bevoelkerung/Bevoelkerungsstand/_inhalt.html.

Statisches Bundesamt. (2021b). *Konsumausgaben der privaten Haushalte 2020 deutlich zurückgegangen.* https://www.destatis.de/DE/Presse/Pressemitteilungen/2021/03/PD21_122_.

Terracciano, A., McCrae, R.R., & Costa, P. (2008). Personality traits: Stability and change with age. *Geriatrics and Aging, 11*(8), 474–478.

Theil, S. (2009, July 17). Germany's technophia is holding it back. *Newsweek*. https://www.newsweek.com/germanys-technophobia-holding-it-back-82013.

Umfrage zur Änderung des Einkaufsverhalten während der Corona-Krise 2020 und 2021. (2021). Statista. https://de.statista.com/statistik/daten/studie/1113346/umfrage/aenderung-des-einkaufsverhaltens-waehrend-der-corona-krise/.

Umfrage zur Nutzung von Online-Anbietern während der Corona-Krise bis Juli 2021. (2021, August 4). Statista. https://de.statista.com/statistik/daten/studie/1113973/umfrage/ verstaerkt-genutzte-online-anbieter-waehrend-der-corona-krise/.

Unterschiede zwischen Frauen und Männern beim Online-Einkauf. (n.d.). eCommerce Magazin. https://www.ecommerce-werkstatt.de/magazin/unterschiede-zwischen-frauen-und-maennern-beim-online-einkauf/.

Veränderungen im Online-Handel durch die Corona-Krise bis November 2020. (2021). Statista. https://de.statista.com/statistik/daten/studie/1104093/umfrage/veraenderungen-im-online-handel-durch-die-corona-krise/.

Weibliche Konsumlust & männliche Qualitätslust. (2020, July 13). *Münstersche Zeitung*. https://www.muensterschezeitung.de/leben-und-erleben/ratgeber/specials/weibliche-konsumlust-and-mannliche-qualitatssucht-838501.

Wer profitiert vom Online-Boom?. (2021, January 6). *Tagesschau*. https://www.tagesschau.de/wirtschaft/verbraucher/profiteure-des-boomenden-onlinehandels-101.html.

Worbs, S. (2010). Mediennutzung von Migranten in Deutschland. *Working Paper 34 der Forschungs-Gruppe des Bundesamtes*. Bundesamt für Migration und Flüchtlinge.

Wulff, C. (2019). Studie: Verbraucher wollen schnell und nachhaltig shoppen: PwCs Global Consumer Insights Survey 2019 zeigt, wie sich der Handel bis 2025 verändert. https://www.pwc.de/de/handel-und-konsumguter/studie-verbraucher-wollen-schnell-und-nachhaltig-shoppen.html.

Zu sorgloser Umgang mit persönlichen Daten. (2020, October 28). Onetz. https://www.onetz.de/oberpfalz/neunburg-vorm-wald/sorgloser-umgang-persoenlichen-daten-id3125589.html.

7 Inside the mind of Italian digital consumers

Alberto Frigerio and Margarita Galagan

Introduction

Compared to other European countries, Italy embraced the practice of e-commerce with a certain delay and the Italian consumers still spend less than half of the European average on online shopping (Morgan, 2019b). Nonetheless, the situation is progressively changing and the common belief is that Italy will align itself with other European countries in the next future. Assessing the Italian case through the lenses of Habermas' system and lifeworld – here, simplified and revisited for explaining the patterns of Italian society – is an innovative approach to clarify what happened and what is happening in this country in the sphere of digital consumption.

According to Habermas, society is characterised by two interactive, but distinct spheres: the system, which is the space of instrumental actions directed toward the realisation of the desired end; and the lifeworld, which is the informal space of those social interactions that contribute to define the knowledge and establish shared meanings (Finlayson, 2005). The system has an impact on the lifeworld by providing new tools for the realisation of diverse goals. Among them, new means for the purchase of products and services. At the same time, the lifeworld has an impact on the system by shaping and spreading new customs and behaviours among the public. Hence, the simultaneous and reciprocal impact between system and lifeworld determines the outcome that, in this case, is the rate of digital consumption in a country (Figure 7.1).

Historically, three different phases of development can be observed by assessing the Italian digital consumers' behaviour through the lenses of Habermas' system and lifeworld model.

Phase 1, a reticent reaction. When the market proposed the novelty of e-commerce, at first and for a certain period of time (arguably, from 1994 to 2008), only a highly-restricted segment of the lifeworld positively responded to it. This result can be explained by taking into account some long-established cultural features of Italian society. First, Italy has a high score on Hofstede's "uncertain avoidance" dimension, which means that, on the whole, Italians are not prone to risk or ambiguity (Hofstede et al., 2010).

DOI: 10.4324/9781003263685-10

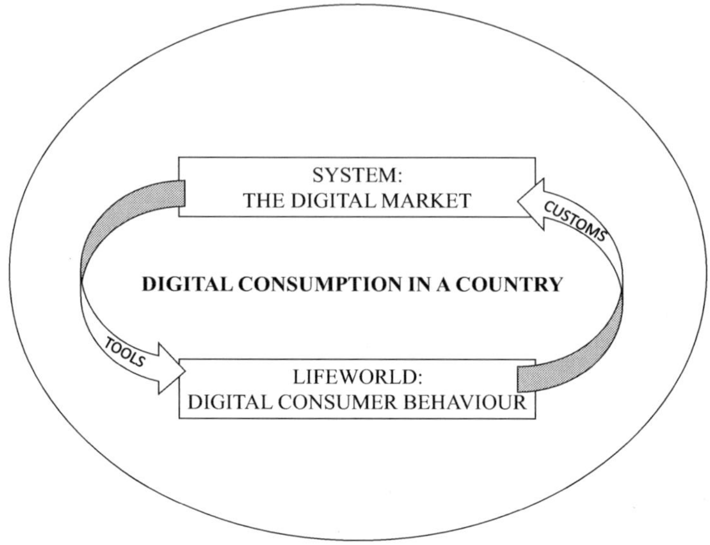

Figure 7.1 The impact of system and lifeworld on the digital consumption of a country

As a result, being unaware about how to proceed with purchase online and/or being scared that something could get wrong (widespread concerns such as, for example, "what if I won't receive my product" or "what if my credit card will get cloned") were factors that significantly constrained the spread of digital consumption among the Italian population. Second, Italy is considered part of Hall's high-context communication countries (Onkvisit & Shaw, 2004). Such countries are characterised by a strong bond between people and a common emphasis toward the context (both physical and cultural) as a key to understanding verbal and non-verbal communication (Hall, 1976). Accordingly, the Italian consumers tend to reveal a certain loyalty toward those trustworthy sellers from whom they regularly buy those commodities or services that are considered of high importance (e.g. medicines, beauty products, or elegant clothes). Likewise, they tend to prefer in-person purchases for those innovative commodities that may demand the consultation of an expert (e.g. computers or other technological devices). Therefore, the impossibility to verbally deal with a physical person while making a purchase online *de facto* slowed down the spread of a digital consumer mentality in the Italian lifeworld.

Additional factors that further contributed to the registered delay in the online purchase in Italy were: an initial diffidence toward novelties, partially dictated by the high average age of the Italian population compared to most of the other European countries – the median age in Italy is 46.7 years, while the median age of the EU-27's population is 43.7 years (Eurostat, 2020); a cultural appreciation of customary routines, which includes, for instance, the practice of personally purchasing food in the supermarket during the weekends; and a relatively limited number of Internet users in the country – in 2009, only 44.4% of the Italian population used the Internet compared to the 70.9% of 2019 (Statista.com, 2021b).

Phase 2, a gradual embracement of the new platforms (approximately from 2009 to 2015). Notwithstanding the cultural barriers mentioned above, the purchase of services and products on the web slowly, but increasingly became more appealing in specific categories of the lifeworld: mainly young adults (ranging from the 20s to 40s) from the North and Central regions more than the South and the islands (Angelini et al., 2018). These people saw in making a purchase online either an opportunity (e.g. in terms of costs, access to otherwise unavailable commodities, or time-saving practice) or a curiosity (e.g. the willingness to try something new). Some of the most important factors that favoured such process of transformation were: an increased popularisation of historical e-commerce websites like, for instance, Amazon and eBay; the rise of the phenomenon of couponing (e.g. Groupon); the development of more user-friendly online interfaces; the practice of sharing experiences through social media platforms (such as Facebook and YouTube); and the securing of online economic transactions through a system like PayPal. These changes favoured the first spreading of digital consumer culture in Italy. Even so, the majority of the Italian population ignored or showed a reluctance to shop online. To a large extent, such a result was dictated by a still restricted number of Internet users and credit cards owners in the country.

Phase 3, a new pathway in the Italian digital consumption (from 2016 to date). The development of mobile commerce represented an important turning point in Italy because customers got the opportunity to shop online by downloading and using simple apps with their smartphones. As a result, an important increase in e-commerce transactions was recorded in such years. In 2016, Italy faced an 18% growth in e-commerce, which produced a turnover of nearly €20 billion (Osservatori.net, 2016). Similar results were recorded in the following years (2016–2019) and, according to Morgan (2019a), the total e-commerce transactions realised through a mobile device in Italy reached a quota of 33%. Likewise, the number of social media users in the country recorded a progressive increase over the years, and, in 2019, Facebook reported 35.7 million active users, followed by YouTube and Instagram, respectively with around 24 and 22.3 million users (Statista.com, 2021a). There is, however, no clear evidence about the impact (if any) played by social media on the development of online shopping in Italy.

The global spread of Covid-19 introduced some additional structural changes. According to Osservatori.net (2020), in 2020 the online purchases in Italy reached a quota of 30.6 billion euro, thus registering a decline of 3% compared to 2019. Nevertheless, the same source reveals that while the number of services purchased online almost halved compared to the former year, the number of products sold online registered a noteworthy growth of 31%. Likewise, in 2020, the number of people in Italy who made a purchase online increased by 13% compared to 2019, thus reaching a quota of 26.9 million (Pontiggia, 2020). Today 65% of the Italian adult population (over 15 years old) claims to make online purchases and/or to pay bills online (Kemp, 2020) and Amazon is the 5th most visited website in Italy (SimilarWeb.com, 2021). So, Italians did not stop purchasing online during quarantine. They just shifted their attention from services to products plausibly due to the restriction imposed by the governments worldwide on the tourism and entertainment industry. There are, therefore, valid reasons to believe that the e-commerce growth will return to (or even exceed) the 2016–2019 rates once the Covid-19 pandemic will progressively get under control.

Since all models are approximations, the systematisation provided here is also an over-simplistic assessment because it does not fully consider the multidimensional aspects of national culture as well as the incongruent behaviour that may occur within similar categories of the population. Moreover, it is an incomplete explanation because it omits a holistic analysis of the problem (e.g. it does not consider the impact of political or economic uncertainty on the behaviour of the Italian consumers). Nevertheless, this schema provides a simple, but cohesive and reasonable overview of the motives behind the moderate spreading of digital consumption in Italy for so many years.

The following sessions try to examine deeper the matter, by offering a critical assessment of the Italian digital consumers' culture. The objective is to address the cultural dynamics that induced some Italians to culturally embrace the idea of shopping online as well as to uncover emerging trends for e-business in Italy. Methodologically, such a study is grounded on the qualitative content analysis of a series of semi-structured interviews, which have been conducted online by the authors between April and June 2021. Each interview consisted of 15 basic questions plus an undetermined series of additional questions that were used to clarify blurred statements and/or to gain some detailed explanations. The respondents were 16 Italian digital consumers, 10 males, and 6 females, living in the northern regions of Italy and aged between 35 and 43 years. What they have in common is the belief that they are Italian digital consumers. The next section reports the main findings from the semi-structured interviews conducted in the course of this study. During the analysis, the collected textual material has been cohesively organised and coded in an attempt to identify relevant patterns. Such information has successively been logically arranged to construct a model where the observed behaviours are related to the underlying attitudes and values of Italian society. Such a model is presented in the third section of this chapter. The conclusive sections sum up the core results of this study and briefly show how they might affect the Italian e-commerce business in the next years.

The Italian digital consumers' behaviour: a qualitative analysis

The literature on the Italian digital consumers' behaviour is largely underdeveloped. Only a few exploratory studies (e.g. Angelini et al., 2018; Kemp, 2020) and online platforms (e.g. Osservatori.net; Casaleggio.it) offer some updated information and in-depth analysis on the emerging customs. At the same time, no comprehensive studies are trying to specifically examine the digital consumer culture in Italy and its system of values. To fill in such a gap of knowledge, the authors of this chapter conducted a series of in-depth interviews with people who identified themselves with the definition of "Italian digital consumers" – here interpreted as a person who claims to regularly purchase a diversified set of assets and services through online platforms. The following analysis will define what Italian digital consumers primarily buy online, how do they proceed before completing a purchase, what factors they value the most, which platforms they tend to use for online shopping, and what kind of actions could further foster the spreading of digital consumer culture in Italy.

Although all respondents defined themselves as digital consumers, the declared number of purchases, as well as the total monetary value of the performed acquisitions, changed drastically from individual to individual. For example, the number of products/services bought online in the last year by a single respondent ranged from 10 to 400, with an arithmetic average of 121 purchases, but a median of only 55 items. Likewise, the amount of money invested on average in a single month for online purchases ranged from 150 to 1,500 euro, with a mean of 587 euro and a median of 325 euro. Therefore, the element of inclusiveness in the "club of digital consumers" is not determined by the number of transitions or the purchasing ability of the buyer, but rather by the confidence and regularity with which online purchases are made. In other terms, the psychological, cultural, and know-how parameters seem to be more relevant than the economic factor.

All respondents identified in hotels and airline tickets the main services commonly purchased online. Several participants made also reference to the purchase of tickets for attending entertaining events of diverse nature (e.g. music concerts, sports competitions, theatres). Therefore, tourism and leisure seem to monopolise the services commonly purchased online. Differently, a more diversified set of products was mentioned by the interviewees. It included: health products (e.g. vitamins and herbal tonics), technological objects (e.g. televisions, computers, and mobile phones), casual clothing, collectibles (e.g. vintage toys and vinyl records), household goods, domestic appliances, sportive items, books, and other articles of "interest, but low economic value".

Notwithstanding such diverse interest in the selections of the products that are commonly purchased online, all respondents claimed that they still prefer to buy food and beverages offline. Such behaviour is, at first glance, justified by the desire "to see and touch the product". However, two factors come to light trying to examine more in-depth the matter: an issue of health-care security that demands control of the purchased culinary product (e.g. freshness, quality, origin, etc.) and a matter of social custom, as purchasing grocery products in person is still viewed as a heartfelt tradition, which must be shared by the whole family.

Around a third of the respondents added clothing among the items they still prefer to purchase offline. The main explanation was the wish to try them (for instance, to check the size and the appearance once worn) before making the purchase. Most of the respondents claimed that such a practice is unfeasible online. Moreover, some interviewees asserted that they do not make online purchases for products over a certain budget (variable from person to person) due to the possible risk of fraud or dissatisfaction with the final product. Actually, the same respondents claimed to trust the system of purchases online, but presumably, there is a boundary after which the perceived risk outweighs the expected benefits.

During the interviews, Amazon and Booking.com resulted from the most popular platforms of e-commerce. Users appreciated their simplicity ("easy to conclude a purchase"), reliability (in terms of money-transfer security as well as final delivery), and competitiveness in prices. Other online platforms mentioned by interviewees were TripAdvisor, Zalando, Subito.it, Ebay – which was, however, highly criticised as the most cumbersome platform – Asos.com, Yoox.com, and Ali Express. Being simplicity still a key condition for online shopping, most of the respondents were relatively unaware of more advanced tools of digital consumption. Only two of them, for example, tried an augmented reality application before making a purchase. In both cases, such experience did not affect their final decision and it was primarily made to satisfy their sense of "curiosity". These results seem to suggest that the Italian way to shop in the digital world is, to a large extent, still limited to online shopping platforms.

All respondents claimed to make preliminary research, mainly on Google and Amazon, before purchasing a product. The objective is to find and buy the searched service or commodity at the lowest possible price. Several respondents stated that searching for the most advantageous price is a sort of "game quest" whose successful completion generates personal satisfaction. Around one-third of the respondents claimed to keep a similar approach for offline purchases too, while the others sustained that such a practice offline would be excessively time-consuming.

So, the consumer decision model for both offline and online purchases seems to be based on the same core structure: problem recognition, search for a solution, evaluation, and comparison of alternatives, decision (Smith, 2020). Online shopping, however, removes the spatial dimension – no need to visit the shop in person anymore – and it exponentially reduces the time to compare prices or products – in a few minutes it is possible to critically assess the features and costs of multiple goods by getting access to a huge quantity of official and unofficial information. As a result, companies now deal with well-informed consumers whose loyalty can only be retained through a focused client-oriented approach (Racolta-Paina & Luca, 2010).

All but one interviewee claimed that their attitudes toward online purchases changed during the Covid-19 pandemic. Specifically, the number of products purchased online significantly increased primarily due to the impossibility to physically access the shops, but also as an effect of the boredom caused by the quarantine restrictions that pushed them to make "tempting, but unneeded purchases". Still, the majority of Italian consumers continued to buy food in person. Differently, the number of services bought online significantly declined due to travel restrictions. Moreover, while the majority of respondents sustained that the average amount of money invested in online purchases did not change in the last year, two interviewees claimed that they had to reduce their investments for online purchases due to the redundancy fund scheme introduced at their workplace during the period of quarantine.

When asked why they make a purchase online and what are the most relevant benefits of shopping online, the following advantages were identified:

- comfort: anyone can purchase whatever he/she wants from his/her home or office just in a few minutes;
- timing: the purchase can be done rapidly, thus saving time for other activities, and most of the products are nowadays delivered home in 48 hours;
- saving: most of the respondents claimed that, after proper research, it is possible to purchase a product online for a price much lower than it is sold offline;
- opportunities: through online platforms, clients can get access to a huge variety of products, including some goods that, otherwise, will be unavailable in their countries.

Although most of the respondents affirmed that social media – mainly Facebook, YouTube, and Instagram – incentivise people to buy online by showing the features of new products, they also showed a low trust toward online reviews. The dominant perception is that most of the comments on social media platforms are biased or made by fake profiles. Therefore, at present, social media are used as platforms to discover new products and services, but they are not used as a direct channel of online purchases and neither as a reliable source of information. Moreover, none of the interviewees claimed to regularly post photos or comments of his/her online purchases on social media platforms. This behaviour, principally justified by a lack of interest and a scarcity of time, is in contrast with the participatory behaviour identified in some studies as a primary factor in the online consumers' decision-making approach (Ashman et al., 2015). Future academic research should investigate deeper this aspect to understand if the Italian digital consumer culture is effectively an exception in this regard.

Proceeding, interviewees commonly agreed that the confidence to shop online has drastically increased in comparison to their first experience. Specifically, the payment system is more secure and the logistics have also been significantly improved. As a result, their number of purchases online has grown over time. Although the current system is viewed as stable and reliable, respondents affirmed that the following actions could be taken to further foster a digital consumption culture in Italy: give customers the possibility to pay in cash upon delivery; enhance the promotion of e-commerce in the traditional channels of communication, and create more platforms that would allow comparing the costs of diverse goods and services.

Moreover, according to respondents, the main factors still constraining the spread of digital consumption in Italy are limited use of the credit card in certain segments of society; a lack of confidence toward the quality of the final product, and/or the safety of operations online due to inexperience or former unsatisfactory events; a still excessively long delivery times for certain zones of Italy (e.g. in the largest cities products are often delivered within 48 hours, while in peripherical areas it might need a whole week or more); a know-how gap and a prevailing scepticism within the eldest population; and the persistence of certain socio-cultural traditions that can hardly be broken (e.g. purchasing of grocery offline).

High perception of risk, fear of financial loss, delivery delays in peripherical areas, rooted cultural traditions, and lack of confidence-knowledge toward e-commerce platforms seem, therefore, the main factors still constraining online shopping in Italy. These considerations are following some of the conclusions already reached by academic literature upon the issue of online shoppers and non-shoppers (Allred et al., 2006).

The underlying attitudes and values of digital Italian consumers

A discrepancy of attitudes comes to light by comparing the cultural features of Italian society that have been identified in the first section and the behavioural approach of the Italian digital consumers as emerging from the interviews examined in the second section. Such difference is, however, explainable considering the ongoing transformations taking place both in the e-commerce system and within Italian society. For instance, Italians are culturally not prone to risk or ambiguity. But the raising confidence in the use of credit cards and the achieved improvements in the system of security for online transactions have progressively fostered digital purchases in the country. Likewise, for Italians in-person communication is an important factor before making a choice. This is still a key issue and, in fact, during interviews respondents show low confidence toward online reviews. However, the combined strategy to recognise the customer's buying behaviour as well as to increase the availability of information online about a product/service (Casaleggio.it, 2021) has partially met the Italian customer's demand for clarity and awareness. Moreover, according to Lewis (1996), Italians show a multi-active behaviour which, *inter alia*, entails the intent of doing several things at once. In this regard, online shopping is a tool that perfectly fits with such a profile in view of its simplicity, immediacy, and versatility.

Still, what needs to be clarified is the system of values supporting the Italian digital consumers' attitude and behaviour. Critical discourse analysis has been conducted on the material collected through in-depth interviews. Figure 7.2 sums up the results of this analysis by connecting behaviours, attitudes, and values.

Looking for comfort is one of the main factors inducing people to make a purchase online. On one side, when describing their experience, the interviewees emphasised the possibility to exploit waiting periods to shop online, thus using such intervals for productive activity. In this regard, the value of convenience, as the capacity to ease the process of purchasing products and services by breaking the barriers of time and space, emerges as one of the core advantages of digital consumption. On the other side, shopping online is defined by respondents as a form of leisure where people can easily compare prices and look for diverse commodities and services. In other terms, e-commerce platforms open a new opportunity for useful entertainment that is appreciated by digital consumers.

A second important – and related – factor in digital consumption is timing consciousness. Digital consumers recognise the values of foresight and resourcefulness in making a purchase online, underlying their ability to

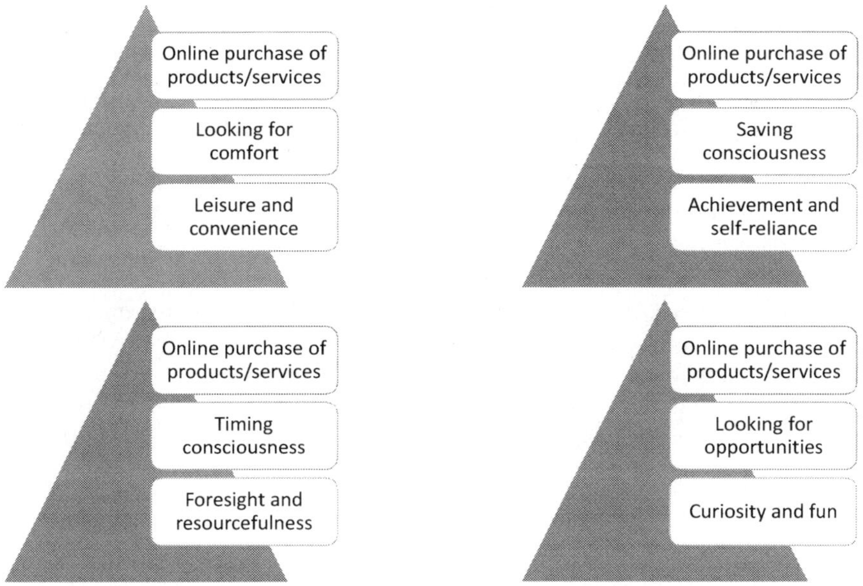

Figure 7.2 Italian digital consumers' behaviours, attitudes, and values

efficiently use their spare time in an optimal way. The emphasis on such values is so stressed by the majority of interviewees to create a binary division between "we", digital consumers, 'who do not have time, but have the digital skills to maximise the outcome by making a purchase online' (reporting the exact words given by an interviewee), and "them", non-digital consumers, 'who have plenty of time, but not the capacity to efficiently operate online and, therefore, prefer to visit several shops in person'.

Likewise, saving consciousness is a third key factor, which drives the respondents to make an online purchase of products and services. Several interviewees underlined the feeling of satisfaction and achievement they get by buying products at a lower price than the one offered in the stores. In this regard, the sense of self-reliance – the capacity to autonomously solve the challenge of looking for the best price – is an added value that provides personal satisfaction and further stimulates the process of preventive research online.

Finally, interviewees claimed to make a purchase online in an attempt to look for opportunities. A sense of adventure and curiosity guide them in the exploration of diverse online platforms. Moreover, most of them claim to have fun in the process due to the "unexpected treasures" they can find on the web. As one of the respondents said,

> sometimes it happens that, while looking for a specific product, you find something else that maybe you do not need, but it is so captivating and tempting that, for a reasonable price, you will be ready to invest a few euro even just for a temporary sense of satisfaction.

The results of this analysis reflect some of the main conclusions already reached in academic literature. First, there is both a hedonic (fun) and utilitarian (goal-oriented) interest behind the individual choice to shop online (Babin et al., 1994). Second, the goal-oriented approach is primarily driven by factors such as convenience, informativeness, selection, and self-control of the process (Sorce et al., 2005; Wolfinbarger & Gilly, 2001). Third, personal values such as self-direction, enjoyment, and self-achievement are directly associated with a positive attitude toward e-shopping (Jayawardhena, 2004). The data extracted from the collected interviews have, nonetheless, shown how such factors must not be viewed as independent elements, but rather as cohesive principles supporting a multi-vectoral consumer approach where fun and utility are interlinked attitudes of the Italian digital consumers. Such a conclusion, which needs anyway to be confirmed by further studies, could represent a distinctive feature of the Italian digital consumption culture.

Conclusions

The status of the Italian digital consumer culture can be briefly but analytically summed up by referring to Sohail Inayatullah's Futures Triangle model (2008). Such a foresight model is based on three parameters: the weight of the past (e.g. resistance to change, traditions, etc.), the push of the present (e.g. trends and driving forces), and the pulls of the future.

Some peculiar socio-cultural features of the Italian society – such as, for example, a low propension to risk and ambiguity, a strong bond between people, the importance of context during the communication process, a diffidence toward novelties, a cultural appreciation of customary routines, and a still relatively constrained number of Internet users – have slowed down for several years the spreading of digital consumer culture in the country. These features represent a legacy of the past that is still rooted in a large segment of the Italian population. However, recent innovations – like, for example, the popularisation of historical e-commerce websites, the spreading of couponing, the creation of user-friendly interfaces, and the development of secure systems of economic transactions online – and unexpected circumstances – as the social restrictions imposed due to Covid-19 – are pushing specific segments of the Italian population (young adults, ranging from the 20s to 40s, mainly – but not exclusively – from the North and Central regions) to explore new opportunities online. At the same time, there are some emerging pull factors – as a wish of comfort, increased attention to price comparison, a better consciousness of time management, and the desire to explore new opportunities – that are progressively extending the range of online shoppers. Hence, the digital consumer scenario in Italy is in an evolving phase, and considering the data reported above, it seems reasonable to conclude that the number of digital consumers, as well as the monetary value of the online purchases, will grow again in the next years.

Moreover, three important features of the forthcoming Italian scenario might be deduced from a cohesive assessment of the statements released during the interviews. First, the Italian e-commerce business has – and it will have – to deal with more demanding and informed customers who are looking for comfort, efficiency, and advantageous deals. The provision of simple, but appealing and efficacious systems to purchase online will, therefore, become an essential condition to get and retain clients. Considering the Italians' "uncertain avoidance" and "customer loyalty" features, few online platforms will get most of the attention, while the others will have to operate in niche businesses to gain consumers. Second, the Italian digital consumers seem to combine utility and pleasure during their research of products/services online and, in addition, they highly value the personal achievements reached during the purchasing process (e.g. saving of time and/or money, capacity to come across unexpected opportunities). As a result, personalised marketing approaches and gamification strategies are likely to become popular and effective tools to catch the attention of experienced digital consumers. Third, a large part of the population who currently do not buy products and/or services online could turn into online shoppers through dedicated interventions aimed at reducing risks and uncertainties, extending the awareness toward the functions of e-commerce platforms, and/or improving technical aspects by, for example, reducing the terms of delivery and realising more user-friendly interfaces. Therefore, from a business perspective, there is still great scope for development.

Altogether, these conditions entail, on one side, the need for more advanced research aimed to address the specific features of those market segments within the Italian population that are not engaged with online shopping yet, and, on the other, upgrading of current online platforms in order to best meet the requests and desires of knowledgeable users. In other terms, the Italian digital consumers' framework will be soon characterised by two different typologies of consumers: a large group of "digital neophytes", who will demand mainly for security and simplicity; and a relatively smaller, but numerically growing group of "experienced users", who will look for both efficiency and enjoyment. Being such consumers driven by diverse goals, business companies will have to expand and differentiate their marketing and selling approaches toward the Italian consumers in order to deepen their customer relationships via digital platforms.

From a technological perspective, search engines and retail websites will keep playing a central role in e-commerce due to their simplicity and capacity to meet customers' needs. Still, experienced users might also get more interested to experience supportive tools like, for example, voice assistant technologies (e.g. Amazon's Alexa) or automated services for regular purchases. Dedicated mobile apps will also further increase their popularity because, arguably, a growing number of online transactions will be completed in the spare time. More exploratory studies are, on the contrary, needed to examine how in-app purchases on social media and augmented/virtual reality tools might introduce innovative shopping experiences in Italy. Although, up to now, Italians have shown a certain scepticism toward these tools, their global popularisation might affect the Italian market too. Likewise, more attention needs to be placed on the rise of diversified online payment systems for e-commerce as well as on the development of personalised advertising and product customisation for regular users.

Bibliography

Allred, C.R., Smith, S.M., & Swinyard, W.R. (2006). E-shopping loves and fearful conservatives: A market segmentation analysis. *Journal of Consumer Marketing, 34*(4/5), 308–333.

Angelini, P.P., Di Nunzio, D., Ferrucci, G., Galossi, E., & Moretti, V. (2018). *Dimensioni e caratteristiche dell'e-commerce in Italia.* Ente Bilaterale Nazionale Terziario.

Ashman, R., Solomon, M.R., & Wolny, J. (2015). An old model for a new age: Consumer decision making in participatory digital culture. *Journal of Customer Behaviour, 14*(2), 127–146. http://dx.doi.org/10.1362/147539215X14373846805743.

Babin, B., Darden, W., & Griffin, M. (1994). Work and/or fun: Measuring hedonic and utilitarian shopping value. *Journal of Consumer Research, 20*(4), 644–656.

Casaleggio.it (2021, March). *E-commerce in Italia 2021. Presentazione della XV edizione della ricerca.* https://www.casaleggio.it/focus/rapporto-e-commerce-in-italia-2021/.

Eurostat. (2020). *Population structure and ageing.* https://ec.europa.eu/eurostat/statistics-explained/index.php/Population_structure_and_ageing#Median_age_is_highest_in_Italy.

Finlayson, J. (2005). *Habermas: A very short introduction.* Oxford University Press.

Habermas, J. (1987). *The theory of communicative action. Lifeworld and system: A critique of functionalist reason* (Vol. 2). Beacon Press.

Hall, E. (1976). *Beyond culture.* Anchor Book.

Hofstede, G., Hofstede, G.J., & Minkov, M. (2010). *Cultures and organizations. Software of the mind. Intercultural cooperation and its importance for survival.* McGraw-Hill.

Inayatullah, S. (2008). Six pillars: Futures thinking for transforming. *Foresight, 10*(1), 4–21. https://doi.org/10.1108/14636680810855991.

Jayawardhena, C. (2004). Personal values' influence on e-shopping attitude and behaviour. *Internet Research, 14*(2), 127–138. http://doi.org/10.1108/10662240410530844.

Kemp, S. (2020, February 13). *Digital 2020: Italy.* https://datareportal.com/reports/digital-2020-italy.

Lewis, R. (1996). *When cultures collide: Leading across cultures.* Nicholas Brealey International.

Morgan, J.P. (2019a). *E-Commerce payments trends: European overview.* https://www.jpmorgan.com/merchant-services/insights/reports/european-overview.

Morgan, J.P. (2019b). *E-Commerce payments trends: Italy.* https://www.jpmorgan.com/merchant-services/insights/reports/italy.

Onkvisit, S., & Shaw, J. (2004). *International marketing. Analysis and strategy* (4th ed.). Routledge.

Osservatori.net. (2016). *L'eCommerce in Italia cresce del 18% e sfiora i 20 milliardi di € nel 2016.* (ECommerce in Italy grows by 18% and reaches € 20 billion in 2016). https://www.osservatori.net/it/ricerche/comunicati-stampa/lecommerce-in-italia-cresce-del-18-e-sfiora-i-20-miliardi-di-nel-2016.

Osservatori.net. (2020). *Nell'Italia post-lockdown gli acquisti online valgono 30,6 mld, con un aumento degli acquisti di prodotto (+31%).* (In post-lockdown Italy, online purchases are worth 30.6 billion, with an increase in product purchases (+31%)). https://www.osservatori.net/it/ricerche/comunicati-stampa/nellitalia-post-lockdown-gli-acquisti-online-valgono-30-6-mld-con-un-aumento-degli-acquisti-di-prodotto-plus31

Pontiggia, V. (2020, December 9). *Il mercato eCommerce in Italia: tiriamo le somme!* https://blog.osservatori.net/it_it/mercato-ecommerce-statistiche-dati-itala.

Racolta-Paina, N.D., & Luca, T.A. (2010). Several considerations regarding the online consumer in the 21st century – A theoretical approach. *Management & Marketing, 5*(2), 85–100.

SimilarWeb.com. (2021). *Top websites ranking.* https://www.similarweb.com/top-websites/italy/.

Smith, A. (2020). *Consumer behaviour and analytics.* Routledge.

Sorce, P., Perotti, V., & Widrick, S. (2005). Attitude and age differences in online buying. *International Journal of Retail & Distribution Management, 33*(2), 122–132. http://doi.org/10.1108/09590550510581458.

Statista.com. (2021a). *Leading social media networks in Italy as of January 2019, ranked by number of active users.* https://www.statista.com/statistics/639777/social-media-active-users-italy/.

Statista.com. (2021b). *Share of individuals using the internet in Italy from 2006 to 2019.* https://www.statista.com/statistics/542279/shares-of-internet-use-in-italy/.

Wolfinbarger, M., & Gilly, M. (2001). Shopping for freedom, control and fun. *California Management Review, 43*(2), 34–55.

8 Social media and mobile tools in consumers' decisions of Polish consumers

Małgorzata Bartosik-Purgat and Ewa Mińska-Struzik

Introduction

The first decades of the 21st century have witnessed sea changes in both technological developments and the needs and behaviour of consumers (Cheng & Guo, 2021; McLean et al., 2020; Wang et al., 2021). Information and communication technologies (ICT) have opened up new opportunities for consumers concerning new types of gathering information and making purchases (Wang et al., 2021). A combination of the expansion of Social Media (SM), the evolution of social commerce (s-commerce), the omnipresence of mobiles phones, and improved artificial intelligence instruments (e.g. augmented reality, virtual assistants, etc.) have all led to new consumer behaviour, ways of purchasing, and communication methods (Marinkovic & Kalinic, 2017; Wang et al., 2021; Woodside & Bernal Mir, 2019). These changes are related not only to the development of technology and industry but also to the level of acceptance and use by consumers. Whilst the latter is generally connected with the cultural backgrounds of societies (Wang et al., 2021; Ziemba et al., 2020), generational changes are also important, as they allow for even greater development of information technologies. In general, younger generations (Y and Z) are more willing to use digital tools to search for information and products and make purchasing decisions (Calvo-Porral & Pesqueira-Sanchez, 2020; Lissitsa & Laor, 2021). However, older consumers likewise seem to want to keep up to date with new products and try to use them (Kesler, 2020).

Poland is one of the most innovative and technologically advanced societies globally. The Bloomberg Innovation Index places Poland 23rd out of the 60 most innovative economies (Chatham, 2021) and the Polish economy ranks 38th among the 131 economies featured in the Global Innovation Index 2020 (Dutta et al., 2020). Thus, the Polish population tries to keep up to date with various innovations and willingly use them both at work and in their private lives, accepting innovative solutions in many fields of their lives, e.g. banking, shopping, education, work, etc. This notwithstanding, data presented in *The Global Competitiveness Report* published by the World Economic Forum in 2019 shows that the process of adopting ICT in Poland is still progressing.

DOI: 10.4324/9781003263685-11

Poland was ranked 51st out of 141 countries surveyed in terms of the level of ICT adoption (Schwab, 2019). The highest level of adoption is associated with Internet use. The newest *Digital Global Statshot Report* for July 2021 indicates that 85% of the Polish population use the Internet (world average is 60.9%) (Kemp, 2021a), and 94.1% of Poles are mobile Internet users (percentage of total Internet users in Poland) (Kemp, 2021b). Other research has found that Poles are innovative and flexible, able to find new ideas and better ways of doing new things, which leads to increased productivity, and thus to a higher standard of living (Bartosik-Purgat et al., 2017). However, this does not mean that all Poles can be described as creative, merely that an essential core within society has emerged which includes, among others, employees from the fields of science, education, computer programming, and also R&D staff, as well as people associated with art, design and the media (Florida, 2002).

It should, though, be noted that behaviour is determined by not only cultural factors. For example, the coronavirus pandemic has contributed to the need to implement new solutions in many areas of life, i.e. work, study, shopping, handling administrative matters, etc. With regard to shopping, people started to buy more products online, even those which they had never bought in such a way previously (e.g. food, medicines, furniture, etc.) (Kissler et al., 2020). The data presented in the report of ExpertSender Institute titled *Online shopping in Poland 2020* indicates that approx. 80% of Poles with Internet access shop online (ExpertSender, 2020). In a study conducted by PricewaterhouseCoopers (PwC), 19% of Poles indicated that they started using online stores more often during the Covid-19 pandemic (PwC, 2020). There is a wide range of digital instruments that may help consumers to make online purchasing decisions, including artificial intelligence such as augmented reality, virtual assistants, and chatbots, cybersecurity devices, and advanced payment methods, as well as SM, and mobile devices (McLean et al., 2020; Rauschnabel et al., 2019; Syrkiewicz-Świtała et al., 2021; Wang et al., 2021). The main focus of this chapter will be on the significance of SM and mobile phones in Polish consumer behaviour. This impact has come about thanks to, first, the development of different SM platforms and the growth of users (Kemp, 2021a); second, the fact that SM is used in s-commerce, which is becoming a fruitful e-commerce channel for many brands, and, third, many Polish consumers use their mobiles while purchasing (Syrkiewicz-Świtała et al., 2021).

This context gives rise to the following two questions:

RQ1: What are the features of Polish society affecting the acceptance of ICT (SM and mobiles) in purchasing behaviour?

RQ2: What is the level of acceptance and usage of SM and mobile devices among Polish consumers?

The main purpose of this chapter is thus two-fold: first, to indicate the characteristics of Polish consumers (divided into generational segments) related to the acceptance and use of SM and mobile devices in their purchasing decisions, and second, to identify the level of usage of these tools in decision-making processes. The main research method used in the chapter is a literature study based on secondary sources. The databases used in the research procedure were Emerald, Elsevier, and Taylor and Francis. Results of research related to the described topics (such as consumer behaviour, SM, mobile devices, etc.) are published in the journals included in these databases. However, the issue of Polish consumers and the Polish market is rarely present in the literature, and so additional journals and online materials relevant to the research problem were also explored. Nevertheless, the main purpose of the chapter also requires statistical data, and to this end, the Statista.com and Eurostat.eu statistical databases were used as well. The following keywords were employed to search for relevant scientific papers and statistical studies: "social media", "mobile devices", "social commerce", "consumer behaviour", "Poland", and "generations".

The chapter first presents the results of the literature review and then moves to an analysis of the level of SM (including s-commerce) and mobile devices usage in consumer decisions. Finally, conclusions are forwarded including business implications and predictions for the future.

Literature review

Polish society in light of cultural, generational, and digital changes

Poland has the fifth largest population in the EU (Europa.eu, 2021). Different generations co-exist and cooperate in Polish society, and all but one have high consumer power (Badowska et al., 2015; Kacprzak & Dziewanowska, 2021) – Baby Boomers and generations X, Y, and Z. The exception is the so-called silent generation, people born before 1946. Baby Boomers born between 1946 and 1964 (Polish Central Statistical Office – PCSO, 2021) and are gradually withdrawing from the labour market, but nonetheless continue to be active consumers. They most often use traditional forms of shopping, i.e. bricks-and-mortar shops, and favour face-to-face contact with salespersons. Outside of the silent generation, this is the least active generation group on the Internet (Badowska et al., 2015), with only every 6th Polish person in this age group using online shopping regularly (Kesler, 2020). Polish Baby Boomers also use Internet banking services less frequently (22%), which results in lower confidence in online purchases (Kesler, 2020). If Baby Boomers do choose online shopping, then they tend to use desktop computers more often than mobile devices (Kesler, 2020). Likewise, Baby Boomers sometimes use Facebook, e-mail, and news portals, but in general, this age group prefers traditional media – the press, television, and radio (Kesler, 2020).

Generation X consists of people born between 1965 and 1976 (PCSO, 2021). Their main generational experience is the systemic transformation in

Poland post-1989. They are also attached to traditional interpersonal contacts and face-to-face communication (Bartosik-Purgat, 2016). As young adults, this generation experienced major economic and political changes on the Polish market (Kacprzak & Dziewanowska, 2021) and for Generation X, having money is a value in itself, and are therefore reluctant to spend it. Generation X constantly have to learn to use new technological solutions, because in their youth there were no advanced technologies, and access to the Internet was limited (Bartosik-Purgat, 2016). They are usually traditionalists, but still try to keep up to date with tech innovations, attempting to use digital tools both at work and in private life, as well as in their consumer behaviours. The most popular communication channel for this group is e-mail, and they also actively search for information on the Internet. Representatives of the Polish Gen X are also gradually entering the world of SM, but more often they are only passive observers rather than active participants (Kesler, 2020). Polish Gen X-ers buy online more often than Baby Boomers (every 1 in 2). They value reliable opinions and product quality guarantees, which is why they compare products offered in different stores more often. In addition, Generation X is the group that shares opinions most often on Internet forums (Kesler, 2020). Generation X is currently the third most numerous group of consumers on the Polish market (Kacprzak & Dziewanowska, 2021; PCSO, 2021).

Generation Y (also known as Millennials) are those born between 1977 and 1997 (PCSO, 2021), and who was brought up in the belief that they are the forge of their own destiny (individual and independent). Their generational experience is related to Poland's accession to the EU, as well as the opening up of the Polish market to the West (Bartosik-Purgat, 2016). Polish Millennials have become eyewitnesses but also participants in the digital and mobile revolution (Kesler, 2020). They were shaped, inter alia, via google and video games. Representatives of Generation Y are eager to buy in online stores, using new solutions regarding, for example, the method of ordering, payment, or delivery methods. As consumers, they are willing to use all-new digital solutions offered by retailers and learn to use new digital tools very quickly (Aikat, 2019; Lipowski & Bondos, 2018). 75% of them regularly shop online, most often using a smartphone (Kesler, 2020), and like to use the latest and newest models of equipment available. Gen Y-ers treat capital very practically and willingly spend their earned money on whatever enables them to achieve their goals. Polish Millennials are also one of the first users of SM – the first portals emerged in their teenage years and have been popular with them from the very beginning (Kesler, 2020). Most have profiles on multiple SM platforms, through which they communicate with both other people and companies (brands). They constitute an important and the most numerous group of consumers on the Polish market (Kacprzak & Dziewanowska, 2021; PCSO, 2021).

Generation Z is those born after 1997 (PCSO, 2021). This social group is sometimes called Generation C from the English words connect, communicate, and change. These are people born in the era of advanced Internet use and mobile telephony, among whom direct contact is being displaced by Internet communication (Król & Zdonek, 2021). Representants of Generation Z are open to new technologies and feel natural in the virtual space, which they treat as a convenient place to search for information, express views, or contact brands (Kacprzak & Dziewanowska, 2021). Generation Z uses mobile devices when making purchasing decisions refer to opinions and comments posted on the Internet, exchanging observations and experiences, and comparing prices and features of goods (Król & Zdonek, 2021). Mobile devices and SM are an essential element of this generation's lifestyle, influencing the way they spend time, the model of maintaining relationships, and the process of making purchasing decisions (Kesler, 2020). Generation Z is very eager to buy online, regardless of the type of product. These are also consumers who are the fastest in incorporating new ICT (Kacprzak & Dziewanowska, 2021). Technological novelties are very quickly, almost naturally assimilated by Generation Z (Kesler, 2020). For Polish Gen Z, money is only another way to fulfil themselves, so they make purchasing decisions efficiently, being aware that in the event of dissatisfaction, they can recover their capital. They are very active online shoppers and mobile users. SM is used very often but they are turning away from the "old" Facebook and prefer SM that more easily transmit visual content – YouTube, Instagram, Snapchat, and TikTok. Generation Z will constitute the largest group of digital consumers in Poland in the next ten years (PCSO, 2021). However, they will be a quite difficult group for the Polish market because their characteristic feature is resistance to traditional advertising messages, instead preferring to rely upon SM and pay attention to the values that a given brand represents.

Social media, social commerce, and mobile in the behaviour of Polish consumers

Social media

The technological development explored many efficient solutions that may be used almost in each part of both companies and consumers' activities. Many digital tools have permanently entered the life of individuals (consumers) and make both professional work and everyday activities, more manageable, and more attractive. One of the most popular digital tools introduced from consumers' perspectives is SM portals (Aikat, 2019; Bartosik-Purgat, 2016).

SM enable the rapid exchange of information and gather users with similar interests and needs. Users of these media can create their profiles, friends lists, and groups and publish posts (entries), music, short videos, or photos (Bartosik-Purgat, 2019). Different types of SM can be used for various purposes and by different segments (types) of users. One classification divides SM into social networks (e.g. Facebook, Twitter, and LinkedIn); media sharing networks (e.g. YouTube, Instagram, TikTok, and Snapchat); consumer review networks (e.g. TripAdvisor, Zomato, and Yelp); discussion forums (e.g. Digg, Reddit, and Quora), bookmarking & content curation networks (Pinterest, Flipboard), and instant messengers (e.g. WhatsApp, Messenger, WeChat).

The *Digital 2021. Poland* report (Kemp, 2021b) indicates that 25.9 million Poles use SM, which is more than half (68.5%) of the country's population (37.82 million people), a year-on-year increase of as much as 2.5 million (10.5%). The most frequently used website in Poland is Google.com, followed by Facebook.com, YouTube.com, Allegro.com, Onet.pl, Interia.pl, Google.pl, Wikipedia.org, Librus.pl, and Olx.pl. Among SM in Poland, YouTube is the leader, used by 92.8% of users, followed by Facebook (89.2%), Facebook Messenger (76.5%), Instagram (60.6%), and WhatsApp (48 2%). Sixth place is taken by Twitter (37.5%), 7th place by Skype (35.2%), then Snapchat (28.9%), Tik-Tok (28.6%), Pinterest (26.4%), LinkedIn (24.6%) , Twitch (18.4%), Wykop.pl (17.9%), Badoo (13.8%), and Reddit.pl (13.7%) (Kemp, 2021b).

The detailed analysis of the data on SM usage presented in Kemp's (2021b) report indicates that YouTube is by far the most popular among Poles, used by 25.9 million users. Advertising on this site reaches 72.9% of the population; there is no gender dominance here. Facebook is used by 18 million Poles, most often people aged 35 and older 96.6% of Facebook users use it on their mobile devices. No more than 3.4% use Facebook only on a desktop computer, and 51.1% only on smartphone applications. Interestingly, ads placed on Facebook are more often clicked on by women – about 23 times a month and about 15 by men. Instagram is used in Poland by nearly 9.2 million people (60.6% of SM users), of which 59.1% are women and 40.9% are men. Every fifth Instagram user in Poland is a woman aged 18–24 (Kemp, 2021b). Snapchat is used by 4.9 million Polish consumers, of which 58.5% are women, and 40.9% are men. Young Polish women also predominate among Pinterest users (80.5% are women, 15.7% men) (Kemp, 2021b).

SM is used for many activities, including, among others: communicating with friends, sharing private photos or videos, seeking advice on thematic groups, seeking information about products, placing advertisements, work purposes, and many others. Bartosik-Purgat et al. (2017) indicated a number of possible SM activities that pertain to consumer behaviour including searching for information about products and services, following the advice of friends on buying a product or using a service, recommending various products (which according to a particular person are worth it) to other users or informing other potential buyers if the purchased product has turned out to be of deficient quality, placing buy/sell offers, watching advertisements placed on SM, and participating in contests organised by companies/brands a particular person is a fan of (Bartosik-Purgat et al., 2017, pp. 88–89). Data presented in Kemp's (2021b) report underlines that 45.3% of Polish SM users employ SM as the main source when researching brands and 30.4% for work purposes. Balakrishnan et al. (2014) indicated that SM influences the consumers' purchase intention and their loyalty according to firms and brands. Similar conclusions were formulated by Nadeem et al. (2015), who emphasised that trust is built between consumer and a brand when there is a possibility to use SM during online shopping. The possibility to gather peer recommendations from other SM users is also very important and impacts purchase attitudes (with a greater impact on women than men). The authors also indicated the importance of online services (ibid.). In previous research, Ruane and Wallace (2013) also showed that SM influence has a greater impact on women's consumer activities than men's.

A report published in 2018 by PwC highlights that Polish consumers trust the reviews and recommendations presented on the Web (PwC, 2018). They often have a more significant impact on their purchasing decisions than direct recommendations of sellers in offline stores, as well as advertising messages. 58% of Polish consumers surveyed indicated that they look for shopping inspiration on SM, and 42% use price comparison websites available on the Internet (PwC, 2018). The conclusions from the report of the ExpertSender Institute entitled *Online shopping in Poland 2020* indicate that advertising on SM is the preferred channel of communication of an offer for almost 44% of Polish online shoppers (ExpertSender, 2020). Elsewhere, research conducted in 2020 by Accenture and Fashionbiznes.pl on a sample of 585 Poles aged 16+ using the CAWI method shows that the coronavirus pandemic, on the one hand, forced new behaviour patterns, and on the other hand, significantly accelerated certain trends in trade, which have already developed in previous years on the Polish market (Accenture. Fashionbiznes.pl, 2020). Consumption of content presented on SM and the Internet increased during the pandemic. Forty-six per cent of respondents emphasised that they are most interested in information about promotions and discounts made available on SM. Forty-one per cent of Poles indicated looking for ideas about spending time at home on SM, 32% for information about new products, and 15% for information about a specific brand, its history, employees, and/or current offer. The report also shows that young consumers (Gen Z, 16–24 years) searched for engaging content published by brands on the Internet or SM to a much greater extent than other generation groups (Accenture. Fashionbiznes.pl, 2020).

Social-commerce

The increasing number of SM users and the number of time people spend on the platforms affects the creation of new functions and possibilities. Kemp's report indicates that the average amount of time per day spent using SM in Poland is almost 2h (Kemp, 2021b), and the observations of the market situation caused by the Covid-19 pandemic lead to the conclusion that the number of hours spent with SM each day is unlikely to decrease soon. Indeed, predictions indicate that the amount of time spent on SM will only continue to grow (PwC, 2020).

The above circumstances affect the development of a new understanding of e-commerce via SM, i.e., s-commerce. There is no single understanding or definition of s-commerce. Many researchers state that it is a general impact of social networks on increasing profits in online sales (e.g. Hu et al., 2021; Jami Pour et al., 2021). S-commerce concerns the building of a positive image of the company based on opinions and comments on their profiles on YouTube, Facebook, TikTok, or Instagram; creating a relationship with SM users; SM groups (e.g. Facebook groups; live-commerce; sales modules built into social platforms like a Facebook shop); and its ability to integrate with e-commerce. Given the purpose of this chapter, this sub-section focuses on the last two elements listed above, namely live-commerce and sales modules incorporated in particular SM.

A live-commerce session is conducted via social platforms by an entrepreneur, celebrity, influencer, or private person (Hu et al., 2021). While streaming, the host offers various items for sale, interacts with potential buyers, and communicates with them in real-time. Live-commerce is used by both professional online stores like Amazon, e-Bay, or Alibaba, and for spontaneous online auctions organised on less adequate apps or live on Facebook.

The concept of live commerce originated in China in 2014, where it is nowadays trendy (Hu et al., 2021; O'Connell, 2020). However, in Poland, live-commerce has become popular only since 2020 (Gładkowski, 2020). The most popular live-streaming platform in Poland is Facebook, where the development and increase in the number of online boutiques can be observed. Many online retailers provide virtual assistants, chatbots, or other online client services, mobile apps, etc. to help clients and increase sales. However, the live-commerce concept combines all of these and also introduces a live broadcast. By getting closer to customers and adding an element of direct experience without leaving home, businesses and customers can access a new, thriving retail environment, even during a lockdown. This form of sale on the Polish market is mainly used by sellers of clothing, textiles, and electronics. On the Polish market, live-commerce helped move popular shops to the Internet during the coronavirus pandemic, and at the same time, has saved many small companies from bankruptcy. However, live-commerce is also used by big, well-known brands, such as Ralph Lauren, Burberry, and Levi's (O'Connell, 2020).

Research conducted in 2021 among Polish e-consumers by the Mobile Institute and the Polish Chamber of Electronic Economy confirms that the importance of shopping on SM is increasing. Two out of ten Polish consumers admit to making such purchases, and 46% of respondents are interested in live-commerce (Mobile Institute, 2020). In 2021, the E-Business Women Foundation (E-BWF) conducted a survey concerning social and live-commerce on a representative sample of Polish consumers (16–75 years). The main conclusions of the study show an upward trend in this matter, with 27% of Poles surveyed having purchased via SM. In turn, 25% of Poles purchased via live streaming on SM, including 10% of respondents who very often make purchases in such a way. Eighteen per cent of respondents indicated that they sell through SM. The main consumer profile on SM is a young woman (<34) from a small town or village. They mainly buy clothes and shoes via Facebook. However, older customers are also familiar with this form of s-shopping, with the survey showing that 24% of people over 50 also had experience with shopping via SM (E-BWF, 2021). Research conducted by Mobile Institute (2021) also has shown that older Polish consumers (the so-called silver consumers) have started buying on SM and are interested in social selling. The most popular social platform through which Poles make purchases is Facebook (82% of people who buy via s-commerce). Apart from Facebook, Poles also use s-commerce on Instagram (19%) and YouTube (16%), TikTok, Snapchat, and Pinterest (7% each) (E-BWF, 2021). The respondents who participated in that research emphasised that shopping with the use of SM is simple, fast, and convenient, as well as personalised and at a reasonable price. Shopping via live-commerce is seen to be attractive due to its form and cost, but most of all, because it emotionally engages with the customer (E-BWF, 2021).

S-commerce in the form of sales modules incorporated in particular SM also refers to the activity of buying and selling on social networking sites and applications. It should be noted that it is not the SM-owning companies that are selling but online retailers (Jami Pour et al., 2021). The s-commerce platform is an SM platform through which online stores (or any business users) can sell their products. Some of the first SM services that offered s-commerce functionality include Facebook, Pinterest, and Instagram. On Pinterest you can use "Shop the Look" pins, on Facebook you can use "Shop/Buy now", and on Instagram, you can use stickers of products (on Instagram, this feature has not yet been introduced around the world, but it is now available in almost all European countries, including Poland). Purchases on Facebook can be made in Facebook stores. These stores function as separate tabs created as part of a company's fan pages. Such SM functions are still in the infancy of their development and as a result, it is challenging to present representative and credible statistics on consumer usage.

The rapid development and increase in popularity of s-commerce have unsurprisingly been led by young consumers. This is due, first, to their higher use of SM platforms in general (especially during the coronavirus pandemic). Second, s-commerce platforms enable the personalisation of customer experiences, such as retargeting, which is attractive and desired by the youngest segment of Polish consumers.

Mobile-commerce

The increase of SM users in Poland and their engagement in online shopping is clearly connected with Internet access, but also with the great number of mobile users (Kemp, 2021b). The research conducted by Mobile Institute (under the patronage of the Chamber of Electronic Economy) on the Polish market in 2016 shows the high dynamism of the growth of mobile commerce (m-commerce). M-commerce concerns, e.g. the buying and selling of products and services via wireless mobile devices such as smartphones, laptops, or tablets. It also applies to both e-shops and subscriptions to various services, mobile banking, and bill payments. With appropriate applications and technical infrastructure, customers can make various types of transactions on the Internet using mobile devices. At the beginning of 2015, 33% of Internet shoppers and 24% of Internet users made mobile purchases. In February 2016, 53% of e-shoppers and 37% of all Internet users were shopping using mobile technology. Forty-three per cent of buyers on the Internet shopped using a smartphone, and 29% used a tablet (Mobile Institute, 2016). However, studies conducted in Poland in 2018 by PwC show a slightly smaller scale of use of mobile technologies by consumers. According to the *Poles shopping* report, in this period, 17% of respondents made purchases via smartphones at least once a week, including 7% every day. In addition, 39% of Polish respondents indicated that they were willing to pay for everyday purchases using mobile payments (PwC, 2018). The newest Kemp's (2021b) report indicates that there were 52.76 million mobile purchases in 2020 (January 2020 – January 2021) in Poland, it is 1.4% more in comparison to the previous year. The percentage of Internet users aged 16–64 that uses a particular mobile app per month shows that the greatest number of people use social networking apps, then communicating apps (e.g. WhatsApp or Messenger), and third place goes to shopping apps (e.g. Allegro, InPost) (Kemp, 2021b). It underlines that mobile device usage affects online shopping behaviour in Poland. 82.5% of the population aged 16–64 had made online purchases (any devices) in the last month, 80.2% used a shopping app on a mobile or a tablet, and 42.9% had purchased a product online in the last month via mobile phone (Kemp, 2021b). What is interesting is that there is no big difference in online shopping among Polish consumers between 16 and 54 years old (an average of around 84%), whilst 74.3% of older consumers purchased products online last month (Kemp, 2021b). Polish customers appreciate shopping via smartphone because of, among others: simple payment processes and/or convenient and easy-to-use shopping applications. In addition, online stores encourage the use of their applications through, e.g. additional discounts and promotions for new users. Data presented by PwC in 2020 showed an increase in m-shopping during the pandemic by 23% for mobile phones and 8% for tablets (PwC, 2020). A study concerning m-commerce indicated that Poles most often make such purchases using a smartphone (60%), 36% of respondents use desktop or laptop, and 4% tablet (E-BWF, 2021).

Data obtained for the last five years shows the development and increase of mobile technology usage in the purchasing decisions of Polish consumers. This situation is related to the dynamics of the modern market in terms of consumer interest in online shopping, but also restrictions and regional lockdowns introduced during the coronavirus pandemic. Nevertheless, the data presented above indicate that Poles can adapt very quickly and can look for smart solutions. Poles want to buy more conveniently, when and how they want – and this is ensured by mobile devices that perfectly combine the offline and online worlds. These devices also allow consumers to dictate the terms and conditions of their purchases – to buy consciously, but also to take advantage of possible shopping opportunities. To this end, convenience is the most frequently indicated advantage of m-commerce (PwC, 2020).

Conclusions, business implications, and directions of future research

The results of the literature review conducted for this study present the situation related to SM and mobile device usage by Polish consumers. In general, Polish consumers constitute a relatively homogeneous group, constituted by the process of virtualisation of consumption. The intensity of this process is influenced by the adoption of digital technologies, not just by one generation but by the whole society. However, there is no doubt that the youngest generation is the fastest and most willing group of consumers to adopt new solutions. However, one should not forget about older Polish consumers who become active buyers in both e- and s-commerce (Mobile Institute, 2021).

The first general conclusion from the study concerns the increase in the number of Polish online shoppers and the transactions they conduct in e-commerce (Kemp, 2021b). This is partly due to the coronavirus pandemic and local lockdowns, during which bricks-and-mortar shops were closed, and people started to buy more products via the Internet. The second issue concerns the popularity of different SM platforms used by different groups of consumers. The situation caused by the coronavirus pandemic was a kind of stimulus for Polish businesses to develop s-commerce in general and live-commerce in particular, saving many small sellers from bankruptcy. The second finding is that the quick development and popularity s-commerce has been supported by mobile devices, which greatly facilitate searching for information about products and making online purchases. It should also be emphasised that a high advancement of mobile technologies and their use by consumers is observed in Poland. Considering the dynamically developing mobile market, it should be stated that the interactive and multimedia nature of consumption appears to be one of the most important directions of its future development. Permanent recognition of this trend is a challenge for companies, who need to react both to the changing mobile technological environment and to consumers who are increasingly using mobile technologies.

With regard to the practical implications of the conducted analysis, it should be indicated that there are slight differences related to the level of participation in the above digital activities among different generations of Polish consumers. The differences mainly relate to the types of SM used by consumers, the level of advancement of the mobile technologies used, and the service needs. Older Polish consumers use Facebook much more than other SM services like Snapchat, TikTok, or Instagram. Younger consumers are more advanced in their mobile technology usage when it comes to online shopping. Retailers offering their products online, especially to younger generations, should consider implementing mobile apps for their stores, which would likely increase availability and online sales.

Polish society is, like much of Europe, ageing on. The segment of the oldest e-consumers is now significant in terms of size, and it will continue to grow in the coming years. Nevertheless, many older customers try to adapt to the digitalisation of various areas of life, including shopping. However, retailers should prepare detailed product information, as well as instructions or guides for offers specifically dedicated to this segment of buyers. They should also properly prepare the store interface, as well as the shopping path. Above all, purchase options must be simple and easy to use, and messages should be clear and specific. Moreover, it is important to ensure the security of transactions (Kesler, 2020). Baby Boomers are the most vulnerable generation in this regard, whereas young people are the least sensitive to cybersecurity activities, not paying much attention to password creation and usually using one or two passwords for all their accounts (Leadem, 2017). By contrast, older generations are afraid that personal information that is provided on the Internet will be misused.

Similarly, the representatives of the Polish Gen X prefer more information about the company and product, therefore such data should be presented in detail in online stores (in particular about the offer addressed to Generation X). Therefore, it is also worth posting extensive and more detailed descriptions, which can sometimes affect the purchase decision. Besides, consumers from Generation X like to compare offers and therefore often use comparison websites concerning competing products (Kesler, 2020). They are still learning about the implementation of new ICT. They were not born in the era of advanced digitisation technologies, but they try to catch up with younger generations. That is why mobile technologies are acceptable during shopping. There is no need to prepare less advanced solutions.

Polish Millennials are active Internet and SM users. Many of them have profiles on different platforms, so the content of the advertising message has to be attractive and delivered through new media. The more the newest solutions are used by online retailers, the better for Generation Y as they are eager to learn and use technological innovations. As such, e-shops should offer different methods of payments, delivery, and others. Millennials care about their relationships and belonging to different communities, which is why producers should communicate with them about trust, loyalty, and other important values. Gen Y consumers like to feel appreciated and valued by sellers, so those that can provide real-time contact with salespersons will have an advantage. This is certainly why live-commerce is developing the fastest on the Polish market in this group of consumers and thus should be considered by retailers offering their products especially to that segment of consumers.

Gen Z consumers are the most technologically advanced e-consumers in Polish e-commerce (mobile apps, payments methods, customisation, etc.). The newer a solution used by an online retailer, the better. E-shops dedicated to the youngest segment of Polish consumers should care about their "technological image". This cohort appreciates interesting and funny content but they also prefer short advertising messages that do require the high involvement of the recipient. Moreover, Generation Z appreciates a simple, but original and credible message and the lack of authenticity of some content negatively affects their confidence. As a result, high-quality communication based on credibility and genuine commitment is growing in importance. Lastly, the youngest Polish consumers like to "stand out from the crowd". Freedom and a wide choice (including shopping) are important to them, which is why the key to success in this segment is the personalisation of products, advertisements and services offered, as well as building comprehensive customer experiences.

It should also be remembered that when communicating with Gen Z consumers, the presence of a firm or brand is also necessary on SM other than Facebook. The analysis of the literature showed that the youngest generation uses YouTube, TikTok, Snapchat, and Instagram more often than Facebook. These are SM that focus on visual content (photos, videos). Thus, firms that want to reach the Polish Gen Z consumers should have a presence on the above SM platforms and prepare appropriate content. Gen Z are also the most active consumers in s-commerce with regard to selling products via SM platforms, e.g. Instagram or Pinterest. Firms should also take into account this possibility to reach this group. In addition, it is worth using virtual assistants or chatbots in online stores (as well as SM shops) because young Poles do not like waiting long for an answer to their questions. Moreover, the use of influencers capable of gaining the trust of young consumers is appropriate, as they like to be appreciated (Kesler, 2020).

There is no doubt that the increase in SM media usage has impacted the development of new ways of their application. One of such method is s-commerce. The study presented in the chapter shows that s-commerce operates in Poland at a fairly advanced and satisfactory level and will continue to grow, with many Polish consumers planning to shop using SM in the near future (E-BWF, 2021; Mobile Institute, 2021). SM platforms should keep this trend in mind and adapt their platforms to s-commerce services. It should also be remembered that different generations use different SM platforms. Therefore, an offer addressed to a particular segment should be presented through those SM which are used by the relevant consumers.

Future research should concern the monitoring of changes in consumer needs and behaviours regarding the use of SM. Retailers may consider (if they have not already done so) including particular SM platforms in their communication channel with consumers. Nevertheless, they should develop the possibilities of buying via SM which are adapted to their potential consumers. Mobile apps should be implemented by e-retailers as well (especially when they offer their products for younger or middle age Polish consumers). In general, online retailers should follow the newest solutions related to ICT and consumer needs. Above all, they should not forget that Polish consumers are among those in Europe who most quickly accept new technological solutions and want to implement them.

Bibliography

Accenture. Fashionbiznes.pl (2020, May 21). *Konsument w nowej rzeczywistości (eng. The consumer in the new reality)*. https://www.accenture.com/_acnmedia/PDF-125/Accenture-Raport-Konsumenci-2020.pdf.

Aikat, D. (2019). Millennials usher a post-digital era: Theorizing how generation Y engages with digital media. In J. Schulz, L. Robinson, A. Khilnani, J. Baldwin, H. Pait, A.A. Williams, J. Davis, & G. Ignatow (Eds.), *Mediated Millennials* (pp. 9–29). Emerald Publishing Limited, Bingley. https://doi.org/10.1108/S2050-206020190000019002.

Badowska, S., Zamojska, A., & Rogala, A. (2015). Baby boomers' attitudes toward innovations: Empirical research in Poland. *Procedia - Social and Behavioral Sciences, 213*, 1050–1056. https://doi.org/10.1016/j.sbspro.2015.11.524.

Balakrishnan, B.K.P.D., Dahnil, M.I., & Yi, W.J. (2014). The impact of social media marketing medium toward purchase intention and brand loyalty among Generation Y. *Procedia – Social and Behavioral Sciences, 148*, 177–185. https://doi.org/10.1016/j.sbspro.2014.07.032.

Bartosik-Purgat, M. (2016). *Media społecznościowe na rynku międzynarodowym. Perspektywa indywidualnych użytkowników* [Social media on the international market. The perspective of individual users]. Difin Publishers.

Bartosik-Purgat, M. (2019). *New media in the marketing communication of enterprises in the international market*. WN PWN Publ.

Bartosik-Purgat, M., Filimon, N., & Hinner, M. (2017). Determinants of social media's use in consumer behaviour: An international comparison. *Economics and Business Review, 3*(2), 79–100. https://doi.org/10.18559/ebr.2017.2.5.

Calvo-Porral, C., & Pesqueira-Sanchez, R. (2020). Generational differences in technology behaviour: Comparing millennials and Generation X. *Kybernetes, 49*(11), 2755–2772. https://doi.org/10.1108/K-09-2019-0598.

Chatham, A. (2021, February 12). *Poland among most innovative countries, says Global Innovation Index*. https://www.thefirstnews.com/article/poland-among-most-innovative-countries-says-global-innovation-index-19801.

Cheng, V.T.P., & Guo, R. (2021). The impact of consumers' attitudes towards technology on the acceptance of hotel technology-based innovation. *Journal of Hospitality and Tourism Technology*, Vol. ahead-of-print No. ahead-of-print. https://doi.org/10.1108/JHTT-06-2020-0145.

Dutta, S., Lanvin, B., & Wunsch-Vincent, S. (Eds.) (2020). *Global innovation index 2020: Who will finance innovation?* Cornell University, INSEAD, and WIPO.

E-BWF. (2021, June 30). *The power of social & live commerce*. https://www.kobietyebiznesu.pl/wp-content/uploads/2021/06/Raport-social-live-commerce-Fundacja-Kobiety-e-biznesu.pdf.

Europa.eu (2021). *Living in EU*. https://europa.eu/european-union/about-eu/figures/living_pl.

ExpertSender. (2020, September 17). *Zakupy online w Polsce 2020* (eng. *Online shopping in Poland 2020*). https://expertsender.pl/blog/zakupy-online-w-polsce-2020-raport-expertsender/.

Florida, R. (2002). *The rise of the creative class*. Basic Books.

Gładkowski, K. (2020, June 26). *Tak się teraz kupuje! Live Commerce podbija świat (eng. This is how you buy now! Live Commerce is conquering the world)*. https://greenparrot.pl/blog/live-commerce-podbija-swiat.

Hu, X., Chen, Z., Davison, R.M., & Liu, Y. (2021). Charting consumers' continued social commerce intention. *Internet Research*, Vol. ahead-of-print No. ahead-of-print. https://doi.org/10.1108/INTR-07-2020-0397.

Jami Pour, M., Hosseinzadeh, M., & Mansouri, N.S. (2021). Challenges of customer experience management in social commerce: An application of social network analysis. *Internet Research*, Vol. ahead-of-print No. ahead-of-print. https://doi.org/10.1108/INTR-01-2021-0076.

Kacprzak, A., & Dziewanowska, K. (2021). Perception of customer retail experiences in Poland. *Journal of Services Marketing, 35*(2), 182–200. https://doi.org/10.1108/JSM-03-2019-0116.

Kemp, S. (2021a, July 21). *Digital audiences swell, but there may be trouble ahead.* https://wearesocial.com/blog/2021/07/digital-audiences-swell-but-there-may-be-trouble-ahead.

Kemp, S. (2021b, February 11). *Digital 2021. Poland.* https://datareportal.com/reports/digital-2021-poland.

Kesler, B. (2020, March 16). *4 pokolenia konsumentów* (eng. *4 Generations of Consumers*), https://www.zentoshop.pl/blog/pokolenia-konsumentow.

Kissler, S.M., Tedijanto, C., Goldstein, E., Grad, Y.H., & Lipsitch, M. (2020). Projecting the transmission dynamics of SARS-CoV-2 through the postpandemic period. *Science, 368*(6493), 860–868, https://doi.org/10.1126/science.abb5793.

Król, K., & Zdonek, D. (2021). Social media use and its impact on intrinsic motivation in Generation Z: A case study from Poland. *Global Knowledge, Memory and Communication, 70*(4/5), 442–458. https://doi.org/10.1108/GKMC-08-2020-0113.

Leadem, R. (2017, July 15). *Cybersecurity habits across generations.* https://www.entrepreneur.com/article/297232.

Lipowski, M., & Bondos, I. (2018). The influence of perceived media richness of marketing channels on online channel usage: Intergenerational differences. *Baltic Journal of Management, 13*(2), 169–190. https://doi.org/10.1108/BJM-04-2017-0127.

Lissitsa, S., & Laor, T. (2021). Baby boomers, generation X and generation Y: Identifying generational differences in effects of personality traits in on-demand radio use. *Technology in Society, 64*, 101526. https://doi.org/10.1016/j.techsoc.2021.101526.

Marinkovic, V., & Kalinic, Z. (2017). Antecedents of customer satisfaction in mobile commerce: Exploring the moderating effect of customization. *Online Information Review, 41*(2), 138–154. https://doi.org/10.1108/OIR-11-2015-0364.

McLean, G., Osei-Frimpong, K., Al-Nabhani, K., & Marriott, H. (2020). Examining consumer attitudes towards retailers' m-commerce mobile applications – An initial adoption vs. continuous use perspective. *Journal of Business Research, 106*, 139–157. https://doi.org/10.1016/j.jbusres.2019.08.032.

Mobile Institute. (2016, March 17). *mShopper 2.0. Polacy na zakupach mobilnych* (eng. *mShopper 2.0. Poles on the mobile shopping*). https://eizba.pl/wp-content/uploads/2018/07/mShopper2.0PolacyNaZakupachMobilnych_marzec2016.pdf.

Mobile Institute. (2020). *Co (u)gryzie e-commerce?* (eng. *What worries e-commerce*?). https://eizba.pl/wp-content/uploads/2021/03/Co_ugryzie_ecommerce_2021_Raport-1.pdf.

Nadeem, W., Andreini, D., Salo, J., & Laukkanen, T. (2015). Engaging consumers online through websites and social media: A gender study of Italian generation Y clothing consumers. *International Journal of Information Management, 35*(4), 432–442. https://doi.org/10.1016/j.ijinfomgt.2015.04.008.

O'Connell, P. (2020, January 20). *Live commerce has risen in the East, will it settle in the West?* https://www.contagious.com/news-and-views/Live-commerce-where-shopping-meets-entertainment.

PCSO. (2021), *Statistical Yearbook of the Republic of Poland*. Statistical Publishing Establishment.

PwC. (2018). *Polacy na zakupach* (eng. *Poles shopping*). https://www.pwc.pl/pl/pdf/polacy-na-zakupach-raport-pwc-2018.pdf.

PwC. (2020). *Nowy obraz polskiego konsumenta. Postawy i zachowania Polaków w obliczu pandemii koronawirusa* (eng. *A new image of the Polish consumer. Attitudes and behaviors of Poles according to the coronavirus pandemic*). https://www.pwc.pl/pl/pdf-nf/2020/raport-pwc-nowy-obraz-polskiego-konsumenta.pdf.

Rauschnabel, P.A., Felix, R., & Hinsch, C. (2019). Augmented reality marketing: How mobile AR-apps can improve brands through inspiration. *Journal of Retailing and Consumer Services, 49*, 43–53. https://doi.org/10.1016/j.jretconser.2019.03.004.

Ruane, L., & Wallace, E. (2013). Generation Y females online: Insights from brand narratives. *Qualitative Market Research: An International Journal, 16*(3), 315–335. https://doi.org/10.1108/13522751311326125.

Schwab, K. (Ed.) (2019). *The global competitiveness report*. World Economic Forum. http://www3.weforum.org/docs/WEF_TheGlobalCompetitivenessReport2019.pdf.

Syrkiewicz-Świtała, M., Detyna, B., Sosada, N., Detyna, J., Świtała, R., Bitkowska, A., & Szkutnik, J. (2021). Mobile applications and eating habits among women and men – Polish experiences. *Biocybernetics and Biomedical Engineering, 41*(3), 1093–1106. https://doi.org/10.1016/j.bbe.2021.07.003.

Wang, Y., Ko, E., & Wang, H. (2021). Augmented reality (AR) app use in the beauty product industry and consumer purchase intention. *Asia Pacific Journal of Marketing and Logistics*, Vol. ahead-of-print No. ahead-of-print. https://doi.org/10.1108/APJML-11-2019-0684.

Woodside, A.G., & Bernal Mir, P. (2019). Clicks and purchase effects of an embedded, social-media, platform endorsement in internet advertising. *Journal of Global Scholars of Marketing Science, 29*(3), 343–357. https://doi.org/10.1080/21639159.2019.1622437.

Ziemba, E., Eisenbardt, M., Mullins, R., & Dettmer, S. (2020, September 11). Consumer engagement in business process innovation–ICT companies cases from Poland and UK. *Journal of Computer Information Systems*. https://doi.org/10.1080/08874417.2020.1808865.

9 Understanding consumers' information power in the digital marketplace

The case of Russia

Ksenia Golovacheva, Maria Smirnova, Olga Alkanova, and Karina Bogatyreva

Introduction

The exchange between consumers and producers depends on the balance of power. In the era of digital transformation, this balance is constantly shifting. In early business history, producers dominated the markets with their supply power; later, the power readjusted between retailers and producers; today, the power balance is shifting again – this time in favour of consumers (Kucuk & Krishnamurthy, 2007). One of the major drivers of power shifts is information. Information empowers consumers in a number of ways. First, it increases the volume and availability of information, thus, helping consumers make more informed decisions. Second, in the era of digital transformation, consumers are endowed with an opportunity to produce content such as product reviews. They may become influencers and set the trends. Finally, consumers have got a variety of opportunities to control the information flows between their devices and business (such as ad-blocking apps, cookie control systems, antiviruses, and personal data management assistants).

To what extent do consumers take advantage of the available opportunities? Have consumers developed the required competencies to effectively manage information and reap the benefits of consumer power in the digital marketplace? These questions are of paramount importance for every market that undergoes a digital transformation. In the context of Russia, they become especially relevant due to the heterogeneous level of market sophistication across regions, social stratification, transitional nature of the Russian economy, and underdeveloped legislation in the area of privacy regulation.

This chapter aims to assess Russian consumers' digital competencies in relation to information consumption, creation, and control and identify potential areas for development. First, we provide an overview of the Russian economy in the era of digital transformation. Second, we outline the stance of consumer information power in Russia. Then, the chapter reports the results of the empirical study of Russian consumers aimed to delineate and measure various information competencies. Finally, we discuss study insights that are of relevance for firms, public policymaking, and consumers themselves.

DOI: 10.4324/9781003263685-12

Socio-economic context of digital transformation in Russia

Russia is one of the major emerging economies in the world ranked 11th by the nominal GDP and 6th by the PPP in 2020 based on the World Bank data. According to the Federal State Statistics Service, the country's population accounted for 146.2 million at the beginning of 2021. The GDP per capita was around 10,126 USD in 2020 (World Bank, 2021). The state of the Russian Federation came into being in 1991 after the Soviet Union collapsed, taking the role of its main successor. Concurrently, the country started a transition from a centrally planned to a market economy. Being the largest country in the world in terms of territory, Russia is richly endowed with natural resources, including natural gas, crude oil, coal, and timber. This leaves a serious imprint on the country's economic structure, making the energy sector one of its main pillars (Sanghi et al., 2021). Apart from being one of the world's largest natural resources producers and exporters, Russia significantly contributes to the global metallurgy industry, as well as chemical and agricultural production, machinery, equipment, and transportation sectors (Federal State Statistics Service, 2020).

Economic diversification has long been a cornerstone of the country's development policy with a view to sustaining a broader range of growth sources (Lyubimov, 2019). In today's reality, this outcome cannot be achieved without the implementation and continuous support of digitalisation processes in each area of social and economic activity. Consequently, the Executive Order on the National Development Goals of the Russian Federation through 2030 declared digital transformation to be a crucial part of Russia's developmental agenda. Such transformation presumes digital maturity of the essential economic sectors as well as a social sphere, including health care, education, and governmental services. It also ensures an increase of the share of households with broadband Internet access up to 97% and a significant intensification of investments into Russian IT solutions. These measures are designed to stimulate digital interaction at all levels, including the relationship between businesses and their clients. The latter is currently being facilitated by the ongoing COVID-19 pandemic that has caused the massive and rapid transfer into online all over the world. It can be therefore inferred that the other side of the digital transformation coin, i.e., the readiness of the country population to rely on digital processes and develop relevant competencies, is to be explored, assessed, and nurtured (Yoo et al., 2018).

In Russia, the phenomenon of digital readiness and competencies development manifests itself through several aspects. The basic one is infrastructural; it covers access to information and communication technologies (ICT) – one of the global competitiveness pillars according to the World Economic Forum. In 2019, Russia ranked 22 of 141 countries of the Global Competitiveness Index on the parameter related to ICT Adoption (Schwab, 2019). In 2018, the overall Internet usage in Russia reached 75.4% of the adult population and continued growing (GFK, 2018).

At the same time, ICT infrastructure development has to be coupled with the digital literacy of the country's population. The notion of digital literacy is broad and comprises such components as information and communication competence, digital content creation, digital security, and skills of problem-solving in the digital environment (Clifford et al., 2020). Despite the emphasis on digital literacy importance within Russia's national developmental projects, evidence suggests that during recent years no significant growth in these regards has been observed. Extant research revealed that in 2018–2019, 26% of the Russian adult population had a high level of digital literacy, while in 2019–2020 this share accounted for 27%, showing only a sluggish growth (NAFI, 2020). Predictably, a notable gap is observed when comparing different age groups: the highest level of relevant competence is attained by those younger than 44 years, while the lowest indication appears within the group of people older than 55. Similar dynamics permeate concerning education, with better digital proficiency among holders of higher education degrees (Dmitrieva et al., 2021). In general, Russian citizens admit the importance of digital skills development in contemporary reality. At the same time, additional training in this field is more often demanded by those who already have the relevant competence at a sufficiently high level (NAFI, 2020).

The development of digital competencies is coupled with the notion of trust. According to the extant research results, in Russia, the level of trust in the digital environment varies from low to moderate (Dmitrieva et al., 2021; Veselov, 2020). At the same time, with regard to the commercial sector, including online shops and services, the level of trust is notoriously high. By some estimates, over 90% of the Russian users generally trust online goods and services providers (Veselov, 2020), which makes the online marketplace a solid foundation for digital competencies development among Russian consumers.

Defining consumer information power

Labrecque et al. (2013) define power in the digital context as the asymmetric ability to exert control over people or valued resources in online social relations and enumerate a number of sources that give consumer power in the digital era, namely demand, information, crowd, and network. Information power is grounded in the ability to consume, produce, and control content (Bandara et al., 2020; Kucuk & Krishnamurthy, 2007; Labrecque et al., 2013). In the current chapter, we suggest considering consumer information power through a set of consumer competencies. As White (1959) defines, competence is a motivational concept, and thus behaviour that leads to the building up of control over objects is not random behaviour produced by a general overflow of energy. Moving from information consumption to creation and then to information control, consumers become empowered through the gradual evolution of their attitudes to information, their knowledge base, and relevant skills.

Consumer power through information consumption

Information search is one of the core stages of the classic consumer decision-making cycle. Consumers are supposed to collect, analyse, and compare information, realising the needs or wants they have (Arora, 1985; Rohm & Swaminathan, 2004). The classic funnel model assumes that consumers narrow down their search, following the collected information available on the market options. The alternative model (Edelman, 2010), on the contrary, assumes that consumers constantly collect information and search out even more options when moving to the next stages in the consumer decision journey.

Increased information availability can lead to the assumption that it becomes easier for the consumer to collect required product information, thus providing the foundation for consumer empowerment. Indeed, as Labrecque et al. (2013) highlight, digitalisation of the economy contributes to consumer power through information consumption which relates to the ease of access to product or service information, which reduces information asymmetry.

At the same time, there might be barriers to the way consumers gain more power through information consumption. The first one relates to limitations of consumers' cognitive ability to process information, leading to potential cognitive bias (e.g. Singh & Giacosa, 2018). Indeed, the most recent approaches (e.g. Keiles & Lieberman, 2019) agree on the frequently chaotic nature of consumer decision-making when facing tremendous amounts of information. The term "information hygiene" is applied to the way consumers deal with available information sources during the information-seeking phase (Edelman Trust Barometer, 2021).

The second barrier stems from consumer sentiments towards the marketplace defined as the general feeling that consumers have for marketing, marketers, and their stance in the marketplace (Mady, 2011). Extant research identified a plethora of marketplace sentiments held by consumers including consumer scepticism, cynicism, trust, self-confidence, marketplace alienation (Helm et al., 2015; Mady, 2011; Pervan & Martin, 2012). These sentiments make consumers develop and adopt particular shopping styles (Sproles & Sproles, 1990), coping strategies (Dommeyer & Gross, 2003), habitual decision-making journeys (Edelman, 2010), and motivation to be engaged in various spectrum of digital activities (Fleming et al., 2017; Mady, 2011). Thus, these sentiments serve as dispositions to act in certain ways and define a consumer's approach to information consumption. For instance, sceptical consumers tend to distrust brand-initiated communications, but pay attention to the information in other sources (Obermiller et al., 2005); alienated consumers tend to consume less information in general (Stewart & Yap, 2020).

Finally, the recent COVID-19 outbreak added to the information balance shift in the market. As one of the pandemic outcomes, consumers moved their purchases online, thus relying more on online information search. These trends affected product categories where consumers preferred offline shopping before – e.g. groceries, fashion items, medical services. Supporting consumers during the information search phase and providing them with decision-making base leads to direct implications for businesses to consider product information seeking as a crucial direction of investments.

Consumers globally are rather pessimistic about the economic recovery, being unsure about the economic prospects (McKinsey, 2020). The uncertainty due to the uniqueness of a situation and lack of precedents, contradicting communication flows from multiple stakeholders contributed to historic drops in the levels of public trust to traditional information sources, including media, government, etc. (Edelman Trust Barometer, 2021). Due to pandemics, consumers face higher uncertainty. This can have additional implications for product information search, raising consumer scepticism even further. On the other hand, there is evidence that consumers realise they need to increase the level of market literacy (Edelman Trust Barometer, 2021), which might shift their attitude and behaviour in terms of product information seeking in the future.

In the case of the Russian economy, there are even further economic sources of uncertainty, affecting consumers and focusing their product information-seeking behaviour on more rational aspects and price. As the trend towards falling real consumer incomes started as early as during politically caused economic downturn in 2014–2015, this tendency continued during the pandemic. As an outcome, consumers face increased pressure to choose smart and rationally. For the first time since Russia turned into a market economy, consumer behaviour was rationalised to such a great extent. In fact, the first decade (1990s) could be called market romanticism, whereas consumers welcomed opportunities, but lacked sophistication. During the 2000s increasing national welfare boosted consumer spending and credits, followed by a slowdown after the world economic crisis in 2008–2009, and ultimately, the hit on consumer incomes during plummeting exchange rates and continued drop in real income after 2014. According to PwC report (2020), consumers in Russia tend to be facing increasing uncertainty in their expectations, which affects their behaviour.

Consumer power through information creation

Consumer power through information creation relates to the ability to produce user-generated content for self-expression, extending individual reach, and elevating the potential for individual opinion to influence markets (Labrecque et al., 2013). With the rise of ICT, consumers steadily increased their role in shaping the information landscape. Consumers express their opinions through complaints, generate e-WOM, advocate for brands (Labrecque et al., 2013). Nowadays, the role of the content generated by consumers represents a solid share of all information available globally. This is the "earner" media that brands are fighting for. As consumers' trust globally has reached historic minimums (e.g. trust to all forms of media) (Edelman Trust Barometer, 2021), there is increased attention to user-generated forms of review and personal WOM – recommendations, and who recommends matters.

Russia has among the lowest positions in the world in terms of trust in the media (Edelman Trust Barometer, 2021). And yet, the strong shift towards digital consumption and digital communications channels leads to increase in variability of information sources and content, available to consumers (PwC, 2020). Moreover, consumers can be motivated to create their content as opposite to already available information sources. The shifts we observe take now less time to change consumer behaviour, e.g. rationalising it and increasing the focus on the role of information (Mérineau, 2019).

At the same time, existing research suggests that there might be differences in consumers' activity in content creation. According to Li and Bernoff (2010), individuals could be clustered as creators, conversationalists, critics, collectors, joiners, spectators, or inactive. For example, the creators are the most active participants on the Internet. They are constantly creating a blog(post)s, websites, videos, audios, and/or other content. The critics are the opposite of the conversationalists. This group responds to status updates, blogs, websites, news, forums, products, and services. For creators and conversationalists, this group is an essential one to maintain online interaction. However, there is a significant overlap in these three segments (creators, critics, and conversationalists). At the same time, those at the end of the ladder of activity (Li & Bernoff, 2010) – the inactive consumers – are not present on social media. Or they may be present but aren't doing anything at all.

Consumer power through information control

The issue of information in consumer behaviour theory has been largely discussed from the perspectives of them having access to information about companies and their products (e.g. Nelson, 1970; Rezabakhsh et al., 2006) and, with the development of the Internet, from the standpoint of information creation (e.g. Labresque et al., 2013; Rezabakhsh et al., 2006). The third (and relatively newer) aspect of consumer power in the digital environment is power through information control, which relates to personal data provision and consumers' privacy concerns (Bandara et al., 2020) as well as to practices in managing communications with organisations (which information to receive, when and how). As communication practices of companies evolve to allow consumer data collection and increased personalisation, information control by consumers shifts more to personal data protection and permission, with related competencies development.

Personal information is one of the most valuable resources that companies may possess. Consequently, this dimension appears in almost all digital competence models and frameworks (e.g. digital safety in the DigComp framework; Carretero et al., 2017) and includes the ability to personal protection, data protection, digital identity protection, security measures, safe and sustainable use. According to National Agency of Financial Studies (NAFI) (2020), Russian citizens demonstrate a good level of understanding of cyber security, including issues related to personal data protection. At the same time, research by Russian Venture Company (RVK) and Institute for National Projects (INP) (2020) showed that Russian consumers consider keeping control of their personal data important and distinctively differentiate government and commercial institutions when it comes to guarantees of personal data security. It is worth mentioning that 59% of respondents admitted trust to large online platforms against only 49% that declared trust in the government in issues related to personal data protection.

With the increase of consumers' information competence, their consciousness regarding third-party access to personal information as well as information control practices evolve. They become selective on how and with whom they would share their personal data. With the wide use of portable and wearable devices that keep track of location, health, and behavioural evidence, consumers may manage this information and decide on providing access to it (Labresque et al., 2013). Lwin et al. (2016) found that consumers who worry about their privacy and sensitive information sharing may take deflective and defensive behaviours. However, according to recent studies (e.g. Anant et al., 2020), few consumers consciously apply sophisticated measures to control the information they provide to companies, often preferring only to manage the browser history and cookies.

Companies need to understand what consumers are ready to do in terms of providing personal information or protecting it. As stated by Mérineau (2019), more than 50% of consumers would be willing to share personal data in exchange for offers or discounts, product recommendations, and personalised shopping experiences. According to Trend Vision by Ipsos (2021), Russian consumers as well realise the positive correlation between the amount of personal data transmitted to companies and the quality of their experience with these companies. Around 50% of consumers demonstrate readiness to share individual information for money or impersonally, and every third would be willing to do that for personalised experience.

Methodology

Sample

To evaluate consumer information competencies, a sample of 561 Russian consumers was surveyed online. Respondents were recruited from an online panel administered by a research company. The respondents live in the two largest metropolitan cities of Russia (Moscow and St. Petersburg) and have made at least one online purchase during the last year. Quota sampling was used to ensure that the sample structure by age and gender complied with the economically active general population between 18 and 55 years old. The sample includes men and women in equal proportions. Forty-four per cent of respondents are between 18 and 34 years old, 56% of respondents are between 35 and 55 years old. The respondents completed an online questionnaire about their information behaviours in the digital marketplace and socio-demographic characteristics.

Operationalisation of variables

To measure consumer information competencies, the research team has generated 22 statements that describe different aspects of behaviour related to information consumption, creation, and control (see Table 9.1). The statements are derived from existing academic literature and empirical reports. Each statement is measured on a frequency scale with five answer options

Table 9.1 Descriptive statistics

Information-related practices	*Mean*	*SD*	*Answer options (share of responses, %)*				
			Never (%)	*Rarely (%)*	*Sometimes (%)*	*Often (%)*	*Almost always (%)*
Information consumption							
1 I read reviews and recommendations on the Internet about brands that are better to buy	4.22	0.73	0	3	7	54	36
2 I spend a lot of time looking for information on various brands before making a purchase	3.81	0.98	2	10	18	45	25
3 I carefully study information about products or services on the Internet before buying	4.35	0.64	0	1	5	51	43
4 I read other users' reviews on products and services before making an online purchase	4.33	0.70	0	2	6	48	44
5 I am looking for coupons and promotional codes on the Internet for the purchase of goods and services	3.06	1.07	7	25	33	27	9
6 I browse sites that collect information about discounts and special offers	3.40	1.01	4	15	31	37	13
7 I use sites and applications that allow comparing prices and characteristics of different products and services	3.49	1.06	6	11	29	38	16
Information creation							
8 I write reviews about companies, products, and services on social networks	2.36	1.10	25	32	27	11	4
9 I leave comments on reviews written by other users	2.30	1.03	26	31	30	10	2
10 I rate the usefulness of product reviews written by other users	2.99	1.11	12	19	36	25	8
11 I publish my photos with brands that I buy	2.08	1.11	40	26	22	9	3

12 I publish my photos of services provided by professionals	2.12	1.12	39	27	21	11	2
13 I write reviews on products and services that I buy	2.20	1.12	34	28	25	10	3
14 I make video reviews on products and services that I buy	1.62	0.94	63	19	12	4	1
Information control							
15 I delete my browser history and clear cookies	3.25	1.17	7	18	35	22	18
16 I use ad-blocking apps and add-ons	3.14	1.27	13	19	29	22	18
17 I check my computer for safety using special programs and applications	3.50	1.19	7	12	30	25	25
18 I read or browse the security policy of websites that ask for permission to access my data	3.00	1.19	12	22	31	23	12
19 I unsubscribe from uninteresting mailings, groups, and channels	3.83	0.93	2	4	28	40	26
20 I subscribe to push notifications and e-mail newsletters if there is such an opportunity	2.31	1.06	26	34	28	9	3
21 I leave information about my preferences on the websites of online retailers and media platforms if there is such an opportunity	2.54	1.09	20	27	35	13	4
22 I log in through social networks when registering on new sites if there is an opportunity	2.80	1.15	*16*	*24*	*31*	*23*	*6*

(Never, Rarely, Sometimes, Often, Almost always). For statements 8–22, the answer option "Regularly" is used instead of "Almost always". The answer options were further converted to a 5-point numerical scale, where 1 represents the rarest category and 5 – the most frequent category.

Analytical approach

To simplify the analysis of 22 statements describing consumer information behaviours, exploratory factor analysis was employed. Twenty-two statements were compressed into five meaningful factors that represent different information competencies. All statements showed high factor loadings on a principal factor, while cross-loadings on other factors were below 0.5 (see Table 9.2). Cronbach's alphas were above 0.7 for three out of five factors, which signifies their high internal consistency (Peterson, 1994). Two factors showed Cronbach's alphas between 0.6 and 0.7. The level is borderline, but still acceptable, although it signifies that information behaviours representing the factors are less correlated (Peterson, 1994). Nevertheless, it is admissible considering that the study was not aimed to develop or validate a new scale, but rather reduce the dimensionality of data representing different information practices to simplify further analysis.

Then, the statements representing each factor were aggregated into five summated variables. To calculate a summated variable, the values of respective answers were averaged for each respondent. The five summated variables associated with each factor were used as clustering criteria. Four consumer clusters with distinct information competencies were identified using Ward hierarchical cluster analysis. The clusters were further profiled on a number of additional variables such as social-demographic parameters and online shopping sentiments.

Findings

Structure and levels of information competences

Exploratory factor analysis delineated five competencies related to information consumption, creation, and control (see Figure 9.1). *Information consumption* practices are divided into two factors: information seeking competence and comparison shopping competence (see Table 9.2). The former includes information practices related to protective behaviours aimed to assure product quality through checking the brand reputation and product reviews on the Internet. The latter is more active with a focus on price comparisons and deal hunting. *Information creation* practices form part of the single competence named accordingly (see Table 9.2). *Information control* practices are divided into two factors: information protection competence and information permission competence (see Table 9.2). The former comprises information practices that help consumers filter and avoid inbound marketing communications and

Table 9.2 Exploratory factor analysis results

Information-related behaviours	*Factor 1. Information seeking*	*Factor 2. Comparison shopping*	*Factor 3. Information creation*	*Factor 4. Information protection*	*Factor 5. Information permission*
Information consumption					
1 I read reviews and recommendations on the Internet about brands that are better to buy	0.82				
2 I spend a lot of time looking for information on various brands before making a purchase	0.69				
3 I carefully study information about products or services on the Internet before buying	0.77				
4 I read other users' reviews on products and services before making an online purchase	0.82				
5 I am looking for coupons and promotional codes on the Internet for the purchase of goods and services		0.78			
6 I browse sites that collect information about discounts and special offers		0.83			
7 I use sites and applications that allow comparing prices and characteristics of different products and services		0.66			
Information creation					
8 I write reviews about companies, products and services on social networks			0.78		
9 I leave comments on reviews written by other users			0.71		
10 I rate the usefulness of product reviews written by other users			0.55		
11 I publish my photos with brands that I buy			0.83		
12 I publish my photos of services provided by professionals			0.82		
13 I write reviews on products and services that I buy			0.82		
14 I make video reviews on products and services that I buy			0.68		

(*Continued*)

Information-related behaviours	*Factor 1. Information seeking*	*Factor 2. Comparison shopping*	*Factor 3. Information creation*	*Factor 4. Information protection*	*Factor 5. Information permission*
Information control					
15 I delete my browser history and clear cookies				0.71	
16 I use ad-blocking apps and add-ons				0.66	
17 I check my computer for safety using special programs and applications				0.75	
18 I read or browse the security policy of websites that ask for permission to access my data				0.57	
19 I unsubscribe from uninteresting mailings, groups and channels				0.52	
20 I subscribe to push notifications and e-mail newsletters if there is such an opportunity					0.72
21 I leave information about my preferences on the websites of online retailers and media platforms if there is such an opportunity					0.50
22 I log in through social networks when registering on new sites if there is an opportunity					0.59
Cronbach's alpha	0.80	0.72	0.88	0.69	0.63
Mean	4.18	3.32	2.24	3.35	2.55
S.D.	0.61	0.84	0.83	0.77	0.84

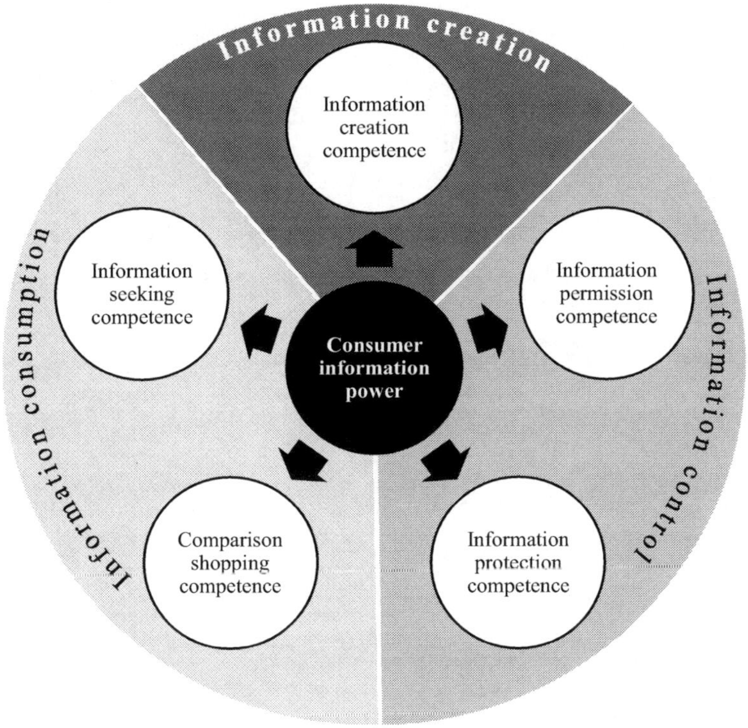

Figure 9.1 Sources of consumer information power

defend their privacy. The latter implies that consumers consciously select the types of inbound communications that they are willing to receive and provide their personal data in exchange for more personalised treatment and other benefits.

The results show that information seeking competence is the most developed one, followed by comparison shopping, information protection, information permission, and information creation competencies respectively (see sample means for all competencies in Table 9.2 or 9.3). However, the development of information competencies is not universal among the population. Rather, there are four distinct clusters with different information competence profiles (see Table 9.3).

Description of clusters

Passive avoiders

Passive avoiders demonstrate the lowest level of information competence development. They are relatively uninvolved in the digital marketplace and do

Table 9.3 Cluster profiles

Profiling criteria	*Passive avoiders*	*Careless searchers*	*Protective searchers*	*Proactive mavens*	*Sample*
Cluster size	200 (36%)	123 (22%)	108 (19%)	130 (23%)	561 (100%)
Information competences (means & standard deviations)					
Information seeking competence	**3.7 (0.6)**	**4.4 (0.4)**	**4.4 (0.4)**	**4.3 (0.5)**	4.1 (0.6)
Comparison shopping competence	2.5 (0.6)	**3.6 (0.5)**	**3.6 (0.5)**	**3.9 (0.6)**	3.3 (0.8)
Information creation competence	1.9 (0.6)	1.6 (0.4)	2.2 (0.5)	**3.2 (0.7)**	2.2 (0.8)
Information protection competence	3.0 (0.7)	2.9 (0.4)	**3.9 (0.4)**	**3.6 (0.7)**	3.4 (0.7)
Information permission competence	2.2 (0.6)	2.1 (0.6)	2.3 (0.4)	**3.5 (0.6)**	2.6 (0.8)
*Online shopping sentiments (means & standard deviations)**					
My online shopping experience lives up to my expectations[a]	*3.9 (0.6)*	4.1 (0.6)	4.0 (0.6)	**4.1 (0.6)**	4.0 (0.6)
My online shopping experience is close to the ideal[b]	3.7 (0.7)	3.7 (0.8)	*3.5 (0.8)*	**3.9 (0.8)**	3.7 (0.8)
I trust online retailers[c]	3.6 (0.6)	3.6 (0.6)	3.5 (0.8)	**3.9 (0.7)**	3.6 (0.7)
I am annoyed by the amount of advertising I encounter on the Internet[d]	3.8 (1.0)	3.9 (0.9)	**4.0 (0.9)**	3.6 (1.1)	3.8 (1.0)
Age structure					
18–24 y.o.	15%	12%	7%	13%	12%
25–34 y.o.	**32%**	24%	**31%**	**42%**	32%
35–44 y.o.	**30%**	**27%**	**35%**	25%	29%
45–55 y.o.	24%	**37%**	27%	21%	27%

Sex structure					
Male	43%	43%	**64%**	**56%**	50%
Female	**57%**	**57%**	36%	44%	50%
Income structure					
Not enough money to buy food	0%	0%	1%	1%	0%
Enough money to buy food, but not clothes	3.5%	2%	1%	1%	2%
Enough money to buy food and clothes, but not household appliances	**36.5%**	**32%**	23%	16%	28%
Enough money to buy household appliances, but not a car	**43.5%**	**49%**	**43%**	**39%**	43%
Enough money to buy everything, except for an apartment or a house	15%	17%	**29%**	**35%**	23%
Enough money to buy an apartment or a house	1.5%	1%	4%	8%	3%
Education structure					
Higher education	56%	**71%**	58%	**66%**	62%
No higher education	44%	29%	42%	34%	38%

[a]Brown-Forsythe (496.50) = 2.79, p = 0.040
[b]Brown-Forsythe (481.90) = 4.47, p = 0.004
[c]Brown-Forsythe (430.75) = 5.80, p = 0.001
[d]Brown-Forsythe (505.88) = 3.19, p = 0.023

not use all the opportunities provided by the technological transformation of shopping. The only way they use consumer power in the digital marketplace is through moderate information seeking which is still below the extent of information seeking demonstrated by other clusters.

Passive avoiders constitute the largest share of the sample (36%). The majority of passive avoiders are women (57%). This cluster is less educated as compared to other clusters (44% do not have a university degree). Their shopping experience is the least satisfactory as compared to the most advanced cluster ($M_{\text{Passive avoiders}} = 3.9$ versus $M_{\text{Proactive mavens}} = 4.1$, Dunnett's test $p < 0.05$).

Their behaviour exhibits a number of contradictions. For instance, passive avoiders have the lowest income in the sample; however, they do not do comparison shopping that can help find better-priced products and lucrative deals. Additionally, they report a relatively low level of trust in online retailers and are irritated by online advertising; however, they do not take any protective actions to establish their consumer power in the digital marketplace. The reason might be the absence of required knowledge that prohibits them from utilising consumer power.

Careless searchers

Careless searchers demonstrate high levels of information seeking and comparison shopping competence. They constitute 22% of the sample. The gender structure is the same as in the previous cluster (57% women); the income distribution is also very similar. However, in contrast to passive avoiders, careless searchers are older (63% are above 35 years old) and more educated (70% have a university degree).

Careless searchers actively consume information both to find better quality products and save on prices. They are equally satisfied with their consumption experience as the most advanced cluster of proactive mavens ($M_{\text{Careless searchers}} = 4.1$ versus $M_{\text{Proactive mavens}} = 4.1$, Dunnett's test $p > 0.05$). Analogously to passive avoiders, they have low trust in online retailers and are irritated by online advertising; but they do not take any precautions measures to mitigate their negative sentiments towards business practices.

Protective searchers

Similar to careless searchers, protective searchers demonstrate high levels of information seeking and comparison shopping competence. The distinctive feature of protective searchers is their strong emphasis on information protection competence. The cluster constitutes 22% of the sample. Protective searchers are predominantly men (64%). The income level is higher than in other clusters. The education level and age structure are similar to the first cluster of passive avoiders.

Protective searchers report that their online shopping experience meets their expectations, but they show the lowest value on the parameter of closeness to ideal ($M_{\text{Protective searchers}} = 3.5$ versus $M_{\text{Proactive mavens}} = 3.9$, Dunnett's test $p < 0.05$). It signifies that protective searchers have high demands in relation to shopping experience (probably because of their larger financial resources) which are not fully met. Additionally, this cluster demonstrates the lowest trust to online retailers and the highest level of irritation by online advertising, which is logically reflected in their active use of ad-blocking apps and other protective behaviours such as cookie control.

Proactive mavens

The cluster consists of consumers who are advanced on all five information competencies. Proactive mavens demonstrate the highest level of online shopping satisfaction, highest trust to online retailers, and the lowest level of irritation by online advertising. In contrast to protective searches, their protective behaviours are balanced by selective permission behaviours: instead of blocking all types of marketing communications, they filter some of them but engage in closer relationships with trusted online retailers. Additionally, proactive mavens exert their consumer power through information creation behaviours.

The cluster accounts for 23% of the sample. Proactive mavens are younger consumers who are active in the digital marketplace. They are more educated than passive avoiders and protective searchers but are behind the educational level of careless searchers (66% have a university degree). The cluster is slightly dominated by male consumers (56%). The income level is higher than in other clusters.

Discussion

This chapter aimed to explore Russian consumers' digital competencies in relation to information consumption, creation, and control and identify potential areas for development. The empirical study of Russian online shoppers produced several insights that are of relevance for firms, public policymaking, and consumers themselves.

First, some competencies are easier adopted by consumers, while others require more effort. In particular, the study delineated five information competencies and showed that information seeking competence is the most advanced one among Russian consumers. The result can be explained by the paramount importance of information-seeking activities in the decision-making processes. The second place is occupied by comparison shopping and information protection competencies. These competencies require greater consumer knowledge and involvement. At the same time, their development can benefit consumers both financially and experientially. Ultimately, information creation and information permission competencies are at the lowest level of development. These competencies are the most sophisticated and imply the mix of consumption and production practices adopted by consumers. Thus, permission and creation competencies establish a completely distinct balance of power in the digital marketplace with the consumer occupying the central position.

Second, information competencies are not universally developed among consumers. There are four distinct clusters with different information competence profiles. We suggest a number of ways each cluster can improve their online shopping experience through competence development.

The cluster of passive avoiders needs advancement of information seeking competence in the first place, as it is the fundamental competence required to effectively manage consumer activities in the digital marketplace. Considering the large share of this cluster and their specific socio-economic stance (lower level of education and lower-income), the government and not-for-profit organisations can pay special attention to passive avoiders through targeted educational programs aimed to improve their basic information competencies.

The careless searcher should pay more attention to protective behaviours. Even though they have a satisfactory online shopping experience, there are risks that they may encounter malignant retailers who are capable of spoiling experience with unfair marketing practices.

Protective searchers have high demands in relation to the online shopping experience. They can take advantage of permission behaviours (such as the provision of personal information to trusted retailers) to allow more personalised treatment and, hence, better customer experience. Moreover, they are lucrative for online retailers due to their higher income and, thus, spending potential. Nevertheless, this cluster is hard to reach for retailers because they actively protect their privacy and resist inbound marketing communications. A managerial application for working with such types of customers is to build trust through demonstrating the transparency of data management practices and respect concerning their privacy. As some authors suggest, consumers who are distrustful of and disillusioned about marketing practices can be more enthusiastic and committed to some brands (Helm et al., 2015; Pervan & Martin, 2012). Hence, protective searchers represent an opportunity to those companies that are able to convince them of their trustworthiness.

Proactive mavens are not only active consumers of information but also content creators who can influence other consumers. Hence, they may inspire the interest of the business as potential influencers and opinion leaders playing with firms at the same battleground. When working with such consumers, businesses should ensure that influencers comply with business values and standards, as these consumers become the voice of the business and represent it in the marketplace.

Third, the study showed that the increase in consumer power does not proportionally improve the consumer experience in the digital marketplace (see Figure 9.2). For instance, protective searchers report less favourable

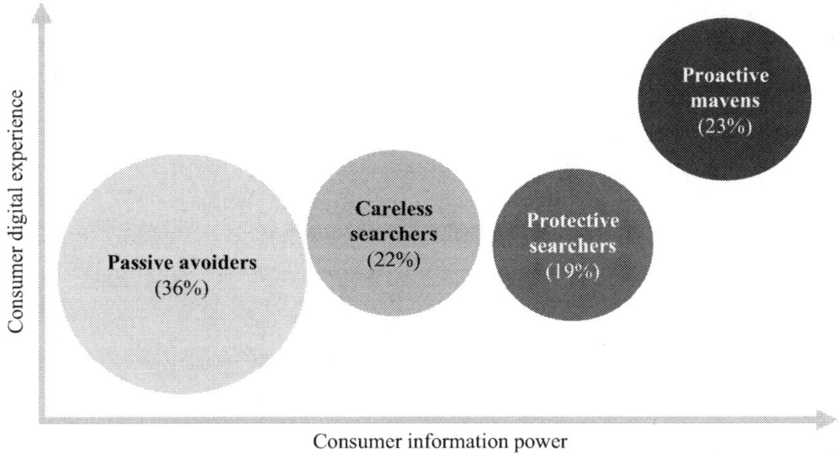

Figure 9.2 Consumer clusters on the power-experience map

online shopping sentiments on some parameters than even the least advanced cluster of passive avoiders (higher irritation with advertising, lower trust to business, and high standards for ideal shopping that are not fully met). These negative sentiments may adversely affect consumer psychological wellbeing and, hence, require some corrective actions. This example makes us assume that the development of information competencies should be balanced: to ensure a better customer experience, advancement of any defensive competence (such as information protection) should be completed with the development of active competence (such as information permission).

The current study offers several managerial implications. It becomes obvious that further transformation of the global marketplace will coincide with the development of consumer power. Among its other sources, information is related to core stages in consumer decision-making and strongly influences the interaction between firms and consumers, as well as between consumers and their peers. Instead of linear, manageable interaction along the funnel stages, both firms and consumers are embedded into a series of "cyclones" (Keiles & Lieberman, 2019), whereas brands and information sources may be added to consideration.

There is no uniform development though. As existing research indicates, being confronted with increasing uncertainty consumers develop various market sentiments – e.g. scepticism and lack of trust, on one side; and tend to overcome uncertainty by increasing their own literacy, on the other side. As suggested in Edelman Trust Barometer (2021), there is a rise in motivation by consumers to be more literate. What kind of strategies can be offered in order to handle diversity in consumers' attitudes and competencies related to information consumption, creation, and control? Adding these criteria to the segmentation process can probably help develop persuasion and education strategies that might help to attract informed consumers, be willing to become loyal customers, and actively participate in positive WOM, as well as other forms of information co-creation. Finally, these new strategies will be relevant for consumers to lift their caution and share user data with businesses. Consumers will decide which businesses they want to share data with, offering them a more competitive angle.

Future research might take this discussion even further. For example, as reported by Labrecque et al. (2013), the next levels of consumer power relate to network interaction and crowd power. Beyond individual proneness, these aspects of consumer behaviour are related to the speed and scale of sharing and exchanging information, goods, and other resources, as well as mobilising for a cause. The latter case might be of particular relevance for such emerging markets as Russia, where consumers have yet to develop their strong voice when indicating priorities to businesses – e.g. ecological initiatives, social and other cause-related steps.

Bibliography

Anant, V., Donchak, L., Kaplan, J., & Soller, H. (2020, April 27). *The consumer-data opportunity and the privacy imperative.* https://www.mckinsey.com/business-functions/strategy-and-corporate-finance/our-insights/the-restart.

Arora, R. (1985, Spring). Involvement: Its measurement for retail store research. *Journal of the Academy of Marketing Science, 13*, 229–241. https://doi.org/10.1007/BF02729717.

Bandara, R., Fernando, M., & Akter, S. (2020). Addressing privacy predicaments in the digital marketplace: A power-relations perspective. *International Journal of Consumer Studies, 44*(5), 423–434. https://doi.org/10.1111/ijcs.12576.

Bandara, R., Fernando, M., & Akter, S. (2021). Managing consumer privacy concerns and defensive behaviours in the digital marketplace. *European Journal of Marketing, 55*(1), 219–246. https://doi.org/10.1108/EJM-06-2019-0515.

Carretero, S., Vuorikari, R., & Punie, Y. (2017). *DigComp 2.1: The digital competence framework for citizens with eight proficiency levels and examples of use. Publications Office of the European Union.* https://doi.org/10.2760/38842.

Clifford, I., Kluzer, S., Troia, S., Jakobsone, M., & Zandbergs, U. (2020). DigComp-Sat. In R. Vuorikari, Y. Punie, J. Castaño Muñoz, I.C. Centeno Mediavilla, W. O'keeffe, & M. Cabrera Giraldez (Eds.), *Publications Office of the European Union.* Luxembourg. doi: 10.2760/77437, JRC123226.

Dmitrieva, N., Zhulin, A., Artamonov, R., & Titov, E. (2021). Assessment of the digital readiness of the population of Russia. In *XXII April International Scientific Conference on the Problems of Economic and Social Development*, Moscow, 13–30 April, 2021. HSE Publishing House, 86 p.

Dommeyer, C.J., & Gross, B. L. (2003). What consumers know and what they do: An investigation of consumer knowledge, awareness, and use of privacy protection strategies. *Journal of Interactive Marketing, 17*(2), 34–51. https://doi.org/10.1002/dir.10053.

Edelman, D.C. (2010, December). Branding in the digital age: You're spending your money in all the wrong places. *Harvard Business Review, 88*(12), 62–69.

Edelman Trust Barometer (2021). Edelman Trust Barometer 2021. Global Report. https://www.edelman.com/sites/g/files/aatuss191/files/2021-03/2021%20Edelman%20Trust%20Barometer.pdf

Federal State Statistics Service. (2020). On foreign trade in 2020. https://gks.ru/bgd/free/b04_03/IssWWW.exe/Stg/d02/32.htm.

Fleming, P., Watson, S.J., Patouris, E., Bartholomew, K.J., & Zizzo, D.J. (2017). Why do people file share unlawfully? A systematic review, meta-analysis and panel study. *Computers in Human Behavior, 72*, 535–548. https://doi.org/10.1016/j.chb.2017.02.014.

GFK. (2018). *Internet connectivity in Russia as of 2018.* https://cdn2.hubspot.net/hubfs/2405078/cms-pdfs/fileadmin/user_upload/dyna_content/ru/documents/press_releases/2019/gfk_rus_internet_audience_in_russia_2018.pdf.

Helm, A.E., Moulard, J.G., & Richins, M. (2015). Consumer cynicism: Developing a scale to measure underlying attitudes influencing marketplace shaping and withdrawal behaviours. *International Journal of Consumer Studies, 39*(5), 515–524. https://doi.org/10.1111/ijcs.12191.

Keiles, E., & Lieberman, M. (2019). *Smash the funnel: The cyclonic buyer journey – A new map for sustainable, repeatable, predictable revenue generation.* An Inc. Original.

Kucuk, S.U., & Krishnamurthy, S. (2007). An analysis of consumer power on the Internet. *Technovation, 27*(1–2), 47–56. https://doi.org/10.1016/j.technovation.2006.05.002.

Labrecque, L.I., vor dem Esche, J., Mathwick, C., Novak, T.P., & Hofacker, C.F. (2013). Consumer power: Evolution in the digital age. *Journal of Interactive Marketing, 27*(4), 257–269. https://doi.org/10.1016/j.intmar.2013.09.002.

Li, C., & Bernoff, J. (2010). Groundswell. Winning in a world transformed by social technologies. Strategic Direction. Harvard Business Review Press.

Lwin, M., Wirtz, J., & Stanaland, A.J.S. (2016). The privacy dyad. *Internet Research, 26*(4), 919–941. https://doi.org/10.1108/IntR-05-2014-0134.

Lyubimov, I. (2019). Russia's diversification prospects. *Russian Journal of Economics, 5*(2), 177–198. https://doi.org/10.32609/j.ruje.5.34753.

Mady, T.T. (2011). Sentiment toward marketing: Should we care about consumer alienation and readiness to use technology?. *Journal of Consumer Behaviour, 10*(4), 192–204. https://doi.org/10.1002/cb.329.

McKinsey: Re-start. (2020). https://www.mckinsey.com/business-functions/strategy-and-corporate-finance/our-insights/the-restart.

Mérineau, E. (2019, May 1). The three levers of consumer power. *Forbes*, https://www.forbes.com/sites/forbesagencycouncil/2019/05/01/the-three-levers-of-consumer-power/?sh=4e0d8a51558d.

National Agency of Financial Studies (NAFI). (2020). *Digital literacy of Russians: Study of the year 2020.* https://nafi.ru/analytics/tsifrovaya-gramotnost-rossiyan-issledovanie-2020/.

Nelson, P. (1970). Information and consumer behaviour. *Journal of Political Economy, 78*(2), 311–329. https://doi.org/10.1086/259630.

Obermiller, C., Spangenberg, E., & MacLachlan, D.L. (2005). Ad skepticism: The consequences of disbelief. *Journal of Advertising, 34*(3), 7–17. https://doi.org/10.1080/00913367.2005.10639199.

Pervan, S.J., & Martin, B.A. (2012). Development and validation of the consumer disillusionment toward marketing activity scale. *Journal of Consumer Behaviour, 11*(5), 339–346. https://doi.org/10.1002/cb.1377.

Peterson, R.A. (1994). A meta-analysis of Cronbach's coefficient alpha. *Journal of Consumer Research, 21*(2), 381–391. https://doi.org/10.1086/209405.

PwC. (2020). Global Consumer Insights Survey: Russia. https://www.pwc.ru/en/publications/consumer-insights-survey-2020.html.

Rezabakhsh, B., Bornemann, D., Hansen, U., & Schrader, U. (2006). Consumer power: A comparison of the old economy and the Internet economy. *Journal of Consumer Policy, 29*(1), 3–36. https://doi.org/10.1007/s10603-005-3307-7.

Rohm, A.J., & Swaminathan, V. (2004). A typology of online shoppers based on shopping motivations. *Journal of Business Research, 57*, 748–757. https://doi.org/10.1016/S0148-2963(02)00351-X

Russian Venture Company & Institute for National Projects. (2020). *Citizens attitude to new technologies in the period of Corona-crisis*. https://inp.ru/.files/358/2_backup.pdf

Sanghi, A., Emelyanova, O., Rostovtseva, I., Wuester, L., Levitanskaya, K., et al. (2021). Russia's economic recovery gathers pace. *Russia Economic Report*, 45. World Bank Group. https://www.worldbank.org/en/country/russia/publication/rer.

Schwab, K. (2019). The Global Competitiveness Report 2019. *World Economic Forum*. http://www3.weforum.org/docs/WEF_TheGlobalCompetitivenessReport2019.pdf.

Singh, P., & Giacosa, E. (2018). Cognitive biases of consumers as barriers in transition towards circular economy. *Management Decision, 57*(4), 921–936. https://doi.org/10.1108/MD-08-2018-0951.

Sproles, E.K., & Sproles, G.B. (1990). Consumer decision-making styles as a function of individual learning styles. *Journal of Consumer Affairs, 24*(1), 134–147. https://doi.org/10.1111/j.1745-6606.1990.tb00262.x.

Stewart, C.R., & Yap, S.F. (2020). Low literacy, policy and consumer vulnerability: Are we really doing enough?. *International Journal of Consumer Studies, 44*(4), 343–352. https://doi.org/10.1111/ijcs.12569.

Trend Vision 2021: Consumers in a Changing World, Ipsos. https://www.ipsos.com/en/russia-trend-vision-2021.

Veselov, Y. (2020). Trust in a digital society. *Vestnik of Saint Petersburg University. Sociology, 13*(2), 129–143. https://doi.org/10.21638/spbu12.2020.202

White, R.W. (1959). Motivation reconsidered: the concept of competence. *Psychological Review, 66*(5), 297. https://doi.org/10.1037/h0040934.

World Bank. (2021). GDP per capita (current US$) – Russian Federation. https://data.worldbank.org/indicator/NY.GDP.PCAP.CD?locations=RU.

Yoo, M., de Wysocki, M., & Cumberland, A. (2018). Country digital readiness: Research to determine a country's digital readiness and key interventions. Cisco Corporate Affairs. https://www.cisco.com/c/dam/assets/csr/pdf/Country-Digital-Readiness-White-Paper-US.pdf.

10 Digital consumption in Spain and the Internet of Things

Nela Filimon and Francesc Fusté-Forné

Introduction

In recent years, intelligent voice devices and assistants have increased their usage by consumers and businesses. This trend is in line with the increasing presence of information and communication technologies (ICTs) and the Internet of Things (IoT), in basically all aspects of people's professional and personal lives. Thus, according to data released by the Digital 2020 reports (Kemp, 2020), 59% of the world population is connected to the Internet, the world user (16–64 years of age) spending online, on average, about six hours and forty-three minutes per day. The same report indicates a daily average of five hours and forty-one minutes spent online, in the case of Spanish Internet users. In the same fashion, the worldwide average time spent on social media, on any device, is of two hours and twenty-four minutes (one hour and fifty-one minutes for Spain), with Facebook, YouTube, and WhatsApp being the top three most used social platforms. Among the devices most used to access the Internet in 2019, mobile phones accounted already for a share of 50.1% of the daily time of the world Internet user (Kemp, 2020).

The data on the usage of intelligent voice assistants shows that 43% of the worldwide Internet users are using voice interfaces monthly, whatever the device, for voice searches and voice commands. In the case of Spain, the proportion stands to 35% of Internet users (Kemp, 2020). As a matter of fact, in countries like the US, existing evidence points to a rather high degree of awareness of "voice technology" among consumers (PwC, 2018). A survey performed by PwC in 2018, found that 90% of the elicited US respondents were familiar with virtual voice assistants (VVA) and devices, of which, 72% used a VVA; among the most used devices, the respondents indicated the smartphone (57%), followed by tablets, laptops, and desktops (29%, for each of them); as for the mobile voice assistants, they were used mainly at home, by 74% of the respondents. Overall, the study highlights the need for the users to acquire more advanced skills to perform also more complex usages of the VVA, as most of the activities done with VVA were about searching, meteorological consulting, news and music listening, and in a smaller proportion, about controlling other home devices or online purchasing (PwC, 2018).

DOI: 10.4324/9781003263685-13

The evidence on the market distribution among the main VVA, shows that in 2020, Apple's Siri and Google Assistant were leading the market, with a 36% share each, followed by Amazon's Alexa (25%) and Microsoft's Cortana, with 19%. Moreover, 58% of the VVA users were employing them for searches on local businesses (Andrienko, 2020). All in all, existing evidence on the usage of the VVA and the profile of the VVA users is rather scarce.

This research aims to contribute to filling in this gap by identifying patterns of consumption emerging from the usage of the IoT, with a special focus on VVA in Spain. The representative data, collected by the Asociación para la Investigación de los Medios de Comunicación (AIMC, 2019) in period October–December 2019, from respondents of 14 years of age or above, are analysed with a latent class approach. Findings show that Spanish VVA users can be structured in four probabilistic segments or clusters, as follows: inactive or non-users of VVA (55% of the sample), occasional VVA users (23%), frequent VVA users (8%), and intensive VVA users, respectively (14%). The data also exhibit a variety of VVAs uses, going from information search, meteorological and traffic checking, to listening to music and radio, alerts/agenda/calendar, or phone calls. The chapter is organized as follows: after a review of the literature on the IoT, we present the methodology and data used in the analysis, followed by findings and discussion, and conclude with some implications for marketers and business managers.

The Internet of Things

The IoT is defined as "an ecosystem that consists of devices equipped with sensors, computing, and networking technologies collaborating to create an autonomous environment in which smart services are delivered" (Bello & Zeadally, 2019, p. 663). Also, the IoT is understood as "a well-defined scheme of interconnected computing tactics, digital, and mechanical devices possessing the capability of transmission of data over the defined network without having any human involvement at any level" (Singh et al., 2020, p. 521). However, previous research also acknowledged the long-term environmental and social impacts of the development of IoT technologies. According to Nižetić et al. (2020), these are the utilization of limited resources, the growing electronic waste because of large volumes of production, and the potential limitation of direct social contacts derived from the overuse of IoT technologies.

The main objective of IoT technologies is not only to improve the efficiency of systems and to simplify processes but also to provide high-quality smart services (Bello & Zeadally, 2019) and to improve the quality of life of humans (Nižetić et al., 2020). Since IoT technologies have an ever-growing impact on humans' daily lives, previous research has investigated the factors that determine the consumers' acceptance of IoT technology (Aldossari & Sidorova, 2020; Gao & Bai, 2014). On one side, Aldossari and Sidorova (2020) argued the customer acceptance is based on factors like effort and performance expectancy, hedonic motivation, and price value. On the other, Gao and Bai (2014) showed the relevance of technology factors (i.e. perceived ease of use), social factors (i.e. social influence), and individual user characteristics (i.e. perceived enjoyment).

Authors such as Bello and Zeadally (2019) reported that smart services are, for example, applied to smart cities (i.e. street lighting), smart homes (i.e. home automation), or smart commerces (i.e. e-payment). In this sense, smart technology based on IoT "has changed human life by providing connectivity to everyone regardless of time and place" (Alaa et al., 2017, p. 48). From a consumer perspective, the IoT is exemplified through a wide range of applications such as personal health, home automation, and wearable devices (Aldossari & Sidorova, 2020). It is obvious that IoT technologies may also lead to digital inequalities among people. As argued by van Deursen et al. (2021),

> those with higher education and those with higher incomes have more positive attitudes and are the first to actually buy IoT. This also means that they are the first to develop the required skills and to engage in a diverse IoT use.
>
> (p. 258)

Among the typologies of smart logistics, previous research has analysed the customer-oriented intelligent logistics whose goal is to provide closeness, flexibility, and accessibility to the customers (Ding et al., 2021; Giannikas et al., 2019). In particular, thc quality of service is a relevant attribute of IoT communication networks, which should exhibit reliability (quality of data), availability (data synchronization), scalability (support users, devices, and services), and security (protection and privacy) (Bello & Zeadally, 2019).

The IoT technologies provide a path to the creation of new technological dimensions (Hassan et al., 2020; Nauman et al., 2020). For example, smartphones are service providers where "technologies such as Siri for iOS or Sherpa for Android have endowed smartphones with a kind of persona" (Miranda et al., 2015, p. 46). Consumers can interact with these smart objects (Hoffman & Novak, 2018). This interaction, in the retail industry, results in value co-creation (Wortmann & Flüchter, 2015) because it offers bidirectional and real-time interaction with customers that improve their experiences (Balaji & Roy, 2017).

The design of IoT products is therefore crucial to anticipate consumer motivation and behaviours during the interactions with businesses to stimulate their decision-making (Chang et al., 2014). In addition,

> the impact which IoT technologies can have is however not limited to the value created by individual connected products. Instead, the functions of one product may be further enhanced if it is connected to related products and thus becomes part of a product system.
>
> (Wortmann & Flüchter, 2015, p. 222)

This system can be accessed both at local and global levels and "almost every object surrounding us can be transformed into smart entities by equipping objects with sensors, actors, and connectivity technologies" (Aldossari & Sidorova, 2020, p. 507).

Methodology

Data and variables

The representative dataset comes from the AIMC (2019) survey which includes 19,973 individuals, all Spanish residents at the moment of the interview, of both genders and age 14 years and older. The information is stratified according to regions and place of birth. For this chapter, we base our analysis only on the subsample of all Spanish natives (85.3% of the total, that is, 17,032 individuals). The other variables characterizing this dataset are presented in the sections below.

Socioeconomic variables

The survey elicited information on several representative indicators for the individuals' socioeconomic and demographic profile. Occupational status was registered with six levels: (1) employed (59.1%); (2) self-employed (10.9%); (3) student (9.2%); (4) housework (2.2%); (5) retired (11.8%), (6) unemployed (6.9%). Education level elicited information on the highest level of completed degrees: (1) primary studies or less (6.3%); (2) second degree (secondary school, bachelor's degree, vocational training) (42.4%); and (3) university (51.2%). The demographic profile is completed with information on gender (men – 69.8%; women – 30.2%); age, structured here in four levels: 14–29 years (16.4%); 30–44 years (34.4%; 45–59 years (36.2%); 60 years or above (12.9%); personal status: single (32.8%); married (47.2%); widowed (1.3%); divorced/separated (6.6%); unmarried couples (12.2%). The type of habitat unfolds in four levels, as follows: below 10,000 inhabitants (14.1%); from 10,000 to 50,000 inhabitants (24.1%); from 50,000 to 200,000 inhabitants (26.0%), and areas with more than 200,000 inhabitants (35.7%). Information about the size of the households is offered through the number of children, as follows: none (70.5%); one (16.6%); two (11.1%); three (1.6%); and four or more (0.2%), respectively.

Equipment and devices used to access Internet

The information on the equipment and devices used by Spaniards to access Internet has been collected with two types of questions: (a) dichotomous type questions (yes/no answers), allowing respondents to select several options, which have revealed the following preferences (yes answers): personal computer (57.6% of the respondents), laptop (72.4%); tablet (51.0%), TV (32.1%), mobile phone (92.7%), video console (11.3%), portable video console (4.7%), smartwatch (10.6%), home assistant (7.7%), and connected car (5.0%); (b) a question that elicited the respondents to indicate only the main device or equipment used to access Internet: mobile phone (44.2%), personal computer (26.2%), laptop (23.1%), tablet (6.0%), and others (TV, smartwatch, connected car, etc.) (0.5%). Overall, the data show that the mobile phone is the most preferred device, followed by personal computers, laptops, and tablets, although smartwatches and virtual home assistants are gradually gaining terrain too.

Internet consumption behaviour

The information collected shows that the greatest part of the Internet users, access it with a high frequency, that is, almost constantly (45.5%) or several times a day (46.3%), while only a small proportion indicated a lower frequency – every day or almost every day (7.1%), several times a week (0.8%) or several times a month or less (0.3%). The daily time allocated to the Internet goes as follows: most of the users spent between two and four hours a day (27.6%), a similar proportion (26.1%) spent between four and eight hours a day, while 13.6% are heavy users, spending more than eight hours per day; other users (18.6%) dedicate only one or two hours at most, 10.1% (from thirty to sixty minutes), while a very small proportion (4% of the users) stay below thirty minutes per day. Overall, the data show a high degree of penetration of the Internet in Spaniards' daily life. Concerning some of the devices used for Internet access, 23.4% of the respondents indicated, for example, that they dedicate one or two hours a day to scroll Internet through the mobile phone, while 22.2% of the respondents use the tablet, between thirty and sixty minutes per day, and 23.6% dedicate only between fifteen and thirty minutes, respectively.

Internet of Things: Virtual voice assistants (VVA)

A special block of the questionnaire was dedicated to collecting information about the most known VVA in Spain, such as Google Assistant, Amazon's Alexa, Apple's Siri, among others. For this purpose, dichotomous type questions (yes/no answers) were used, for example, to know which VVA were used by the respondent during the month before the interview, with the following results: Google Assistant goes first, being selected by 51.8% of the respondents (yes answer), followed by Apple's Siri, 38.5% and Amazon's Alexa, with 24.5%. Other VVA, such as Microsoft's Cortana (10.4%), Samsung's Bixby (5.7%), and Movistar's Aura (3.0%) all have much lower usage rates among the Spaniards.

Concerning the VVA's users behaviour, this information was captured with a question on the frequency of their usage, which returned interesting results: basically, more than half of the respondents (55.3%), stated that they never or almost never used VVA while the remaining half, indicated the following usage frequencies: 9.6% uses VVA almost constantly or several times a day, 4.7% every day or almost every day, 7.8% only several times per week, and 22.5% uses VVA only occasionally, several times a month or less. Among the most used devices to employ VVA, the mobile phone goes first, with 77.9% (yes answer reported, for the dichotomous question), followed by the intelligent speaker (31.5%), personal computer (16.7%), laptop (15.5%), the car (11.2%), TV (8.0%), and smartwatch (7.9%). A Likert-type question (1-completely unsatisfied and 5-very satisfied) measured the degree of satisfaction among the VVA users (mean 3.6 and median 4.0): the big bulk of the VVA users (90.2%) indicated an above the average level of satisfaction, of which, 15.1% were very satisfied.

A special block of dichotomous questions (yes/no, multiple choices allowed) focused on the main activities performed with the VVA, during the month before the interview, with the following feedback: 61.0% (yes answer) of the VVA users indicated the usage of VVA for general searches on the Internet, 50.0% pointed to meteorological and traffic consulting, 47.6% preferred to listen to music or the radio, 46.4% used VVA mainly for alerts, calendar planning and lists making, while 38.6% made phone calls, listen to the news (25.6%), or send messages (24.3%). A smaller proportion of the respondents indicated that the VVA was related to home automation control (19.5%) or online purchases/food delivery at home (7.2%).

Research design and data analysis

In this chapter, we set to identify latent profiles of IoT's users, with a special focus on the use of VVA. For this purpose, we apply latent class analysis (LCA; Lazarsfeld & Henry, 1968), an exploratory approach that can also be applied to categorical variables (see e.g. Cuadrado-García et al., 2018; Daenekindt & Roose, 2014). LCA is structuring the sample in clusters or segments and estimates, for each observation, the likelihood of belonging to only one cluster, conditioned on the set of variables used in the analysis (Magidson & Vermunt, 2001). The frequency of using VVA (codified in three levels), a proxy for the VVA users' behaviour, was employed here to segment the sample: (1) constant or almost daily users (14%); (2) several times per week (8%); (3) several times per month or less (22%); and (4) never or almost never (55%).

Intuitively, LCA procedure starts by estimating the so-called null model (1-class LCA) and, if this model is not a good fit for the data, the number of latent classes is gradually increased on a one-by-one basis each time, until it fails to reject the null model. LCA was performed with Latent Gold 4.5 (Vermunt & Magidson, 2008). Table 10.1, shows the goodness of fit statistics usually employed to select the LCA model for the analysis: the Bayesian Information Criterion (BIC), the Akaike Information Criterion (AIK), the Consistent Akaike Information Criterion (CAIC), and the chi-squared likelihood-ratio statistic (L2), this last statistic accounting for the unexplained association among the variables analysed (see Dayton, 1998; Raftery, 1986).

Table 10.1 The goodness of fit statistics for the LCA model

LCA model	L^2	*BIC(LL)*	*AIC(LL)*	*CAIC(LL)*	*No. par*	*df*	*p-value*	*Class. Error*
1-class	26,045.855	64,911.4718	64,880.5033	64,915.4718	4	11	1.0e-5639	0
2-class	11,6954.957	50,609.8233	50,540.144	50,618.8233	9	6	3.9e-2533	0
3-class	48,918.873	43,854.9256	43,746.5356	43,868.9256	14	1	6.3e-1065	0
4-class	2.9944	39,014.7434	38,867.6427	39,033.7434	19	−4	.	0
5-class	2.7501	39,063.2099	38,877.3984	39,087.2099	24	−9	.	0.2767

Source: Own estimation based on data from AIMC (2019).
Note: The model with 4 latent classes is the best choice as it has the lowest values for the BIC, AIC, and CAIC statistics.

The model selected is the one with four latent classes as it shows the lowest values for these criteria.

The parameters of the selected model

In Table 10.2, the first row stands for the relative size of each segment or cluster, thus indicating the proportion of individuals belonging to each cluster: cluster 1 (55% of the sample), cluster 2 (23%), cluster 3 (14%), and cluster 4 (8%), respectively. Furthermore, we present the row profiles of the LCA estimates due to their intuitive interpretation. In this fashion, the values in Table 10.2 indicate, for example, whether the individuals classified in a cluster are over- or under-represented among the individuals with similar behaviour (see bold values). Thus, VVA user in cluster 3 (14% of the sample) are over-represented among the VVA user who answer *Yes* to using VVA on a constant or almost daily manner, and *No* to the remaining alternatives (several times a week, several times a month, or less, and those who never use VVA). The estimates in Table 10.2 indicate the following probabilistic patterns of behaviour for the Spanish VVA users: more than half of the sample (cluster 1, 55%) never uses VVA (inactive VVA users); 23% of the sample (cluster 2), are occasional users of VVA devices, as they use them several times a month or less; cluster 3 (14%) represents the constant or daily users of VVA (intensive users), while in cluster 4 (8%) are overrepresented the individuals who use VVA devices several times a week (frequent users).

Results and discussion

VVA preferences and devices used

The results presented in Table 10.3 allows identifying the following probabilistic patterns emerging from the types of VVA preferred by the respondents: thus, the intensive VVA users (cluster 3), give the first preference to local VVA, such as Aura (Movistar), followed by Alexa (Amazon), Bixby (Samsung), and Cortana (Microsoft); on average, they also appear to be more

Table 10.2 Probabilistic patterns of VVA usage behaviour (row profiles, %)

	Cluster 1 (inactive VVA users)	*Cluster 2 (occasional VVA users)*	*Cluster 3 (intensive VVA users)*	*Cluster 4 (frequent VVA users)*	*Sample*
Cluster size	55%	23%	14%	8%	100%
(s.e.)	(0.0038)	(0.0032)	(0.0027)	(0.0021)	
VVA's frequency of use					
Constant or almost daily					
Yes	0%	0%	**100%**	0%	100%
No	**65%**	**26%**	0%	**9%**	100%
Several times a week					
Yes	0%	0%	0%	**100%**	100%
No	**60%**	**24%**	**16%**	0%	100%
Several times a month or less					
Yes	0%	**100%**	0%	0%	100%
No	**71%**	0%	**19%**	**10%**	100%
Never or almost never					
Yes	**100%**	0%	0%	0%	100%
No	0%	**50%**	**32%**	**17%**	100%

Source: Own estimation based on data from AIMC (2019).
Note: The probabilistic profile of each cluster is determined by the individuals overrepresented (see bold values which highlight the percentages greater/equal than the cluster size) among the individuals with a similar pattern of behaviour in that cluster.

skilled in terms of the equipment used to activate the VVA, as they prefer the intelligent speakers, smartwatches, smart TV, and tablets. The frequent VVA users (cluster 4), are more likely to choose Siri (Apple) and Google Assistant, followed by Cortana (Microsoft) and Bixby (Samsung), and in terms of equipment and devices, their main preferences go for the mobile phone, followed by the smart TV and smartwatch. The occasional VVA users (cluster 2), show a higher probability for using Google Assistant and Siri (Apple), and they exhibit a clear preference for the mobile phone as a device.

Activities performed with VVA

According to the results displayed in Table 10.4, the main activities for which VVA are employed, are the following. The intensive VVA users (cluster 3) are overrepresented for all the activities listed in the table (yes answer), although in terms of preferences, they have a higher likelihood to use VVA for more specific activities, such as house automation control, online purchases and home-delivered food, and news, music, and radio listening. The frequent VVA users (cluster 4), are more oriented towards the use of VVA for more common activities like, for example, phone calls and general searches on the Internet, alerts/agenda/calendar/lists, messages, and meteorological and traffic consulting. The occasional VVA users (cluster 2) instead, are rather inactive in terms of activities performed with the VVA, using the VVA mainly of general searches on the Internet, most likely also because of their lower level of awareness and skill about VVA and their usage.

Table 10.3 Types of VVA and the equipment or devices they are used with

	Cluster 1 (inactive VVA users)	*Cluster 2 (occasional VVA users)*	*Cluster 3 (intensive VVA users)*	*Cluster 4 (frequent VVA users)*	*Sample*
Cluster size	55%	23%	14%	8%	100%
Types of VVA used in the last month					
Alexa (Amazon)					
Yes	0%	10%	**71%**	**19%**	100%
No	0%	26%	44%	30%	100%
Google Assistant					
Yes	0%	**23%**	**49%**	**28%**	100%
No	0%	21%	52%	27%	100%
Aura (Movistar)					
Yes	0%	7%	**74%**	**18%**	100%
No	0%	23%	50%	28%	100%
Bixby (Samsung)					
Yes	0%	19%	**58%**	**23%**	100%
No	0%	22%	50%	28%	100%
Cortana (Microsoft)					
Yes	0%	21%	**53%**	**26%**	100%
No	0%	22%	50%	28%	100%
Siri (Apple)					
Yes	0%	**24%**	**47%**	**29%**	100%
No	0%	21%	52%	26%	100%
Equipment with which the VVA is used					
Personal computer or laptop					
Yes	0%	19%	**59%**	**22%**	100%
No	0%	23%	49%	28%	100%
Tablet					
Yes	0%	16%	**62%**	**22%**	100%
No	0%	23%	48%	28%	100%
Mobile phone					
Yes	0%	**24%**	**48%**	**28%**	100%
No	0%	18%	58%	24%	100%
Television					
Yes	0%	14%	**63%**	**24%**	100%
No	0%	23%	49%	28%	100%
Intelligent speaker					
Yes	0%	11%	**69%**	**21%**	100%
No	0%	28%	42%	30%	100%
Car					
Yes	0%	21%	**58%**	**21%**	100%
No	0%	22%	49%	28%	100%
Smartwatch					
Yes	0%	14%	**63%**	**23%**	100%
No	0%	23%	49%	28%	100%

Source: Own estimation based on data from AIMC (2019).

Note: The probabilistic profile of each cluster is determined by the individuals overrepresented (see bold values which highlight the percentages greater/equal than the cluster size) among the individuals with a similar pattern of behaviour in that cluster. To simplify the interpretation of each cluster's profile, we focus only the Yes answers.

Table 10.4 Probabilistic patterns of the activities performed with VVA

	Cluster 1 (inactive VVA users)	*Cluster 2 (occasional VVA users)*	*Cluster 3 (intensive VVA users)*	*Cluster 4 (frequent VVA users)*	*Sample*
Cluster size	55%	23%	14%	8%	100%
Types of activities for which VVA was used					
General searches					
Yes	0%	**23%**	**49%**	**28%**	100%
No	0%	21%	52%	27%	100%
Meteorological or traffic consulting					
Yes	0%	17%	**57%**	**25%**	100%
No	0%	27%	44%	29%	100%
House automation control					
Yes	0%	6%	**79%**	**16%**	100%
No	0%	26%	44%	30%	100%
Phone calls					
Yes	0%	19%	**53%**	**28%**	100%
No	0%	24%	49%	27%	100%
Send messages					
Yes	0%	16%	**58%**	**25%**	100%
No	0%	24%	48%	28%	100%
Alerts/agenda/calendar/lists					
Yes	0%	15%	**60%**	**26%**	100%
No	0%	29%	42%	29%	100%
Music or radio listening					
Yes	0%	14%	**62%**	**24%**	100%
No	0%	30%	40%	30%	100%
News listening					
Yes	0%	12%	**67%**	**21%**	100%
No	0%	26%	45%	30%	100%
Purchase/ask for food delivery at home					
Yes	0%	11%	**71%**	**18%**	100%
No	0%	23%	49%	28%	100%

Source: Own estimation based on data from AIMC (2019).

Note: The probabilistic profile of each cluster is determined by the individuals overrepresented (see bold values which highlight the percentages greater/equal than the cluster size) among the individuals with a similar pattern of behaviour in that cluster. To simplify the interpretation of each cluster's profile, we focus only the Yes answers.

Sociodemographic profiles of the VVA users

The sociodemographic variables used to characterize the profiles of the VVA users are presented in Table 10.5. The estimates show that the intensive VVA users (cluster 3) are, on average, more likely to be men, below 44 years of age, single or living in couple (married or unmarried), and belonging to a

Table 10.5 Sociodemographic profiles of the VVA users and non-users

	Cluster 1 (inactive VVA users)	*Cluster 2 (occasional VVA users)*	*Cluster 3 (intensive VVA users)*	*Cluster 4 (frequent VVA users)*	*Sample*
Cluster size	55%	23%	14%	8%	100%
Gender					
Female	**56%**	**25%**	12%	7%	100%
Male	**55%**	22%	**15%**	**8%**	100%
Personal status					
Single	54%	**24%**	**14%**	**8%**	100%
Married	**56%**	22%	**15%**	**8%**	100%
Widowed	**62%**	19%	12%	7%	100%
Divorced/separated	**61%**	19%	12%	7%	100%
Couple not married	52%	**25%**	**15%**	**8%**	100%
Type of habitat (thousands of inhabitants)					
>10	**57%**	**23%**	14%	6%	100%
10–50	**56%**	**23%**	14%	7%	100%
50–200	**55%**	**23%**	14%	**8%**	100%
>200	54%	21%	**16%**	**8%**	100%
Number of children in the household					
None	**58%**	22%	12%	**8%**	100%
One	49%	**24%**	**18%**	**8%**	100%
Two	50%	22%	**19%**	**9%**	100%
Three	41%	**28%**	**24%**	7%	100%
Four or more	36%	21%	**36%**	7%	100%
Age					
14–29 years	44%	**28%**	**18%**	**9%**	100%
30–44 years	52%	**23%**	**17%**	**8%**	100%
45–59 years	**59%**	22%	12%	7%	100%
<=60 years	**68%**	18%	8%	6%	100%
Education level					
Primary or less	55%	**23%**	**15%**	7%	100%
Second grade	54%	**23%**	**15%**	**8%**	100%
University	**56%**	22%	14%	**8%**	100%
Occupational status					
Self-employed	52%	22%	**17%**	**8%**	100%
Employed	54%	**23%**	**15%**	**8%**	100%
Student	46%	**29%**	**15%**	**10%**	100%
House works	**59%**	**23%**	11%	7%	100%
Unemployed	**62%**	21%	11%	7%	100%
Retired	**68%**	17%	9%	6%	100%

Source: Own estimation based on data from AIMC (2019).

Note: The probabilistic profile of each cluster is determined by the individuals overrepresented (see bold values which highlight the percentages greater/equal than the cluster size) among the individuals with a similar pattern of behaviour in that cluster.

household with children; they exhibit an active occupational status, being either employed, self-employed, or studying; educational level and the type of habitat are two variables that do not seem to play a relevant discriminant role here, as the intensive VVA users are likely to be found in all types of living areas and across all educational profiles. The frequent VVA users (cluster 4) share some common features with the intensive VVA users in terms of genre (more likely to be men), personal status (single and married or unmarried couples), age (below 44 years of age), and occupational status (self-employed, employed, or students); in terms of education, they are more likely to have finished the second grade or hold a university degree; on average, they belong to smaller size households, either with no children or no more than two; in the same fashion, they have a higher likelihood of living in a medium and large urban area (above 50,000 inhabitants). The occasional VVA users, segment (cluster 2) are, on average, women, below 44 years of age, either single or unmarried couples, and live in areas no larger than 200,000 inhabitants; they belong to households with one or three children and their highest educational degree don't go beyond the second grade; concerning the occupational status, they are either working (employed or house works) or still studying. As for the non-VVA users (cluster 1), on average, they are older (45–59 years and above) and reported no children in the household; their educational background is rather mixed, including both university graduates and primary studies, and their occupational status is lower, being either retired, unemployed, or dedicated to house works; they are more likely to be found in living areas with less than 200,000 inhabitants and in terms of personal status, they are either single or live as an unmarried couple. Last but not least, while gender does play a discriminant role for the VVA users, in the case of the non-VVA users, the estimates show that they could be either men or women. Overall, the sociodemographic variables appear to be more important for the segmentation of the sample in VVA users and non-VVA users, respectively, with gender playing a more significant role.

Conclusions

This research has focused on the usage of VVA in Spain with the purpose of identifying clusters of VVA users emerging from the frequency of VVA's usage habits. The LCA method has returned three segments of active VVA users (intensive, frequent, and occasional), representing 45% of the sample, and one inactive segment, accounting for the remaining 55% of the sample size. The results show that the VVA awareness and their usage could play a discriminant role when comes to individuals' social and cultural status. Thus, intensive and frequent VVA users are likely to be, on average, more skilled and knowledgeable about a greater variety of VVA (Alexa Amazon, Google Assistant, Aura Movistar, Cortana Microsoft, Bixby Samsung, and Siri Apple), about all the devices available to be employed with the VVA (Tablet, PC, mobile phone, TV, intelligent speakers, cars. and smartwatches), and the whole range of activities performed with the VVA and measured in the survey (general searches, weather/traffic checking, house automation control, phone calls, messaging, music, news, and radio listening, purchases/food ordering, and alerts/calendar/lists).

This said, each segment nevertheless, has a clear preference when comes to the VVA used (intensive VVA users prefer most Aura Movistar and Alexa Amazon, while the frequent VVA users have Siri Apple and Google Assistant as main preferences), the devices employed (intensive VVA users prefer the intelligent speakers, smartwatches, TV, and tablets, while the frequent VVA users put in the first place the mobile phones, followed by TV and smartwatches), and the type of activities performed (intensive VVA users give preference to more complex activities such as house automation control, purchases/food ordering, and news, music, and radio listening, while the frequent VVA users segment use VVA general searches, phone calls, and alerts/calendar/lists issues). The degree of awareness and knowledge about VVA is much lower in the case of the occasional VVA users' segment: the only VVA used are Siri Apple and Google Assistant with the mobile phone as the unique device and only for general searches.

In the same fashion, the results also indicate that sociodemographic variables are important social status markers, especially when comes to the distinction between VVA users and non-users, a special role being played by gender and age. In this respect, women have a higher likelihood of belonging to the clusters of occasional and non-VVA users, while men are either intensive or frequent users. Also, generational differences are clearly differentiating the VVA active users (on average, younger, between 14 and 44 years of age) from the inactive ones (45–59 and above 60 years of age). Personal status' discriminant role is less relevant, compared to gender and age: the inactive segment reunites individuals either married, divorced, or separated and the three segments of active VVA users are characterized mainly by single and couples (either married or unmarried). As for the size of the households, the estimates support the generational gap between VVA users and non-users: while the intensive VVA users reported the presence of children in the household (from one to four or more), the frequent and the occasional VVA users' segments reported either none or no more than two/three children in the household. Occupational status has a stronger discriminant power in distinguishing the VVA users (on average, active in the labour market or studying) from the non-users (unemployed, retired, or dedicated to house works). Finally, the educational level does not seem to play a significant role in the characterization of the four clusters. One potential reason could be that, according to international evidence, 58% of the US VVA users employ them on smartphones to find information on local businesses, of which 46% do so daily (Murphy, 2018), thus overcoming the potential barriers imposed by the level of finished studies.

Finally, this research has focused on the VVA (type of VVA, devices, activities, frequency of usage), leaving aside other variables in the characterization of the segments, such as the frequency of using the Internet, the time spent online, or the main devices used to access the Internet, satisfaction with the VVA, most used social networks, privacy and security concerns, among others. For some of these variables, we only present descriptive statistics, although their employment in the characterization of the clusters could offer additional insights.

Business implications

All in all, the results indicate that more resources and efforts must be made, to popularize VVA, their usage, and the devices used to employ them, both by policymakers and firms. Existing evidence for other countries, like the US (see Murphy, 2018) or worldwide (see Kemp, 2020), on the use of VVA, also highlights the gender gap, in favour of men (see Kemp, 2020; Murphy, 2018) and the age gap, with older individuals, above 55 years of age more likely to be non-users of VVA, although some of them would not be reluctant in doing it (see Murphy, 2018). In terms of the most popular VVA devices, our findings are in line with the existing evidence showing that smartphones are taking over personal computers and laptops, in the US, for example, the mobile voice search being ranked second after the mobile browser (Sterling, 2019). Overall, VVA are also gaining market share in Spain, inviting businesses to adapt their business models and the customer relationship management strategies to better communicate the value proposition of their products and services, given that VVA are called to change the way customers interact with products and brands.

Bibliography

AIMC (2019). Navegantes en la red – Encuesta AIMC a usuarios de Internet / Internet surfers – AIMC survey of Internet users. *Asociación para la Investigación de los Medios de Comunicación*. Online. https://www.aimc.es/otros-estudios-trabajos/navegantes-la-red/

Alaa, M., Zaidan, A.A., Zaidan, B.B., Talal, M., & Kiah, M.L.M. (2017). A review of smart home applications based on Internet of Things. *Journal of Network and Computer Applications, 97*, 48–65.

Aldossari, M.Q., & Sidorova, A. (2020). Consumer acceptance of Internet of Things (IoT): Smart home context. *Journal of Computer Information Systems, 60*(6), 507–517.

Andrienko, O. (2020, August 27). Leveraging voice search for local business (study). https://www.semrush.com/blog/voice-search-local-seo/

Balaji, M.S., & Roy, S.K. (2017). Value co-creation with Internet of things technology in the retail industry. *Journal of Marketing Management, 33*(1–2), 7–31.

Bello, O., & Zeadally, S. (2019). Toward efficient smartification of the Internet of Things (IoT) services. *Future Generation Computer Systems, 92*, 663–673.

Chang, Y., Dong, X., & Sun, W. (2014). Influence of characteristics of the Internet of Things on consumer purchase intention. *Social Behavior and Personality: An International Journal, 42*(2), 321–330.

Cuadrado-García, M., Filimon, N., & Montoro-Pons, J. (2018). Picturing Spanish filmgoers: Motives, barriers and film theatres. *Regional Science Inquiry, 10*, 45–60.

Daenekindt, S., & Roose, H. (2014). Ways of preferring: Distinction through the 'what' and the 'how' of cultural consumption. *Journal of Consumer Culture, 17*(1), 25–45.

Dayton, C.M. (1998). *Latent class scaling analysis*. Sage University Paper Series on QASS, 07–126. Sage Publishers.

Ding, Y., Jin, M., Li, S., & Feng, D. (2021). Smart logistics based on the Internet of Things technology: An overview. *International Journal of Logistics Research and Applications, 24*(4), 323–345.

Gao, L., & Bai, X. (2014). A unified perspective on the factors influencing consumer acceptance of internet of things technology. *Asia Pacific Journal of Marketing and Logistics, 26*(2), 211–231.

Giannikas, V., McFarlane, D., & Strachan, J. (2019). Towards the deployment of customer orientation: A case study in third-party logistics. *Computers in Industry, 104*, 75–87.

Hassan, R., Qamar, F., Hasan, M.K., Aman, A.H.M., & Ahmed, A.S. (2020). Internet of Things and its applications: A comprehensive survey. *Symmetry, 12*(10), 1674.

Hoffman, D.L., & Novak, T.P. (2018). Consumer and object experience in the internet of things: An assemblage theory approach. *Journal of Consumer Research, 44*(6), 1178–1204.

Kemp, S. (2020, January 30). *Digital 2020: Global digital overview*. https://datareportal.com/reports/digital-2020-global-digital-overview.

Lazarsfeld, S.J., & Henry, N.W. (1968). *Latent structure analysis*. Houghton Mifflin Company.

Magidson, J., &Vermunt, J.K. (2001). Latent class factor and cluster models, bi-plots, and related graphical displays. In M. Sober & M. Becker (Eds.), *Sociological methodology* (Vol. 31, pp. 223–264). Blackwell Publishers.

Miranda, J., Mäkitalo, N., Garcia-Alonso, J., Berrocal, J., Mikkonen, T., Canal, C., & Murillo, J.M. (2015). From the Internet of Things to the Internet of People. *IEEE Internet Computing, 19*(2), 40–47.

Murphy, R. (2018, April 26). Voice search for local business study. https://www.brightlocal.com/research/voice-search-for-local-business-study/.

Nauman, A., Qadri, Y.A., Amjad, M., Zikria, Y.B., Afzal, M.K., & Kim, S.W. (2020). Multimedia Internet of Things: A comprehensive survey. *IEEE Access, 8*, 8202–8250.

Nižetić, S., Šolić, P., González-de, D.L.D.I., & Patrono, L. (2020). Internet of Things (IoT): Opportunities, issues and challenges towards a smart and sustainable future. *Journal of Cleaner Production, 274*, 122877.

PwC. (2018). *Consumer intelligence series: Prepare for the voice revolution*. https://www.pwc.com/us/en/services/consulting/library/consumer-intelligence-series/voice-assistants.html.

Raftery, A.E. (1986). Choosing models for cross-classifications. *American Sociological Review, 51*, 145–146.

Singh, R.P., Javaid, M., Haleem, A., & Suman, R. (2020). Internet of Things (IoT) applications to fight against COVID-19 pandemic. *Diabetes & Metabolic Syndrome: Clinical Research & Reviews, 14*(4), 521–524.

Sterling, G. (2019, December 23). Nine voice search stats to close out 2019. Search Engine Land. https://searchengineland.com/nine-voice-search-stats-to-close-out-2019-326884.

van Deursen, A.J., van der Zeeuw, A., de Boer, P., Jansen, G., & van Rompay, T. (2021). Digital inequalities in the Internet of Things: Differences in attitudes, material access, skills, and usage. *Information, Communication & Society, 24*(2), 258–276.

Vermunt, J.K., & Magidson, J. (2008). *LG-syntax user's guide: Manual for Latent GOLD 4.5 syntax module*. Statistical Innovations Inc.

Wortmann, F., & Flüchter, K. (2015). Internet of things. *Business & Information Systems Engineering, 57*(3), 221–224.

11 Digital Trends of European consumers' behaviour

Forecasts and predictions

Małgorzata Bartosik-Purgat and Nela Filimon

Introduction

Information and communication technologies (ICT) impact a wide range of areas of behaviour and activities, of both individual consumers and businesses (including suppliers, manufacturers, distributors, and post-selling services). The recent development and increase in the use of the Internet and digital communication tools was also due to global factors, e.g. the COVID-19 pandemic and the related restrictions on the movement of people around the world (Dvorak et al., 2021; Sharma & Kapoor, 2021). Other influential factors include generational changes and different digital skills and preferences of consumers of various age cohorts, increasing access to Internet resources, the rapid development of mobile telephony and devices, and changes in people's lifestyles (Berraies et al., 2017; Verma et al., 2021). All these factors have led to not just changes in people's lives but also to the emergence of new business models based mainly on digital technologies. This new situation is thus challenging for consumers, producers, and retailers alike.

The significance of ICT's impact on consumers' behaviour may be considered, as mentioned above, from the perspective of the individual consumer, producer, and retailer. The main contextual factors and activities involved have been presented throughout the chapters in this book. However, the main objective of this chapter is to identify and indicate the direction of future developments in the use of ICTs by these three above-mentioned groups of actors. A literature review of the newest scientific publications on the topic reveals several trends expected in relation to ICTs' influence, e.g. e-commerce development, increased social media, and mobile usage, eco-trends, online communication between consumers and retailers, increased personalisation of the firms' customer-relationship management strategies, usage of virtual voice assistants (VVA), home automation, and other aspects of consumer behaviour.

E-commerce in Europe

The global situation caused by Covid-19 pandemic has led to more European consumers making purchases in online stores. Many of them have even started to buy products in online shops that were previously only purchased

DOI: 10.4324/9781003263685-14

in brick-and-mortar stores and forecasts of retail e-commerce revenue from 2017 to 2025 indicate a permanent increase. Expectations of e-commerce revenue in Europe show growth to 569.2 billion U.S. dollars in 2025 (Statista.com, 2021a). Likewise, forecasts about the number of e-commerce users in Europe by 2025 indicate an increase to 569.8 million in 2025 (Statista.com, 2021b). These increased numbers are likely to be due to not only the COVID-19 pandemic but also to a wider customer preference for online shopping. The features and advantages of e-commerce are also important to note here, including the convenience of such form of shopping, time employed to compare products and services, usually lower prices for many products and services, return options, convenient and technologically developed methods of payment and delivery, and the use of new tools such as virtual voice assistants (VVA), or chatbots, among others (Nogueira et al., 2021).

Communication with e-customers (including social media and mobile phones)

Good customer service, and above all, proper communication is an important challenge for the retailers. Good communication and customer-relationship building and management are, and will continue to be, the main avenue to increasing the number of new consumers and maintaining the loyal ones (Collin-Lachaud & Diallo, 2021). In the case of online communication – which will certainly be the main channel for contacting and sharing information – VVA and chatbots will play an important role, alongside traditional channels like social platforms and instant messengers (Chen et al., 2021; Chesney et al., 2017; Collin-Lachaud & Diallo, 2021). Communication through these instruments is, first of all, attractive especially for young customers, and second, it also contributes to accelerating business–customer interaction, and to reduce costs in comparison to manual solutions (Hsieh & Lee, 2021). What is more, an increasing number of young consumers are using, for example, VVA when making online purchases (voice commerce), such as Amazon Alexa (Hsieh & Lee, 2021; Jiménez-Barreto et al., 2021). Furthermore, generally, younger people usually prefer to be involved in the vlogosphere rather than in the blogosphere when applying online tools. When using v-commerce, consumers can give the appropriate command to the virtual voice assistant and indicate what they want to buy and how they want to pay. They should also have their payment card connected with the smartphone. Then the payment for purchases done by the virtual voice assistant will be made automatically through this card (Chen et al., 2021). Therefore, retailers, wishing to enable v-commerce for these consumers, should enable such technology. Digital technologies are also expected to increase even further the interaction between consumers and companies or brands, through online mass collaborations (e.g. prosumers) or the use of collective intelligence to solve specific problems (e.g. crowdsourcing) or to submit ideas to create new products/services.

Producers and retailers should also follow the new trends and developments in the social media realm, first because the number of social media users keeps increasing (Kemp, 2020, 2021); and, second, because social media are one of the most widespread instruments for maintaining communication between retailers and consumers. This trend is likely to continue thanks to an increase in the use of mobile devices, which account for most social media activity (Ju et al., 2021). A few years ago, it was not even possible to run Facebook on a phone smoothly. Currently, almost all consumers have a combination of Facebook, YouTube, LinkedIn, Snapchat, Instagram, and TikTok applications on their smartphones. This means that in the future people are expected to be more divided between the various social networking portals. What can be seen now, and what may increase in the future, are the differences between the communities of individual social platforms. As a result, producers and retailers have to use not only the "old" and the most widespread social platforms like Facebook, but also those platforms that are used by particular segments of consumers (e.g. generation Z) like TikTok, Snapchat, and others, which might not be widely used or even present yet in many business sectors. In other words, companies using social media to promote their activities will have to choose the platforms which most of their customers use. What is more, while communicating with the customers, companies should use the correct form of the content. Nowadays, content posted on social networks is often in the shape of short films, because even the best text cannot compete with video reach, especially when it comes to selling products and services online (García-de-Frutos & Estrella-Ramón, 2021; Rohde & Mau, 2021); consumer guides, visualisations, tutorials, reviews, arrangements all become more understandable in short films format. In addition, video marketing also allows for coverage and live broadcast, which, combined with influencer marketing, offers powerful audience engagement with the commercial message (Rohde & Mau, 2021). This trend is likely to be maintained in the future (especially in the next few years) but will certainly also evolve and reach not just the youngest consumers but also the older ones, who are using these new forms of obtaining information more and more often. Nevertheless, with the usage of the video for content presentation, the companies should also emphasise in the messages the problems the customers are struggling with. Such expectations were observed during COVID-19 pandemic (Rohde & Mau, 2021). They should also focus on providing reliable information and on building a long-term, continuous relationship with their customers, which will help to expand the number of loyal customers and increase performance.

Social media not only allow contact between people, and gathering and sharing information, but may also be used as an efficient platform for e-commerce (Jami Pour et al., 2021; Saarijärvi et al., 2018). Consumers can now conveniently and quickly buy products via social media platforms, e.g. Facebook and Instagram. In addition, new business models such as live-commerce (also called live-streaming) – which started in China in 2014 and has now begun to expand in many European markets (Gibreel et al., 2018;

Qin & De-Juan-Vigaray, 2021) – is developing rapidly. It should be underlined that the increase of such new activities and possibilities through social media is usually impacted by the growth of mobile devices' use. They allow a faster and more comfortable access to social media platforms. These ways of social media usage will certainly continue to grow in the future not only in Europe but also in other world's markets (China was the pioneer of this method of selling). Such solutions give an opportunity especially for small businesses that can use social platforms or marketplaces, such as LiveMarket (a marketplace available in Poland that is a combination of Allegro and TikTok) (Mokrzycka, 2021).

The next issue associated with social media, as already mentioned above, is the increasing use of mobile devices (e.g. smartphones, tablets, etc.) by consumers. Producers and retailers should be prepared for a scenario in which an even greater importance will have to be attached to the optimisation of content for mobile devices (Kim & Kim, 2021) and it seems likely that a large part of the social media market will be dedicated exclusively to smartphones. Indeed, the future of social media is inextricably linked to mobile devices (Collin-Lachaud & Diallo, 2021), which is why mobile applications for mobile sales will be a must-have option for all e-retailers in the coming years.

Gathering information about consumers and personalisation

On top of communication, both producers and retailers should constantly monitor the market and try to identify the needs and capabilities of their potential buyers. For this purpose, it seems necessary to use solutions based on data collection, processing, and marketing automation. These activities include, among others, big data analysis (BDA), machine learning (ML), and artificial intelligence (AI) (Gupta et al., 2021; Jiménez-Barreto et al., 2021). Skilful data analysis allows companies to better reach customers, understand their needs and behaviours, and build engagement. Marketing automation tools and their associated functions (e.g. tracking visitors on the website, autoresponders, email marketing, lead nurturing and lead scoring, forms and pop-ups, landing pages, dynamic content, analytics, and reports, etc.) can also help reach customers and improve retailers' communication with them (Gupta et al., 2021). They can likewise help to identify users on websites and help to match the correct message to address to them. Marketing automation tools also help to segment potential customers and define their preferences, and thus retailers can create campaigns targeted at specific groups.

By knowing what the client is guided by during making purchasing decisions, retailers can not only personalise their offer but also make better business and strategic decisions. Some researchers emphasise that personalisation is, and will continue to be the key to "customers' hearts and wallets" (Huang & Zhou, 2019; Tran et al., 2020, 2021) as many customers who shop online are currently irritated by content and offers that are not adjusted to them. Personalisation of products and services – e.g. adaptation to the customers' needs and situation – should be based on an analysis of their behaviour history on the website, previous transactions, payment methods, and other data from the network, including personal data from social media. Proper adaptation for consumers' needs may also be achieved by the implementation of AI tools (Jiménez-Barreto et al., 2021), as they can encourage customers to make a specific purchase by providing them with perfectly matched products. In the near future, e-commerce (e-commerce 4.0) will likely develop using virtual and augmented reality, and the possibility of making voice purchases (Hsieh & Lee, 2021), as it was mentioned above. Some online stores already use the possibilities offered by augmented, and virtual reality (Castillo & Bigne, 2021), thanks to which customers can, for example, virtually try on clothes, choose cosmetics or check how a certain piece of furniture or paint colour will look in their apartment (Herrero-Crespo et al., 2021).

Eco-consumers' awareness and green marketing

In the near future, consumers will expect the main business players in the e-commerce industry to reduce the negative impact of their activities on the natural environment and to seek and implement environmental-friendly methods of doing business (Calderon-Monge et al., 2020; De Canio et al., 2021). In the coming years, these expectations will surely increase as consumers become more eco-aware and will be less reluctant to, for example, buy products with excess plastic packaging. It is also worth mentioning that many young consumers underline that they already take into account the environmental impact of the product and production process when making a purchase (Eastman & Iyer, 2021; Göçer & Sevil Oflaç, 2017).

The growing popularity of plant-based meals is also a manifestation of concern for the natural environment (Borusiak et al., 2021). In practice, more and more restaurants specialising in vegetarian and vegan cuisine are opening and, year by year, consumers are more and more willing to declare their readiness to limit meat consumption or even eliminate it from their diets (Armstrong Soule & Sekhon, 2019; Borusiak et al., 2021). Furthermore, in the next few years, in addition to plant-based lifestyles, the food industry will likely be influenced by the growing popularity of climatarianism (Dakin et al., 2021), e.g. consumers who are guided not so much by the ingredients, but rather by the origin of the ingredients (Dakin et al., 2021; Milfont et al., 2021). They do not have strict rules about what kind of food they buy and can eat, but it is important instead, what path a particular ingredient "travelled" before it reached the table and what carbon footprint has left during production and transportation (Milfont et al., 2021). As such, climatarians focus primarily on local food and on buying organic products, and by so doing, they try to keep the production of waste and pollution to a minimum.

Due to the growing eco-awareness of consumers, it is also worth considering how businesses care and should care for nature in the future.

Nowadays, eco-awareness belongs to one of the most widespread elements of companies' strategies, and especially firms that are perceived as non-ecological and which litter the environment may experience even greater declines in sales in the future (Amoako et al., 2021a; Papadas et al., 2017). Communication to consumers (the potential buyers) about eco-awareness and eco-activities may thus be a good element of a company's social responsibility programme and green marketing (eco-marketing) plan (Ali, 2021; Amoako et al., 2021a; Eastman & Iyer, 2021). Green marketing is based on the belief that in increasingly conscious societies, consumers will be more likely to choose products and services from those companies that are perceived as "more eco-friendly" (Ali, 2021; Papadas et al., 2017). However, sometimes companies promote themselves as allegedly green, when in fact, they continue to pollute the environment on a massive scale. In this case, we are dealing with the so-called greenwashing (Kurpierz & Smith, 2020). Such unethical actions can lead to brand image loss and the subsequent loss of those customers who take environmental issues very seriously. The basis of green marketing should be honesty, or at the very least, it must correlate with real actions aimed at improving the situation of the planet (Sun & Wang, 2020).

Payments and delivery in e-commerce

According to both e-commerce firms and e-consumers, the possibility of using diverse digital payments is an absolute must-have for an online retailer. A narrow offer of payment methods applied by an e-retailer is one of the reasons why customers will withdraw from a transaction (Grüschow et al., 2016). Nowadays, the possibility of paying by credit card or fast transfer may not be enough. Mobile payments are the future: a service configured to complete the purchase with almost one click (Flavián et al., 2020) as, for example, the Polish mobile payments BLIK, which offers a distinct advantage to its users. Next, deferred payments are still a developing option in e-commerce, but they may be used by many consumers in the future (Cicala, 2021).

Regarding delivery options, online retailers offer now more often better conditions for purchased products' delivery than during the pre-pandemic times. These areas will become even more important in the future. For example, one-day delivery – which for several years has been one of the most important factors influencing the decision to purchase – is becoming even more popular, especially in larger urban agglomerations, because it is physically possible, due to the closer proximity to logistics centres (Bergmann et al., 2020; Kandula et al., 2021). It will still be a significant issue for online retailers that, in addition to traditional delivery forms, use lockers that facilitate the pickup of parcels. In addition, the largest e-commerce firms (e.g. Amazon) have already rolled-out the use of drones to deliver purchases (Cokyasar, 2021).

Finally, another very important element in the e-commerce process is the possibility of returning goods (Rintamäki et al., 2021). During the

COVID-19 pandemic, many brands were determined to give customers the possibility of withdrawing from their purchasing decision and thus decided to allow customers to return online purchased goods. Additionally, some online retailers have extended the possible return time from 14 days to 30 days (and in many cases even longer).

Cross border e-commerce and international e-consumers

Consumers in the 21st century very often cross not only the physical borders of countries but also virtual borders when they buy products in online shops. The COVID-19 pandemic caused lockdowns in many countries of the world, meaning that consumers could no longer travel and shop abroad. This situation caused an increase of purchases from international online platforms, available in many countries (e.g. E-bay, AliExpress, and Amazon).

Due to e-consumers' growing interest in shopping on international online platforms, middle and small producers and e-retailers may consider the possibility of selling their products in the international arena (Cassia & Magno, 2021). The given online platform through which a company sells needs to be properly prepared and equipped with additional functionalities to which consumers from a particular market are accustomed to (Cassia & Magno, 2021; Goldman et al., 2020). For example, it should present prices in the local currency, handle foreign payments (e.g. via PayPal), and offer courier deliveries. Additionally, after deciding to start an e-business on a foreign market, a company should look at not only the cultural conditions but also the purchasing habits of potential customers, which often differ significantly in terms of the products themselves, the method of their presentation, and also the payment system (e.g. use of mobile devices, instalment purchases) and method of delivery. It is likewise very important to prepare product descriptions in the language of a particular society, making it easier for consumers to find out more about an offer and make an informed purchase decision (Mou et al., 2020). In the same fashion, an international survey on global consumers from 29 countries, run by CSA Research (2020) states that 76% of the consumers are more likely to purchase a product if the information is presented in their own language and 40% prefer the local-language sites. Conversely, incorrect translations and linguistic errors will dissuade customers and arouse distrust and a feeling of lack of credibility on a particular e-shop (Huang & Chang, 2019; Mou et al., 2020).

In addition to the above-mentioned factors, another very important element in international e-commerce is getting to know the specific context of foreign countries in which the company intends to operate. Knowledge of the customs of a particular market will help firms to properly prepare the offer and other promotional activities in the e-shop. For example, China's biggest e-consumption holiday is not Black Friday, but Singles' Day (November 11), when Chinese consumers spend enormous amounts of money shopping for all kinds of products (BusinessInsider, 2021).

All the companies' activities indicated above and associated with the implementation of innovations will certainly contribute to improving the customer experience (Amoako et al., 2021b). Customer experience's significance grows more and more and will also gain more importance in the future because it relates to consolidating and deepening the relationship with the client (Jami Pour et al., 2021). Customer experience aims to ensure that the entire experience related to the product offer and the company is as pleasant as possible and effectively influences customers' purchasing decisions (Marmat, 2021).

In conclusion, the COVID-19 pandemic has forced consumers to change their habits, and online shopping has been a way for them to fulfil their shopping needs in almost every area of their lives. Moreover, many consumers are aware that their purchases should start with looking at Internet sources, even if they make the final purchase offline. E-commerce will certainly develop and increase in the future; it will be popular form shopping for many consumers, especially those from younger generations. But, retailers should also not forget about those consumers who still prefer (and will continue to prefer in the future) doing shopping in stationary stores. Some researchers underline that the future (pandemic and post-pandemic times) of commerce will be seen in the blurring of lines between online and offline sales (e.g. Dvorak et al., 2021; Kannan & Kulkarni, 2021). As such, omnichannel strategies and the diversification of sales methods will be important solutions. The omnichannel strategy complements and drives different forms of reaching potential customers, e.g. online store, website, promotion and sales via social media (s-commerce), sales platforms, and sales by phone. All of these should dovetail with the others (Mahadevan & Joshi, 2021). Nevertheless, retailers will have to constantly monitor the development of new technologies and try to implement them in their stores (Herrero-Crespo et al., 2021). What is more, they will have to also check the level of acceptance of these new technologies by their potential customers and as such will have to permanently gather information about the needs and preferences of purchasers.

Bibliography

Ali, M. (2021). A social practice theory perspective on green marketing initiatives and green purchase behavior. *Cross Cultural & Strategic Management, 28*(4), 815–838. https://doi.org/10.1108/CCSM-12-2020-0241.

Amoako, G.K., Doe, J.K., & Dzogbenuku, R.K. (2021a). Perceived firm ethicality and brand loyalty: The mediating role of corporate social responsibility and perceived green marketing. *Society and Business Review, 16*(3), 398–419. https://doi.org/10.1108/SBR-05-2020-0076.

Amoako, G.K., Doe, J.K., & Neequaye, E.K. (2021b). Online innovation and repurchase intentions in hotels: The mediating effect of customer experience. *International Hospitality Review*, Vol. ahead-of-print No. ahead-of-print. https://doi.org/10.1108/IHR-02-2021-0008.

Armstrong Soule, C.A., & Sekhon, T. (2019). Preaching to the middle of the road: Strategic differences in persuasive appeals for meat anti-consumption. *British Food Journal, 121*(1), 157–171. https://doi.org/10.1108/BFJ-03-2018-0209.

Bergmann, F.M., Wagner, S.M., & WInkenbach, M. (2020). Integrating first-mile pickup and last-mile delivery on shared vehicle routes for efficient urban e-commerce distribution. *Transportation Research Part B: Methodological, 131*, 26–62. https://doi.org/10.1016/j.trb.2019.09.013.

Berraies, S., Ben Yahia, K., & Hannachi, M. (2017). Identifying the effects of perceived values of mobile banking applications on customers: Comparative study between baby boomers, generation X and generation Y. *International Journal of Bank Marketing, 35*(6), 1018–1038. https://doi.org/10.1108/IJBM-09-2016-0137.

Borusiak, B., Szymkowiak, A., Kucharska, B, Gálova, J., & Mravcová, A. (2021). Predictors of intention to reduce meat consumption due to environmental reasons – Results from Poland and Slovakia. *Meat Science, 184*, 108674. https://doi.org/10.1016/j.meatsci.2021.108674.

BusinessInsider. (2021, August 20). *E-commerce: oto pięć zagranicznych rynków, na które powinni zwrócić uwagę polscy sprzedawcy* [E-commerce: here are five foreign markets that Polish retailers should pay attention to]. https://businessinsider.com.pl/finanse/e-commerce-oto-piec-zagranicznych-rynkow-na-ktore-powinni-zwrocic-uwage-polscy/ql4tvhs.

Calderon-Monge, E., Redondo-Rodriguez, R.G., & Ramírez-Hurtado, J.M. (2020). Narrowing the gap between consumer purchasing intention and behaviour through ecolabelling: A challenge for eco-entrepreneurism. *British Food Journal*, Vol. ahead-of-print No. ahead-of-print. https://doi.org/10.1108/BFJ-09-2020-0874.

Cassia, F., & Magno, F. (2021). Cross-border e-commerce as a foreign market entry mode among SMEs: The relationship between export capabilities and performance. *Review of International Business and Strategy*, Vol. ahead-of-print No. ahead-of-print. https://doi.org/10.1108/RIBS-02-2021-0027.

Castillo, S.M.J., & Bigne, E. (2021). A model of adoption of AR-based self-service technologies: A two country comparison. *International Journal of Retail & Distribution Management, 49*(7), 875–898. https://doi.org/10.1108/IJRDM-09-2020-0380.

Chen, J.V., Thi Le, H., & Tran, S.T.T. (2021). Understanding automated conversational agent as a decision aid: Matching agent's conversation with customer's shopping task. *Internet Research, 31*(4), 1376–1404. https://doi.org/10.1108/INTR-11-2019-0447.

Chesney, T., Chuah, S.-H., Dobele, A.R., & Hoffmann, R. (2017). Information richness and trust in v-commerce: Implications for services marketing. *Journal of Services Marketing, 31*(3), 295–307. https://doi.org/10.1108/JSM-02-2015-0099.

Cicala, S. (2021). The incidence of extreme economic stress: Evidence from utility disconnections. *Journal of Public Economics, 200*, 104461. https://doi.org/10.1016/j.jpubeco.2021.104461.

Cokyasar, T. (2021). Optimization of battery swapping infrastructure for e-commerce drone delivery. *Computer communication, 168*, 146–154. https://doi.org/10.1016/j.comcom.2020.12.015.

Collin-Lachaud, I., & Diallo, M.F. (2021). Smartphone use during shopping and store loyalty: The role of social influence. *International Journal of Retail & Distribution Management, 49*(5), 678–697. https://doi.org/10.1108/IJRDM-03-2020-0109.

CSA Research. (2020, July 7). *Can't read, won't buy – B2C*. CSA Research Press Releases. https://csa-research.com/Blogs-Events/CSA-in-the-Media/Press-Releases/Consumers-Prefer-their-Own-Language

Dakin, B.C., Ching, A.E., Teperman, E., Klebl, C., Moshel, M., & Bastian, B. (2021). Prescribing vegetarian or flexitarian diets leads to sustained reduction in meat intake. *Appetite, 164*, 105285. https://doi.org/10.1016/j.appet.2021.105285.

De Canio, F., Martinelli, E., & Endrighi, E. (2021). Enhancing consumers' pro-environmental purchase intentions: The moderating role of environmental concern. *International Journal of Retail & Distribution Management, 49*(9), 1312–1329. https://doi.org/10.1108/IJRDM-08-2020-0301.

Dvorak, J., Komarkova, L., & Stehlik, L. (2021). The effect of the COVID-19 crisis on the perception of digitisation in the purchasing process: Customers and retailers perspective. *Journal of Entrepreneurship in Emerging Economies, 13*(4), 628–647. https://doi.org/10.1108/JEEE-07-2020-0260.

Eastman, J.K., & Iyer, R. (2021). Understanding the ecologically conscious behaviors of status motivated millennials. *Journal of Consumer Marketing, 38*(5), 565–575. https://doi.org/10.1108/JCM-02-2020-3652.

Flavián, C., Guinaliu, M., & Lu, Y. (2020). Mobile payments adoption – Introducing mindfulness to better understand consumer behavior. *International Journal of Bank Marketing, 38*(7), 1575–1599. https://doi.org/10.1108/IJBM-01-2020-0039.

García-de-Frutos, N., & Estrella-Ramón, A. (2021). You absolutely (don't) need this! Examining differences on customer engagement components for (anti)haul youtubers' videos. *Journal of Research in Interactive Marketing, 15*(1), 86–103. https://doi.org/10.1108/JRIM-11-2019-0181.

Gibreel, O., AlOtaibi, D.A., & Altmann, J. (2018). Social commerce development in emerging markets. *Electronic Commerce Research and Applications, 27*, 152–162. https://doi.org/10.1016/j.elerap.2017.12.008.

Göçer, A., & Sevil Oflaç, B. (2017). Understanding young consumers' tendencies regarding eco-labelled products. *Asia Pacific Journal of Marketing and Logistics, 29*(1), 80–97. https://doi.org/10.1108/APJML-03-2016-0036.

Goldman, S.P., van Herk, H., Verhagen, T., & Weltevreden, J.W. (2020, October 24). Strategic orientations and digital marketing tactics in cross-border e-commerce: Comparing developed and emerging markets. *International Small Business Journal, 39*, 350–371. https://doi.org/10.1177/0266242620962658.

Grüschow, R.M., Kemper, J., & Brettel, M. (2016). How do different payment methods deliver cost and credit efficiency in electronic commerce? *Electronic Commerce Research and Applications, 18*, 27–36. https://doi.org/10.1016/j.elerap.2016.06.001.

Gupta, S., Justy, T., Kamboj, S., Kumar, A., & Kristiffersen, E. (2021). Big data and firm marketing performance: Findings from knowledge-based view. *Technological Forecasting and Social Change, 171*, 120986. https://doi.org/10.1016/j.techfore.2021.120986.

Herrero-Crespo, A., Viejo-Fernández, N., Collado-Agudo, J., & Sanzo Pérez, M.J. (2021). Webrooming or showrooming, that is the question: Explaining omnichannel behavioural intention through the technology acceptance model and exploratory behaviour. *Journal of Fashion Marketing and Management*, Vol. ahead-of-print No. ahead-of-print. https://doi.org/10.1108/JFMM-05-2020-0091.

Hsieh, S.H., & Lee, C.T. (2021). Hey Alexa: Examining the effect of perceived socialness in usage intentions of AI assistant-enabled smart speaker. *Journal of Research in Interactive Marketing, 15*(2), 267–294. https://doi.org/10.1108/JRIM-11-2019-0179.

Huang, S.L., & Chang, Y.-C. (2019). Cross-border e-commerce: Consumers' intention to shop on foreign websites. *Internet Research, 29*(6), 1256–1279. https://doi.org/10.1108/INTR-11-2017-0428.

Huang, J., & Zhou, L. (2019). The dual roles of web personalization on consumer decision quality in online shopping: The perspective of information load. *Internet Research, 29*(6), 1280–1300. https://doi.org/10.1108/INTR-11-2017-0421.

Jami Pour, M., Hosseinzadeh, M., & Mansouri, N.S. (2021). Challenges of customer experience management in social commerce: An application of social network analysis. *Internet Research*, Vol. ahead-of-print No. ahead-of-print. https://doi.org/10.1108/INTR-01-2021-0076.

Jiménez-Barreto, J., Rubio, N., & Molinillo, S. (2021). "Find a flight for me, Oscar!" Motivational customer experiences with chatbots. *International Journal of Contemporary Hospitality Management*, Vol. ahead-of-print No. ahead-of-print. https://doi.org/10.1108/IJCHM-10-2020-1244.

Ju, X., Chocarro, R., & Martín Martín, O. (2021). Value creation in mobile social media: A systematic review and agenda for future research. *Baltic Journal of Management*, Vol. ahead-of-print No. ahead-of-print. https://doi.org/10.1108/BJM-04-2021-0157.

Kandula, S., Krishnamoorthy, S., & Roy, D. (2021). A prescriptive analytics framework for efficient E-commerce order delivery. *Decision Support Systems, 147*, 113584. https://doi.org/10.1016/j.dss.2021.113584.

Kannan, P.K., & Kulkarni, G. (2021). The impact of Covid-19 on customer journeys: Implications for interactive marketing. *Journal of Research in Interactive Marketing*, Vol. ahead-of-print No. ahead-of-print. https://doi.org/10.1108/JRIM-03-2021-0078.

Kemp, S. (2020, July 21). *Digital use around the world in July 2020.* https://wearesocial.com/blog/2020/07/digital-use-around-the-world-in-july-2020.

Kemp, S. (2021, July 21). *Digital audiences swell, but there may be trouble ahead.* https://wearesocial.com/blog/2021/07/digital-audiences-swell-but-there-may-be-trouble-ahead.

Kim, Y., & Kim, B. (2021). Effects of young adults' smartphone use for social media on communication network heterogeneity, social capital and civic engagement. *Online Information Review*, Vol. ahead-of-print No. ahead-of-print. https://doi.org/10.1108/OIR-08-2020-0332.

Kurpierz, J.R., & Smith, K. (2020). The greenwashing triangle: Adapting tools from fraud to improve CSR reporting. *Sustainability Accounting, Management and Policy Journal, 11*(6), 1075–1093. https://doi.org/10.1108/SAMPJ-10-2018-0272.

Mahadevan, K., & Joshi, S. (2021). Omnichannel retailing: A bibliometric and network visualization analysis. *Benchmarking: An International Journal*, Vol. ahead-of-print No. ahead-of-print. https://doi.org/10.1108/BIJ-12-2020-0622.

Marmat, G. (2021). Enhancing brand experience in the online social media network context: A contingency perspective. *Qualitative Market Research*, Vol. ahead-of-print No. ahead-of-print. https://doi.org/10.1108/QMR-07-2020-0096.

Milfont, T.L., Satherley, N., Osborne, D., Wilson, M.S., & Sibley, C.G. (2021). To meat, or not to meat: A longitudinal investigation of transitioning to and from plant-based diets. *Appetite, 166*, 105584. https://doi.org/10.1016/j.appet.2021.105584.

Mokrzycka, K. (2021, March 24). *Wkrótce rusza LiveMarket – polska platforma internetowa do sprzedaży na żywo. „To połączenie Allegro i Tik-Toka*" (eng. *LiveMarket - a Polish online platform for live sales - will be launched soon. "It's a combination of Allegro and Tik-Tok*").

https://300gospodarka.pl/wywiady/wkrotce-rusza-livemarket-polska-platforma-internetowa-do-sprzedazy-na-zywo-to-polaczenie-allegro-i-tik-toka.

Mou, J., Zhu, W., & Benyoucef, M. (2020). Impact of product description and involvement on purchase intention in cross-border e-commerce. *Industrial Management & Data Systems, 120*(3), 567–586. https://doi.org/10.1108/IMDS-05-2019-0280.

Nogueira, G.P.M., Rangel, J.J.A., & Shimod, E. (2021). Sustainable last-mile distribution in B2C e-commerce: Do consumers really care? *Cleaner and Responsible Consumption, 3*, 100021. https://doi.org/10.1016/j.clrc.2021.100021.

Papadas, K.K., Avlonitis, G.J., & Carrigan, M. (2017). Green marketing orientation: Conceptualization, scale development and validation. *Journal of Business Research, 80*, 236–246. https://doi.org/10.1016/j.jbusres.2017.05.024.

Qin, L., & De-Juan-Vigaray, M.D. (2021). Social commerce: Is interpersonal trust formation similar between U.S.A. and Spain? *Journal of Retailing and Consumer Services, 62*, 102642. https://doi.org/10.1016/j.jretconser.2021.102642.

Rintamäki, T., Spence, M.T., Saarijärvi, H., Joensuu, J., & Yrjölä, M. (2021). Customers' perceptions of returning items purchased online: Planned versus unplanned product returners. *International Journal of Physical Distribution & Logistics Management, 51*(4), 403–422. https://doi.org/10.1108/IJPDLM-10-2019-0302.

Rohde, P., & Mau, G. (2021). "It's selling like hotcakes": Deconstructing social media influencer marketing in long-form video content on YouTube via social influence heuristics. *European Journal of Marketing*, Vol. ahead-of-print No. ahead-of-print. https://doi.org/10.1108/EJM-06-2019-0530.

Saarijärvi, H., Joensuu, J., Rintamaki, T., & Yrjölä, M. (2018). One person's trash is another person's treasure: Profiling consumer-to-consumer e-commerce in Facebook. *International Journal of Retail & Distribution Management, 46*(11/12), 1092–1107. https://doi.org/10.1108/IJRDM-04-2017-0091.

Sharma, A., & Kapoor, P.S. (2021). Message sharing and verification behaviour on social media during the COVID-19 pandemic: A study in the context of India and the USA. *Online Information Review*, Vol. ahead-of-print No. ahead-of-print. https://doi.org/10.1108/OIR-07-2020-0282.

Statista.com (2021a, May 20). Europe: Retail e-commerce revenue forecast from 2017 to 2025. https://www.statista.com/forecasts/715663/e-commerce-revenue-forecast-in-europe.

Statista.com (2021b, May 20). Online retail users in Europe 2017–2025. https://www.statista.com/forecasts/715683/e-commerce-users-in-europe.

Sun, Y., & Wang, S. (2020). Understanding consumers' intentions to purchase green products in the social media marketing context. *Asia Pacific Journal of Marketing and Logistics*, Vol. 32 No. 4, pp. 860–878. https://doi.org/10.1108/APJML-03-2019-0178.

Tran, T.P., van Solt, M., & Zemanek Jr, J.E. (2020). How does personalization affect brand relationship in social commerce? A mediation perspective. *Journal of Consumer Marketing, 37*(5), 473–486. https://doi.org/10.1108/JCM-12-2017-2499.

Tran, T.P., Muldrow, A., & Ho, K.N.B. (2021). Understanding drivers of brand love – The role of personalized ads on social media. *Journal of Consumer Marketing, 38*(1), 1–14. https://doi.org/10.1108/JCM-07-2019-3304.

Verma, D., Tripathi, V., & Singh, A.P. (2021). From physical to digital: What drives generation Z for mobile commerce adoption?. *Journal of Asia Business Studies*, Vol. ahead-of-print No. ahead-of-print. https://doi.org/10.1108/JABS-05-2020-0207.

Index

Note: **Bold** page numbers refer to tables, *italic* page numbers refer to figures.